THE ULTIMATE SCOTTISH CYCLING BOOK

ACKNOWLEDGEMENTS

Special thanks to the following for their help and patience: John and May Lamarra, Hugh Murray, Stewart Love. Thanks also to Charles and Janice Soane, Tom and Margo Andrew, Yvonne Huntly, James MacMillan, Argyll, the Isles and Loch Lomond Tourist Board, SUSTRANS, Calmac Ferries and Historic Scotland.

The **Ultimate**
Scottish Cycling Book

Paul Lamarra

MAINSTREAM
PUBLISHING
EDINBURGH AND LONDON

FOR
CATHERINE, BETH AND CLAIRE

First published in Great Britain in 2003 by
MAINSTREAM PUBLISHING (EDINBURGH) LTD
7 Albany Street
Edinburgh EH1 3UG

ISBN 1 84018 617 8

A catalogue record for this book is available from the British Library

Maps: Jeremy Semmens

Typeset in Berkeley and Copperplate

Printed in Great Britain by
Mackays of Chatham plc

CONTENTS

LOCATION MAP

AN INTRODUCTION TO CYCLE TOURING IN SCOTLAND

There should be more to travel than just working your way through a list of places to see. Satisfying travel involves all of the senses and it takes time. Touring by bicycle, I believe, is one of the most satisfying ways to travel because you are exposed to everything, there is no question of rushing, and when you arrive by bicycle people will generally react positively – after all, you're not going to take off without paying.

Also, don't underestimate the sense of achievement. No matter how many miles you cover you'll always feel you deserve that warm bath, drink by the fire or that comforting dessert. On a bike, exploring Scotland becomes a much more subtle experience and you will be amazed at what catches your eye.

Scotland is hilly and is one of the rainier places in the world, so don't come to Scotland expecting to completely avoid either. All of the routes in this book do involve hills but I think that all of them can be justified. There is however no obligation to cycle up them all – just get off and push if you feel the need. Hopefully you will find from this book that Scotland is a country well suited to being toured by bike. There are many hundreds of miles of lanes that are all but free of traffic; added to this there are not that many people living in Scotland and fewer people have cars here than elsewhere in Europe.

I hope that the narrative on each route will show you exactly what to expect and, crucially, motivate you to give it a try. The Essentials section attached to each narrative should provide all the information needed to plan a successful trip. I wouldn't recommend taking this book with you; it is probably best to read the narrative at your leisure and copy the important details to take with you.

Neither do I recommend a daily schedule to keep to – I leave that to you. Use the information provided to plan a route according to your own priorities. Take as long as you want, indeed the longer you take the better. When planning your route don't be over prescriptive or try to take in all of the sights on offer, as you'll find that this becomes an onerous task. By all means pencil in the must-see sights but just take the rest as they come.

Don't be put off or cowed by those who shave their legs, are too keen to don lycra and brag that they can do 60 miles to the cream cracker. This book is not about earnest cycling or developing a backside as leathery as your saddle, it's about pleasure. So take your time, get off the bike frequently, dine well, cycle safely and cycle on the left.

GETTING TO SCOTLAND

BY AIR

Each airline has a different policy on bicycle carriage. Some want them boxed, others want you to waive your rights to compensation for any damage caused, some will charge, some won't; however, you should find that this is the easiest way of travelling anywhere with a bike.

It is important, no matter who you fly with, that you deflate the tyres, reverse the pedals and turn the handlebars so that they are in line with the frame. Basically, make the bike as flat as possible.

There are a number of bicycle boxes on the market that will make your bike easy to handle and reduce or eliminate the chances of damage. These tend to be expensive and can only really be justified for the most expensive bikes. Some airlines provide cardboard boxes but some would say that this can encourage rougher treatment of your bike. Bear in mind that if you have your own bike box you'll have to find somewhere to store it. I have travelled many times by air with my bike unprotected and have only experienced minor damage. At www.bikeaccess.net you'll find other cyclists' experiences of travelling with some airlines. Contact each airline for further details.

UK AND EUROPE TO SCOTLAND
British Airways: 0845 773 3377; www.ba.com
British Midland: 0870 60 70 555; www.flybmi.com

British European: 08705 676 676; www.british-european.com
EasyJet: 08706 000 000; www.easyjet.com
Ryanair: 0871 246 0000; www.ryanair.com

CROSSING THE ATLANTIC
Airlines that offer direct flights to Glasgow
Air Canada: 1-800 663 3721; www.aircanada.ca
British Airways: (US) 1-800 247 9297; (Canada) 1-800 668 1059;
   www.ba.com
Northwest Airlines: 1-800 447 4747; www.nwa.com

Via Dublin
Aer Lingus: 1-800 223 6537; www.aerlingus.ie

Via Iceland
Icelandair: 1-800 223 5500; www.icelandair.com

Via London
All of the above airlines and many more fly via London. In fact most people
   wanting to fly to Scotland will have to come via London. Fortunately
   there are several flights every hour out of London for Scotland.

AIRPORTS

Information on all flights to/from Aberdeen, Edinburgh and Glasgow at
www.baa.com

ARRIVING AT GLASGOW
There is a signed cycle route to Paisley Gilmour Street Station from where
you can catch a train to Glasgow Central, Ardrossan (Firth of Clyde route),
Wemyss Bay (end of FoC route) or Ayr (end of Galloway route). It is about
two miles from the airport to Paisley Gilmour Street Station.

ARRIVING AT PRESTWICK
There is a dedicated railway station at Prestwick from where you can travel
to Glasgow Central or Ayr. There is also a signed cycle route into Glasgow
via Ardrossan. It is about 40 miles to Glasgow and 15 miles to Ardrossan
(Firth of Clyde route).

ARRIVING AT EDINBURGH

There is a signed cycle route which follows the A8 into Edinburgh. Make your way out to the A8 from the airport following signs for Edinburgh. The cycle path is on the far side of the A8, so go under the A8 to the next roundabout following cycle signs for Edinburgh and Newbridge to join the cycle path. From the Gogar Roundabout onwards cyclists are expected to use the bus lanes; you can if you wish catch a train from The Gyle. Distance from the airport to Edinburgh Waverly Railway Station is nine miles.

ARRIVING AT ABERDEEN (DYCE)

Dyce railway station is adjacent to the airport. The Aberdeenshire route starts from Dyce railway station. You can catch trains for Aberdeen, Glasgow, Edinburgh and Inverness from Dyce.

RAIL

There are three companies operating services from England to Scotland. All carry bicycles.

GNER operate the East Coast Mainline from London King's Cross to Glasgow, Edinburgh and Aberdeen. GNER can carry up to five bicycles per train and do not make a charge.

Virgin Rail operates in the west with services from London Euston, Bristol, Birmingham and Manchester Piccadilly to Glasgow Central. Virgin Rail will carry a maximum of three bicycles and charge £3 each way. Tandems are charged £6 each way.

Caledonian Sleepers operate overnight services from London Euston to Glasgow, Inverness, Aberdeen and Fort William. Bicycles may be booked no more than 12 weeks in advance.

GNER: 08457 225 225; www.gner.co.uk
Virgin: 08457 222 333; www.virgintrains.co.uk
Caledonian Sleeper: www.scotrail.co.uk
National Rail Enquiries: 08457 48 49 50
Online booking and information: www.thetrainline.com

FERRY

FROM EUROPE

Superfast Ferries operate a daily crossing from Zeebrugge, Belgium, to Rosyth on the Firth of Forth. The crossing takes about 17 hours. Online bookings and a list of booking agents can be found at www.superfast.com.

To get to Rosyth Railway Station for a train to Edinburgh leave the port and go straight through the first roundabout. At the second roundabout follow signs for Forth Road Bridge, Glasgow, Edinburgh, A90, M8, M90. At the next roundabout follow signs for Rosyth and Dunfermline. Follow King's Road (becomes a dual carriageway) straight through each of the roundabouts to the top of the hill. The station is on the right. It is about one-and-a-half miles from the port to the railway station. These roads are likely to be busy with traffic.

FROM IRELAND
Stena Line: 028 9074 7747; www.stenaline.co.uk; Belfast–Stranraer
P&O Irish Ferries: 0870 242 4777; www.poirishsea.com; Larne–Cairnryan
Seacat: 028 9032 9461; www.seacat.co.uk; Belfast–Troon, Ayrshire.

Onward travel by rail is straightforward from Stranraer and Troon to Glasgow but not from Cairnryan. Journey times: Stranraer to Glasgow takes two hours; Troon to Glasgow takes 40 minutes.

GETTING AROUND SCOTLAND

SCOTRAIL
Scotrail operate most train services in Scotland. Glasgow suburban trains do not have any dedicated cycle space but bicycles can be conveyed in the passenger compartments. For these services it is best to avoid peak periods. For all other services it is essential that you book in advance. Bookings can be made eight weeks before travel and no later than two hours before travel. Most services carry only two bicycles but the Glasgow to Oban service will carry six. Scotrail will not carry tandems or trailers.

Scotrail bookings and enquiries: 08457 55 00 33; www.scotrail.co.uk
Online booking and information: www.thetrainline.com
National Rail Enquiries: 08457 48 49 50

CALMAC
Calmac operate all ferry services on the west coast. For individual ferry journeys there is a charge for bicycles but this is waived if the passenger purchases an Island Hopscotch Ticket or an Island Rover Ticket. There are 26 pre-planned routes for which Island Hopscotch tickets are available. The Island Rover tickets allow unlimited use of Calmac ferries for an eight- or fifteen-day period. Both offer excellent value.

Calmac general enquiries and information: 01475 650 100; www.calmac.co.uk

Travel information specific to each route can be found in the Essentials section of each chapter.

ACCOMMODATION

The Essentials section of each chapter lists accommodation for most of the places visited along the way. These lists are by no means exhaustive. Some of those listed have signed up for the *Cyclists Welcome Scheme* operated by VisitScotland; ask when booking. Participants in the scheme should offer flexible meal-time options, drying facilities and secure cycle storage. I cannot vouch for all of the accommodation listed in Essentials and you should contact each provider before travelling to check cost, vacancies and meals offered. In some areas the availability of accommodation is limited, especially in the remoter areas of the Highlands and it is best to book ahead.

HOSTELS
The Scottish Youth Hostel Association (SYHA) has around 70 hostels in Scotland that are among the best places to stay. Hostels range from simple crofts to grand houses and castles. You have to be a member of the International Youth Hostel Federation (IYHF) in order to use their hostels.

Central reservations service: 08701 55 32 55; www.syha.org.uk

Hostels in the Outer Hebrides are operated by the Gatliff Trust; these hostels are under the umbrella of the SYHA but do not receive bookings – it's on a first-come-first-served basis.

More information at www.gatliff.org.uk

There are many independent hostels in Scotland although the vast majority are in the cities or in the Highlands.

More details at www.hostel-scotland.co.uk

CAMPING
Campsites are generally available throughout Scotland but in wild areas wild camping is tolerated. In the Western Isles it is actively encouraged. It is best to ask, however, although this is not always possible. Never camp within sight of someone's home or farm and take care to leave the site as you found it. A campfire is never appropriate.

For up-to-date information on accommodation contact the relevant tourist board.

Aberdeen and Grampian: 01224 632727; www.agtb.org

Argyll, the Isles, Loch Lomond, Stirling and Trossachs: 01369 703785; www.scottish.heartlands.org

Ayrshire and Arran: 01292 288688; www.ayrshire-arran.com
Dumfries and Galloway: 01387 253862; www.dumfriesandgalloway.co.uk
Edinburgh and Lothians: 0131 473 3800; www.edinburgh.org
Greater Glasgow and Clyde Valley: 0141 204 4400; www.seeglasgow.com
Highlands: 01987 421160; www.host.co.uk
Perthshire: 01738 627958; www.perthshire.co.uk
Scottish Borders: 01835 863435; www.scot-borders.co.uk
Western Isles: 01851 703088; www.witb.co.uk

WEATHER, MIDGES AND TOURISTS

Yes, Scotland can be wet, but it isn't as wet as it is perceived. Out of the ten weeks or so that I spent cycling to research this book it only rained on nine days and then never for the whole day. In the summer the days are so long that it is possible to wait and see what the weather will be like later on. The prevailing wind in Scotland is from the south-west and each route has been constructed to take advantage of this fact.

Scots will tell you that May is the best month for good weather. I find this to be the case more often than not, but you'll be taking a chance on the weather whenever you go. The summers are not necessarily drier but they are usually warmer.

The summer menace is the midges. Underestimate them at your peril. If you intend to camp then purchase a midge net. A mosquito net will *not* do – the holes are too big and all you'll be doing is providing indoor feeding for the blighters. When you're on the coast, a breeze will usually keep them at bay. They like damp and still conditions so don't camp anywhere too sheltered or close to boggy ground. Midges are not usually a problem at the margins of the cycling season when it is too cold.

You'll find that if you travel outwith the months of July, August and bank holiday weekends you'll have your pick of the accommodation and the roads will be deserted. However, you may find that opening hours for shops, hotels, pubs and attractions are curtailed.

EATING

Places to eat are thick on the ground in most of the areas in this book, except in Sutherland where there are big distances between locations. The times between which meals are served seem to be enshrined in some UN catering charter that only Scotland has signed up to. They are rarely up for discussion. This is largely due to difficulties in attracting staff to remote areas and the fact that staff have to have a break.

Therefore it is worth trying to make sure that you are stopped somewhere around lunchtime. I find that a picnic lunch is much more in the spirit of free and easy cycle touring. With regard to dinner, ask when you book your accommodation about the availability of meals.

SUSTRANS

SUSTRANS is the charity responsible for the National Cycle Network (NCN). Their heroic efforts have vastly increased the number of safe cycle touring options available by providing an alternative to the busiest and most dangerous roads. Some cycle paths are excellent but others are not quite up to the mark yet. Their sign-posted routes, which a couple of the routes contained in this book follow at times, allow you to switch off and forget about the map. They also provide excellent maps for their routes.

SUSTRANS always need more money, so if you can be of any assistance or would just like to purchase their maps, contact them at SUSTRANS (Scotland), 3 Coates Place, Edinburgh EH3 7AA; 0131 652 0187; www.sustrans.org.uk.

ENJOYING YOUR CYCLING

The cyclist and bicycle should be well prepared for the trip. There is frequently no other option than to continue in the event of a malfunction of rider or bike. So have the bike serviced and cycle as much as you can beforehand.

It is a good idea to be able to carry out basic repairs, as problems that do occur tend to be minor (that's if the bike is well maintained in the first place). The most likely catastrophic failures are a cable snapping or a tyre shredding, so replace these if they show signs of wear. I have had a chain come apart and now carry spare chain links and a link extractor. It should go without saying that spare inner tubes, a puncture-repair kit and a pump are the first things to be packed. You should also carry the relevant spanners and Allen keys.

Simple things like properly inflated and smooth tyres that are designed for road use will increase your pleasure immeasurably. Persevering with the knobbly tyres that the bike came with when you bought it is a false economy, so replace them!

Take as little as possible. I mean it – some people manage to tour with nothing more than a change of clothes and a credit card. At the very most take three sets of clothes (that includes your clothes for cycling in) but try to make do with two, and if you absolutely have to, take a lightweight change of footwear. Always dry wet cycling gear and put it on every day. Don't be tempted to wear your change of clothes on the bike.

The best way to carry your kit is in panniers. For those who choose to camp, front and rear panniers may be necessary. If you're staying in hotels or B&Bs, a set of rear panniers is more than enough. A backpack is not a good idea as it restricts your movement and upsets your balance. Clothes, maps and books stored in panniers should always be wrapped in plastic bags.

Specialised cycle clothing can keep you comfortable for longer and improve your aerodynamics. You don't have to wear the fashion equivalent of cling film as there is a range of cyclewear that looks normal enough for you to wear even when you're not in the company of a bicycle. Otherwise avoid clothes that are loose and don't cope well when wet. I always prefer to cycle in shorts.

You'll definitely need a waterproof but remember it will be packed away most of the time so it can't be too bulky. A lightweight fleece for when the temperature drops is a good idea, as are gloves. Believe it or not, keeping the sun off can be a more serious problem and sun-block for the backs of your hands, face and neck is essential even on overcast days. Wear a helmet that has a skip on it and wear sunglasses.

It is imperative that you remain hydrated and that you keep your energy levels up. Drink regularly and always have an emergency supply of chocolate or dried fruit or one of those instant energy chemical concoctions. Finally, be bright and wear a helmet.

EMERGENCIES

In the event of an accident remain calm and dial 999 if an ambulance is required. Being tired is *not* an emergency. Travel Insurance is always a good idea.

SECURITY

Take a lock and attach the key to an item of clothing such as a zip or the zip on a handlebar bag. An easily removed handlebar bag is a good idea for carrying valuables, cameras, maps and passports. In general, theft is not a big problem except in the cities, where you should always keep an eye on your kit.

MAPS

I use a combination of the Ordnance Survey's *Landranger* Maps (1:50,000) and their *Road Maps* (1: 250,000). The *Road Maps* give me an overview of the route whereas the *Landranger* allows me to home in on the detail. Each route requires at least four *Landranger* maps. *Landranger* maps are about £6 each and available widely. They are worth it in areas where there are lots of lanes and back roads. For the Western Isles, the Firth of Clyde and Sutherland the *Road Maps* will suffice. SUSTRANS produce very good cycle maps for their national cycling routes that could come in handy for parts of some of the routes.

CYCLE HIRE AND HOLIDAY OPERATORS

Biketrax, Edinburgh, (0131 228 6333; www.biketrax.co.uk) hire out everything that you could possibly need, including kiddy trailers, panniers and roof racks.

If you fancy cycle touring in Scotland but would rather someone else ironed out the wrinkles then contact any of the following:
Bespoke Highland Tours: 0141 334 9017; www.highland-tours.co.uk
Scottish Youth Hostelling Association: 01786 891 400; www.syha.org.uk
Scottish Cycling Holidays: 01250 876 100; www.scotcycle.co.uk

USEFUL CONTACTS AND OTHER ROUTES

The Cyclists' Touring Club have a wealth of information on touring in Scotland available to members. Membership benefits also include third-party insurance and travel discounts.
CTC: 01483 417217; www.ctc.org.uk
Adventure Cycling Association (North American equivalent of the CTC): 1-800 755 2453; www.adv-cycling.org
VisitScotland has created a website devoted to cycling in Scotland at www.cycling.visitscotland.com
Cyclecover Cycle Rescue: 0800 212 810 – a rescue service similar to that available to motorists; £30 per year

Notable other cycle routes in Scotland include the Border Loop (250 miles) and the Four Abbeys – details from the Scottish Borders Tourist Board (*see* Accommodation). The Kingdom of Fife has an extensive network of cycle ways and a 104-mile tour; details from the Kingdom of Fife Tourist Board: 01334 472021; www.standrews.co.uk. Details of the Great Glen Cycleway that runs from Fort William to Inverness can be obtained from Highland Tourist Board (*see* Accommodation).

1

THE WEATHER
MULL AND ARDNAMURCHAN

Oban is the Grand Central Station of the world of Western Isles ferries. It has a buzz and a sense of purpose that many towns envy. It has that indescribable atmosphere of a jumping-off point. Oban is one of those places where I get a shivery goosebump feeling, just as when watching the destinations of Berlin, Warsaw and Beijing click round on the board at Gare du Nord in Paris, or in Banff in the Canadian Rockies before setting out on a trail that leads deep into the mountains. It is probably the presence of like-minded souls and there were at least 60 cyclists waiting on the pier for the arrival of ferries to take them to Barra or to Mull. Ferries travel to destinations where Gaelic rather than English is spoken but can be reached without crossing time zones or producing passports. They are as different to Oban as Paris is to Warsaw; the Hebrides are another world in another time.

Oban is also famous for its folly. It is no doubt folly to be famous for a folly but they're rather proud of it. McCaig, a local banker, made a well-meaning attempt to recreate Rome's Coliseum on the hill overlooking the town but it is no more than an exterior wall. From the pier, McCaig's Folly is an intriguing structure and offers much promise but from up there on the hill it is the view of down here on the pier that is the attraction.

The Barra ferry was late so the Mull ferry would be late, so the pier was crowded with impatient travellers. It wasn't just the folk up at the folly who were looking down on us on the pier. The *Hebridean Princess* was occupying her priority berth and the well-heeled viewed the developing mêlée from their teak deckloungers whilst sipping aperitifs. Dainty sea delicacies purchased from the quayside fishmonger were the unofficial *hors d'oeuvre*. I wondered if they knew that I was eating a crab sandwich purchased from the self same fishmonger. 'No ordinary cyclist this,' I mouthed up to them.

Ferries, it seems, are just like buses – they all come at once. *The Clansman* from Barra and the *Isle of Mull* from the Isle of Mull were manoeuvring in the bay, tooting to each other in that *Thomas the Tank Engine* way. The *Hebridean Princess* didn't toot back to her former colleagues, as she had moved on. In her new role as a luxury and bijou cruise ship she has eschewed the black, white and red of the state Calmac line for a shiny royal-blue hull and a dignified white superstructure. She no doubt thought herself too good, like the kid on the street who wins a place at grammar school and no longer comes out to play.

The Clansman's gaping mouth swallowed up the Barra-bound and made way for the Mull ferry. The Calmac ferries once again tooted to each other, and once again the *Hebridean Princess* remained aloof – perhaps they were flirting with her, each hoping for a response.

Oh, my God! Would it be like this for a whole week? I am unaccustomed to travelling alone and already I was inventing personas for inanimate objects. Perhaps I should have attached myself to the many more cyclists who were making their way to Barra. I resolved to seek out lots of company.

The biological configuration of my ferry was all wrong: we were to enter via the stern to be spewed out at Craignure. I know old habits die hard. 'I must find lots of company,' I was reciting to myself as I wheeled my bike down the ramp at the boson's insistence, into the belly of the ship, sorry, the car deck.

The contrast with the *Hebridean Princess*, I imagine, extends to the inside. The queue at the self-service restaurant was already 50 deep. I decided to skip it. Indigestion was the only likely outcome of queuing for half-an-hour and then eating in under ten minutes. Anyway, self-service doesn't quite work for the solo diner, as it is necessary to buy one's meal and then find a table to eat it at. Instead I decided to go up on deck and let the passengers of the *Hebridean Princess* know that I was not partaking of lasagne and chips, state-subsidy style.

Duart Castle posts the Mull lookout, a fairytale edifice that looks so much the castle. Its location on a black headland, overlooking the once strategically important Firth of Lorne, is perfect for dramatic effect. A group of Americans rose to stand at the rail and dutifully photographed it. Their mutterings conveyed relief that they had finally seen a castle that looked like a castle and what's more it had a roof on it. Duart is the seat of the Clan MacLean, even though they had their behind firmly booted off it by the Campbells for several hundred years. The MacDougalls had it first, then the MacDonalds, followed by the MacLeans, who lost it to the Campbells for their unstinting support of the Jacobite cause. Sir Fitzroy MacLean purchased and restored it in 1911, proudly replacing his buttocks on behalf of the Clan MacLean on their ancient seat.

Coughed up at Craignure it was too late to make any progress towards Iona, so my day's cycling amounted to the few hundred yards to the campsite. As campsites go this was a good one. Impressively comfortable and thoughtfully laid out, little patches of astro-turf were the tent-pitching stations. Not easy to get pegs into, I have to say. My tent did look small among the giants that could probably house whole Bedouin clans. It felt very suburban and far too many campers were washing cars or caravans. The caravan washers, with long brushes brought along for the purpose, gently foaming and washing their little homes, resembled zookeepers washing their elephants – a Radio 2 listener's fantasy.

The next day started with a short stiff climb that was already familiar to me from the evening before. I had salved my conscience and taken precautions against the onset of a deep-vein thrombosis by cycling the 14 miles to Loch Buie. Unfortunately the logic of hair of the dog that bit you does not extend to tired muscles. Oh, it was a struggle!

I had returned to the campsite just before sunset, aglow with my evening's achievement only to fall over at the tent, having forgotten to disengage my feet from the pedals. A woman tutted and sniffed the air and no doubt curtains twitched. The gossip probably featured the drunken cyclist in the small tent at Pitch 52.

Craignure is a tourist honey-pot. On the road out of Craignure there are many signs to tempt the traveller in a scene reminiscent of a *Road Runner* cartoon. You know: 'Two Hundred Yards to Bird Seed', 'Get Your Free Bird Seed' – only the signs advertise a jewellery centre, a birds-of-prey centre and spend-your-money-here centres. Duart Castle was one such attraction. But it involves a mile detour. It is just about worth the trip, but if the weather is fine then get on with it and leave it until you return to Craignure at the end of the trip; that's if the cosy Craignure Inn doesn't seduce you. However, these many attractions soak up most of the traffic before you are very far out of Craignure. The best time to set off is just after the ferry disgorges its load.

The day before had ended with a fine evening. A very light wind barely ruffled Loch Spelve and the low sun picked out the glinting granite on Beinn Bearnaich and Dun da Gaoithe. Today they were hiding under a blanket of cloud and they were in no hurry to start the new day. Clumps of thrift, foxgloves, bluebells and bog myrtle lined the road. The warm humid air accentuated their aroma, creating a pungent fug. It wasn't a great day but there were no elemental hindrances; indeed, the wind was gently pushing at my back.

The road to Iona, like most of the roads on Mull, is single track with passing places. This type of highway slows everyone down and the best way to avoid frustration is to take it slowly so that you never fly past a passing place only to have to retreat or bump off the road. Just be ready to stop.

It wasn't a vehicle that prompted my first enforced halt but rather a flock of jaywalking fowl. As my experience only extends to the dead and plucked variety, I could not, with any certainty, identify them. They clucked and clinked their way across the road without a thought. I say clinked because they resembled cognac bottles with legs, seeming to lack wings, and all their weight was at the bottom end. It was while I was ruling out the varieties of game that they couldn't possibly be that I ran into my first cyclist. She introduced herself as Robin from New Zealand and made it clear she was female. She had even tied a teddy bear to her handlebars as a feminine touch. Her name might not give anything away but I was in little doubt that she was right.

Robin was peeved that her companion was dawdling and not even wearing a helmet. Granted she was wearing the go-faster variety but I thought it was unlikely that similar headwear would make much difference to his progress. I kept my own cycling philosophy to myself.

As well as fuming, she was contemplating the eight-mile detour to Loch Buie. She enquired after its worth. I felt it was entirely worth it and told her so. I added that I had gone off in search of Boswell and Johnson, a couple of eighteenth-century travellers who spent their last night on Mull at Loch Buie. Neither of them makes much mention of the journey except that Boswell reported it as 'tedious'.

Certainly the hill that blocks the way is tedious from the point of view of the self-propelled cyclist. Beyond the very stiff climb, tempered by the pleasantly light woodland that surrounds it, Loch Spelve is regained. The hills seem to want to conspire to keep this sea loch from the Firth of Lorn, only allowing it a narrow opening. The seaweed-matted shores are a giveaway, as are the lobster creels that are dumped along the shore. The road to Loch Buie rather gratifyingly has turf growing up the middle, suggesting that this is a road less travelled.

It is an ancient community that occupies the sheltered and verdant bay at the head of Loch Buie. The nearby stone circle is the best to be found on Mull and the overgrown Moy Castle is as secluded as Duart Castle is prominent and must have been built by a particularly introspective branch of the MacLeans. I am told that Boswell and Johnson's lodgings are now incorporated into outbuildings of Loch Buie Lodge and they are not at all evocative of their stay.

Robin had not heard of either Boswell or Johnson – perversely it was the hill that appealed to her. I left her to it and began my own climb over the pass between Ben Buie and Beinn Taliadh.

However, my departure was delayed by a dubious – or just a very early – version of a motor vehicle. It had no sides or roof and a very basic-sounding engine. All sorts of quaint artefacts were hanging off various hooks. A jolly couple in period dress and their presumably ancient car made me doubt for a moment my place in time, as the only way of knowing in this timeless landscape is by the vehicles that pass. I was content to hold onto the notion of inadvertently travelling through time until the next internal-combustion-propelled vehicle presented itself – a Hillman Imp. Oh well, it wasn't all the way back.

The well-graded hill pauses briefly at Torness. Not as menacing as its east-coast namesake, Torness Nuclear Power Station, but it is just as desolate. I stood among the ruins of the tumbledown cottages with their moss-covered stones and roofless gables trying to imagine the bloody deeds of the nineteenth-century Clearances, in that Hollywood way. However Liam Neeson as 'Rob Roy' was the only unpleasant image involuntarily popping up in my mind's eye.

It was during my Neeson moment that a big green thing with flapping arms came running over. Was it the dragon that is said to have lived in these hills? Was it someone or something that had seen the dragon and was running for its life? No, it was an ornithologist who wanted to share with me his golden-eagle moment. He tentatively held out his binoculars and pointed to the sky but withdrew them and returned them to his eyes, obviously itching to see the birds again. His guidebook said there would be eagles here and so there were. I told him that my guidebook had warned of a dragon and a headless horseman. He hadn't seen either but he had seen a White Tailed Sea Eagle by Loch Spelve. He puffed out his chest to give me an idea of its dimensions. I decided to go off and take my chances with the dragon.

The road that followed was certainly haunting if not haunted by a headless horseman. An internecine war between the Loch Buie and the Duart MacLeans resulted in the instigator, allegedly spurred on by his ambitious wife, losing his head, literally. In a battle to settle matters his head was severed from his body and his horse galloped off with its now headless rider still in the saddle. His body finally fell off the horse at Torness and a small cairn now marks the spot.

The top of the pass is an intimidating spot. Ben Buie on the left, which translates as 'yellowish hill', was showing none of that hue. It is as wild as the Highlands can be. Johnson reports that Boswell 'thought no part of the Highlands equally terrifick'. Black bulbous crags, formed by lava cooling and solidifying as it dripped, overhang the pass. Large glacial erratics sit like petrified sheep grazing on piles of moraine. Ancient locals perceptively noticed that the rocks were alien and explained their presence by telling tales of giants hurling them at one another. Tales of dragons and giants are inevitable in such an awesome spot.

The descent back to sea level promised to be a fast one. I could see well into the distance and so I wouldn't have to restrain my momentum for fear of being surprised by a car. I wasn't very far into the descent before I couldn't see a bloody thing, as my eyes were watering with the speed at which the countryside was flying by.

It seems as though I was some way along the side of Loch Scridain before I felt the need to pedal again. I failed to stop in the tiny hamlet of Pennyghael at the head of the loch as I didn't want to waste a drop of the potential energy I had built up on the ascent.

Loch Scridain marks a change. The mountains are left behind for the low-lying Ross of Mull peninsula. The Ross is a granite tongue that licks out into the Atlantic with Iona a morsel on its very tip. From now on Mull shows its Hebridean side. Crofting communities, current and abandoned, litter the Ross.

The road was initially level, undemanding and hugged the shore. I constantly scoured the view for signs of otters, seals or a sea eagle but the black rocky shore made verifying movement impossible. However, the orange-billed oystercatchers and the occasional curlew were easy enough to spot as they hopped along, as were the statuesque herons. Across the loch the Ardmeanach peninsula runs parallel to the Ross. It is a black mass of ancient lava, its successive lava flows as easy to spot as layers in the cliffs. Eventually the road gives up the water's edge and a pattern develops of ascending over a headland to descend into a bay – a characteristic of coastal cycling the world over.

It didn't seem long before I reached the typically Hebridean village of Bunessan. An informal museum on the way out of the village has tried hard to document the life of the crofter on the Ross and also keeps tabs on the diaspora with very detailed family trees. Most of the cleared families in this area settled in Canada, founding their own Bunessan near Toronto. It is a peculiar irony that it is the new Bunessan that is now struggling to survive, while in contrast the original seems to be vital and thriving. Volunteer curators will point you to the spots where evidence of the life that was once lived can still be seen.

Fionnphort is land's end for Mull – the road literally just runs into the sea. Fionnphort has an uncompromising on-the-edge feel to it and until recently didn't have anything to encourage you to linger. In order that it didn't exist just to service Iona, the Columba Centre was built. You will find out a lot more about Columba and the Celtic Church here than on Iona itself. Apparently Columba forbade the presence of women or cows on the island. Cows were forbidden because Columba believed that wherever you found a cow you found a woman – or was it the other way round? I wonder which tempted him more?

I had to give up my plans to spend the night on Iona. The last ferry is quite early and it was already tied up for the night. I cycled a windswept mile further south to Fidden. A semi-official campsite sits on a particularly beautiful spot on the machair. I pitched my tent on the edge of a tiny bay of silver sand. The hope was that the gently sibilating Atlantic Ocean would lull me to sleep. The short grass that characterises the machair also means no midges. Sheep shit, though, comes at no extra charge.

The tidal island of Erraid can be reached at low-tide from Fidden. On the lee of the island facing the campsite is a neat row of lighthouse keepers' cottages, once home to the off-duty custodians of the Skerryvore and Dubh Artach lighthouses. The little cottages are typical of the architecture of the Northern Lighthouse Board. For someone brought up on a diet of *Blue Peter*, they are wonderfully evocative of the human age of lighthouses. Square gardens are marked off by perfect stone walls enclosing small patches of order in an otherwise wild landscape. Perhaps for those who faced down the chaotic elements daily it was best to start at grassroots.

Erraid was the base for Robert Louis Stevenson's uncle while he was building the two lighthouses already referred to. This was maybe the island where Stevenson actually wrote his book *Kidnapped*, as the island is referred to explicitly as the one onto which Robert Balfour was washed up. Today the Findhorn Foundation tends the island; the foundation is a spiritual organisation that attracts soul searchers – and what a place in which to soul search. I wonder if you have to admit when you've found it and have to leave.

It wasn't so much a night of being lulled to sleep as it was one of being blown awake. The morning wasn't looking much better, although the wind had eased and had considerably swung round to the west, so once again I would have the wind at my back – uncommon luck. The sky was grey and barely able to lift itself off the ground. This is the default position. It is this kind of weather that produced this wild, boggy and uninhabited landscape. Today, I imagined, would be just how a cinematographer would have requested it to show the drama and the struggle of life here. It was like viewing the world in Panavision or through an elongated picture frame, as if nothing above 500 ft existed, obliterated by the heavy cloud. It was difficult to decide whether it was rock interspersed with grass or grass interspersed with rock.

Even on a dull day, the translucent sea lapping into the granite coves around Fionnphort looks incredible. The almost lurid pink of the granite and the green of the sea could have been painted on by Dali himself.

Fionnphort's windward shore looks onto Iona's fairer lee shore and the contrast is stark. The rocky coves face gentle sandy bays, but it is more than that. Stepping onto Iona there was a palpable sense of purpose beyond subsistence farming. Freed from the mundane daily struggle it has a more relaxed atmosphere. Hero of the Enlightenment, Voltaire, reacted with horror when Boswell told him of his plans to tour the Highlands of Scotland with Johnson. However I think that Voltaire would have approved of Iona and agreed that it does display a certain degree of urbanity and sophistication.

Relieved that no one felt it necessary to check for bovine or feminine attributes, I set off in search of nourishment for the body rather than the soul. Voltaire would definitely have approved of the Argyll Hotel. Scottish food with a French twist may be a bit of a cliché but they do it extraordinarily well. To sample a *bouillabaisse*, the famous Mediterranean fish stew, is a long-standing ambition of mine. If you attempt to order it in France, chefs will huff and puff in that Gallic way and tell you to return the next day, which is not ideal when you are a touring cyclist. Delightfully, the Argyll Hotel has concocted a Hebridean version, a deep bowl of Queen Clams with their bright orange roe still attached, cod, haddock, salmon and other *fruit de mer*. It must be at least as good if not better than its southern inspiration. I look forward to making the comparison one day.

It was difficult to leave the art-deco dining room of the Argyll. Not only because of its faintly colonial air and view of the bay but also because the large lunch washed down with Fraoch Heather Ale was having a soporific effect. A wet saddle and a full stomach are not conducive to cycling. The short distance to the abbey via the ruined nunnery was barely achieved and thankfully traffic free. I stopped first at the graveyard to visit the grave of Labour Party leader John Smith. I thought I should because I'd met him once, walking alone in the Cairngorms. Many political pilgrims have literally beaten a path to his grave but it is not only the grass that has become worn. The inscription on his simple gravestone was barely discernible – rather ironic when you consider the very much older inscriptions that are still clear today.

The abbey itself didn't really do it for me, though I can accept that it is the presence of this building that has created the special atmosphere on the island. It is plain and simple in the Scottish tradition but I prefer the grand cathedrals of France and Spain where I can marvel at the wonder of their construction.

Despite the ruinous state of the abbey (it was being used as a cattle barn when Johnson visited), he wrote 'that man is little to be envied . . . whose piety would not grow warmer among the ruins of Iona'. Perhaps then it should have been left in ruins.

For me, it is the Road of the Dead, the roadway of marble cobblestones that leads from St Oran's Chapel, that provides the strongest link with the time when Iona was at the centre of the Celtic Church. It is said that 60 kings of Scotland, France and Norway were carried along this road to their final resting place.

It would have been easy to spend the night on Iona and I fancied a spot overlooking the magnificent white sandy beach at the northern tip of the island. On a previous visit the weather was hot and sunny and the view of the beach truly resembled a scene that would not have been out of place on the cover of *Condé Nast Traveller*. Today the wind was too strong for coastal camping and another night on Iona would mean I would run the risk of another visit to the Argyll Hotel and thus run the risk of another night on Iona.

The strong wind was still blowing from the west when I finally set off again to retrace part of the previous day's journey to Pennyghael. I hadn't intended to stop at Pennyghael but 17 miles was far enough in the pouring rain. I arrived in double-quick time without having to pedal very hard. I was cold, soaked through and slightly demoralised and there was no way I was camping. Instead I chose the first B&B I encountered.

I chose in haste. The accommodation was adequate but the atmosphere was frosty. The cheap toilet paper prepared me for the breakfast ahead. It just fitted the description of breakfast and no more. My host assessed two child guests with a stare, as though they were Hansel and Gretel. Judging by the mean breakfast, she had clearly decided they were fat enough already.

The Mull weather sages, and there are many, make two assertions. One, when the wind blows from the west the pattern will be one good day followed by one bad day. Two, Iona would always be clear but Ben More would be in mist. On this day the first was holding true, as it was looking promising, but it was Ben More rather than Iona that was clear of mist, rising its full height from the shore of Loch Scridain.

Ben More and the surrounding mountains that huddle between Loch na Keal and Loch Scridain are the remains of volcanoes, and the Ardmeanach peninsula was obviously formed by their lava flows. The awesome black cliffs would seem to indicate violent eruptions with copious amounts of lava.

Very few places can have their geology as well documented as Mull. It has been a Mecca for geologists since 1819 when Dr John MacCulloch discovered a fossilised tree 40 ft tall that had been enveloped by a lava flow. Known as MacCulloch's Tree it can be viewed at Burg on Ardmeanach. A National Trust property, it is signposted from the road.

To cross from Loch Scridain to Loch na Keal inevitably involves a climb. It was not a difficult climb but it was a claustrophobic one, through dense conifer forest. After days of open views it was frustrating to be able to hear what sounded like an impressive water flow but not to be able to see it. Views to the hills beyond the trees were elusive, flicking between trees like an early cinema reel.

Leaving the conifer forest at the top of the climb was like being led out of the house wearing a blindfold to have it whipped off in the driveway to reveal a shiny new car tied up with an oversize bow. Initially, the craggy hillsides seemed to suggest that I was deep in the remains of a volcano's crater but once through the narrow gap the view was stupendous. It was so good that I imagined I was experiencing something of the elation that the first settlers in America would have experienced when they finally reached the Pacific coast, despite it being less than an hour since I'd left the shore of Loch Scridain.

On my left was the empty and rugged landscape of Ardmeanach's north shore. Black and brooding, there would appear to be no easy way to explore it. Clouds travelling fast overhead constantly changed the light. The tone of green hillsides constantly changed from dark and wild to light and almost lawn-like.

The road dived away to the right, somehow managing to twist its way back to sea-level, and the descent promised to be much faster than the ascent. Therein lay the dilemma: to enjoy the adrenalin of a fast descent or to show restraint and soak in the views around every bend? Cliffs tower and waterfalls cascade in deep chasms. I found that I had to stop round every corner for a photograph.

The green island lying in the loch far below is Inchkenneth. Boswell and Johnson stayed the night there with the island's laird. Johnson, on stepping ashore, expressed his delight at the impression of a carriage wheel in the sand, a poignant reminder of the comforts of London after so long in a land where no roads existed. Today, the most striking feature on the island is the large white suburban home that could be just as poignant to the modern traveller from the south of England.

The house and island were for a time the retreat of the Mitford family, a family that attracted much notoriety, in particular for the Fascist sympathies of Unity Mitford. Unity became good friends with Hitler and was accepted into his inner circle. At the outbreak of war she attempted to kill herself with a pistol that Hitler had gifted to her. She failed and her attempt rendered her an invalid. She died on Inchkenneth in 1948, hidden from public view, I imagine.

The cycle along the southern shore of Loch na Keal was simply sensational. Not only do you maintain an exhilarating momentum for what seems like forever but the cliffs bear down on you, almost squeezing you and the road off the shore and into the loch. The road literally clings onto the end of ancient lava flows and it doesn't take too big a leap to visualise the lava sizzling as it came into contact with the sea. I did at times feel intimidated by my seemingly precarious position between the cliffs and the sea and I felt slightly queasy at the amount of rock scattered on the road.

The countryside eventually eases, the hillsides relax and lie back from the road. Ben More to my right had its impressive ridges on display. Stony beaches littered with giant boulders and the occasional upturned boat at least put some distance between the road and the water – although judging by the scraps of dried seaweed lying on the tarmac, this is not always the case.

At the head of Loch na Keal, I paused to regain my composure. I can say that those were among the most satisfying and spectacular miles I have ever cycled.

Company had been scarce up to this point and it was for company that I stopped prematurely at Killiechronan at the head of Loch na Keal. An unofficial campsite with few facilities, it is in a stunning location looking down the length of Loch na Keal and over to Ben More.

It was a good night spent with like-minded people singing round a campfire and swapping anecdotes. Dick, an octogenarian Australian and an enthusiastic folk singer, told stories of being shipwrecked off Sudan with his five children. Fellow cycle tourists told rather more earnest tales of cycling through 23 countries. They were so keen on cycling I reckoned they probably had a theme house with a bicycle bell for a door-bell. Veterans of so many cycle trips, it was pleasing to note that Mull had certainly not disappointed them.

Despite the previous day ending with a glorious sunset, the Mull weather was true to form. It was atrocious. I set myself two mini targets: to cycle the short distance across Mull's narrowest point to Salen to buy fuel for the stove and later round to Ulva to catch a boat trip to Staffa and Fingal's Cave. I had booked my Staffa trip as advised at Oban but I was now regretting the obligation I was under to cycle the seven miles to Ulva Ferry in the pouring rain.

A lugubrious Yorkshireman with his hood pulled up met me on the forecourt of his tiny petrol station in Salen. 'Fill it up,' I said, holding out my fuel bottle only at the last minute. It was a mistimed joke and he sullenly filled my fuel bottle.

It was a laborious struggle uphill into the wind, which for the first time fought against me. Only the prospect of hot tea and carrot cake from the tea-room on Ulva kept me going. A 60-second ferry crossing to Ulva and the tearoom is available on demand. It is, to say the least, the most expensive ferry crossing I have ever encountered and consequently the most expensive cup of tea. The ferry ticket does however include a visit to a thatched black house and displays on island wildlife, geology and history.

In the past Ulva and its tidal neighbour of Gometra supported 800 people who were mainly employed in kelping, i.e. obtaining sodium bicarbonate from seaweed. When the price of kelp collapsed, the islands were to be the scene of some of the most brutal forced evictions. Now only a handful of people live on the islands.

Abandoned communities and spectacular coastal rock formations can be seen all round the island from the boat on the way out to Staffa. Unfortunately, Staffa itself was nowhere to be seen, hidden under an angry mass of cloud. Beyond Ulva, the sail across the open sea was not a comfortable one, but as the boat rounded the tip of Staffa to face Fingal's Cave the weather lifted and Mendlessohn's 'Hebridean' Overture was piped over the tannoy, much to the amusement of the foreign passengers. Clichés are what we Scots do best.

As soon as Joseph Banks revealed the cave to the world at the end of the eighteenth century, literary and musical greats fell over themselves, and no doubt the basalt columns, to visit Fingal's Cave. These greats used up all the best metaphors, describing the cave as a cathedral or the columnar scenery as the pipes of an organ, so I will say no more about it. The view of the whole island from slightly further away is truly breathtaking. A visit to the island involves a tight squeeze through rocky reefs and a climb up a very steep cliff, aided by steel staircases, but a chance to get up close to the puffins is worth it.

The sun was shining strongly by the time I returned to the saddle so I enthusiastically set off northwards from Ulva. This section of coast has the fairest aspect of all Mull's seaboard. The road flows through sporadic woodland and the wild fruit and flowers return to the verges. The road is set on top of a raised beach that elevates you 100 ft above the sea. With waterfalls plunging into the sea, broadleaf woodland and lush green fields, it was a scene reminiscent of an idealised bible picture. It looked like a landscape just out of the wrapper – brand new. With the warm sun on my back it wasn't too far away from paradise.

The road, however, does not always follow a benign course and a couple of times it turns steeply up the way. The longest climb past Burg was tempered only by the cottage named 'Burg Bear'. It must belong to people from Furth of Mull as locals would insist on a sensible Gaelic name that would translate to white house or something like that.

With a swish and swoosh from the high point I was overlooking the idyllic Calgary Bay. Some would say it is the finest beach on all of Mull or perhaps even the west of Scotland. Seeing it on a beautiful day, I couldn't disagree. It is a sandy bay with a hinterland of extensive machair sheltered from the open sea by a volcanic dyke. Calgary, Mull, did indeed give its name to the Canadian city but no more than a couple of houses and an ancient graveyard make up the original.

I wanted to get to Tobermory, Mull's capital, but I couldn't go on. I sat on the perfect green and apparently sensitive machair not quite knowing how to fully take in the beauty of such a spot in a short space of time. Rushing on went against the grain, so to resolve my anguish I stayed. A small area has been set aside for camping in an attempt to persuade people not to camp on the machair. It seems to be working.

It was not an altogether undisturbed night. A group of campers sat themselves on the highest point of the machair hoping to spot whales. Inevitably they did. 'Whales, whales, whales in the bay!' This would make up for not seeing anything other than the commonplace up until now. A whale sighting just seemed so apt in this little idyll, no doubt these intelligent beasts appreciated Calgary's charms. So, with a T-shirt on inside out and untied shoelaces I stumbled up to the viewpoint. Blurry eyes were pointed out to the end of the bay where waves were breaking over rocks. Lots of theories were espoused as to why they weren't moving. They weren't moving because they weren't whales. I left the still-insisting hoaxers and returned to bed. Perhaps this was the first recorded incidence of 'crying whale'.

The next morning heavy moist air that would spontaneously burst into rain was sitting down on Calgary. Reluctantly I sat my dry bottom onto a wet saddle. The day was either reflecting or inducing my mood and it was a disinclined cyclist that set off that morning. Even the grass and flowers were lolling about, heavy with damp.

Dervaig was the first village and supply post I had encountered en route since the post office at Pennyghael. I had passed there on a Sunday and it was therefore shut. This was now Wednesday. Dervaig has to be the wettest-looking village in all creation. It is built in a bog. Thank God there are no mosquitoes at this latitude. Mind you, the Dervaig midge has a ferocious reputation.

On the inside, Dervaig is a pretty, quintessentially Hebridean village. Each side of the main street is neatly lined by low whitewashed cottages. The film-location people obviously don't know about Dervaig or they would have shot something here – or maybe they have.

The local shop and post office specialises in food of the frozen, vacuum-packed or dried variety. This was not really surprising but not quite what I was hoping to get my teeth into so I left with a multi-pack of crisps. It was too early for the cosy and atmospheric Bellachroy Hotel or for 'Coffee and Books'.

The Old Byre Heritage Centre, about half a mile up a hill and down a hill out of Dervaig was open. It is a self-confessed Aladdin's Cave. The only difference is, Aladdin found something he wanted. The shop must hold a record for the twee. Everything from deerstalkers to thistle-adorned ashtrays. I am sure the *Sunday Post* was on sale despite it being a

Wednesday. The atmosphere inside was thick with the smell of those perfumed wood shavings, incomprehensibly named potpourri.

I purchased my ticket for the film show but declined the invitation to wait in the tea room as my taste buds were so tainted with the perfume of potpourri that not even smoky-bacon crisps could get rid of the taste. The film show is excellent for those weary of reading labels attached to display cabinets. It covers the history, flora and fauna of Mull. Narrated by Nick Heskith, it is very well done. The film was, as it boasted, an excellent introduction to Mull. Pity I was only hours away from departing the island for Ardnamurchan.

From the film I learned that the road to Tobermory was constructed to enable the lame daughter of a local laird to ride her pony and trap. The grade is even and has ameliorated the climb as much as is possible but, jings, the top was a long time coming. The whole way up I was trying to guess the line of the road. I knew where I hoped it would go but a passing car confirmed my worst fears. Don't be fooled by the viewpoint – it's by no means the top.

Up to this point I had found myself at odds with the curmudgeon Johnson, but when he describes the journey from Tobermory as 'a most dolorous journey', I feel I have to add that the journey to Tobermory is equally dolorous. My objectivity was seeping away with the dye from my clothes. Some form of human rusting seemed possible. I am sure the journey across this featureless tract has its merits. There were attractive sections through mature deciduous woodland and an intriguing graveyard. Two climbs in succession did nothing for my spirits and the downhills that followed only served to let the rain penetrate to my skin bullet style. I am sure it can be beautiful on a good day!

Newdale Campsite heralds the outskirts of Tobermory. You may choose to stay here but believe me, if you descend to Tobermory by bike there will be no question of you cycling back up. The road into Tobermory is long and steep.

Tobermory is definitely a great port in a storm. An influx of sailors hasn't traditionally stimulated the kind of trade that a town would want, but the crews of the hundred or so pleasure yachts that are regularly anchored in the harbour have led to the opening up of upmarket restaurants, speciality food stores, a designer-chocolate maker and shops for artisans of every craft. Oysters and speciality breads are the order of the day.

Tobermory was bustling and vibrant even on this wet day. The bright colours of the harbour buildings that make Tobermory instantly recognisable on pictorial calendars were undimmed. It was good to be somewhere and my mood began to lift.

The hordes of sailors seemed to be glad of the bad weather. For these seagoing parrots it meant they could continue wearing their colourful waterproofs so relieving themselves of the need to talk in loud voices about their big boat in the bay. Unfortunately for cyclists, the Lycra gear that many prefer must be worn in the company of a bike, otherwise it sends out an altogether different message – one that sailors of old might have preferred.

Historically, though, Tobermory's reputation was for boats sinking rather than boats floating. A ship believed to be the treasure ship *Florencia* of the Spanish Armada found itself in Tobermory after the defeat by Raleigh. The ship was mysteriously blown up while at anchor. Efforts to find the treasure of mythical proportions have at times been on a par with those to detect the Loch Ness Monster. Disappointingly, the ship has been identified as the more mundane *San Juan de Sicilia* with no treasure on board. Exhibits detailing this wreck and the numerous others around Mull's coast are to be found in the homely Tobermory Museum – a good place to spend an hour out of the rain.

It was a silent and uneventful crossing of the Sound of Mull to Kilchoan, the thick mist deadening the senses. An eerie silhouette slowly came into focus as the mean-looking Mingary Castle, an imposing and battle-worn fastness that stands guard over Loch Sunart and the Sound, a chilling welcome to Ardnamurchan.

Dry land is in short supply at Kilchoan. The sea comes up to its high watermark and stays lying in pools on the exposed peat. Low white houses are scattered over hillsides on probably the only available patches of terra firma. There isn't a cosy corner anywhere. The damp chill pushed me on.

The road that for most of its length hugs the shore of Loch Sunart is forced high to avoid Ben Hiant. The pain of reaching the 600 ft-summit of the pass was not as bad as I'd feared. It was a relatively gentle climb and there are level sections on which to recover. Over the trip I made several notes to myself about the loneliness of various roads but none were more so than this road. It was almost possible to believe that I was in a post-car era. I fantasised about some great petroleum shortage and that the day of the car was over, for it would be possible not to hear about it out on the westernmost fringes of the British mainland.

High above Loch Mudle in the midst of an almost tundra-like landscape a stag blocked my way. He eyed me confidently. Would he let me pass? Our stand-off lasted a few minutes before he then stepped aside, nonchalantly flicking his head like an Italian customs officer, as if to say, 'Hurry up, before I change my mind!'

Despite the gradual nature of the climb the miles were not clicking by very quickly. An age seemed to pass between mileposts. However, this was all about to change, as miles of uninterrupted descent stretched before me. Before my freewheel ended I had doubled my distance from Kilchoan.

The Sunart Oakwoods that line the banks of the loch took me by surprise. I wasn't expecting such magnificent and extensive woodlands. These stately trees civilised what had been, up to now, a wild journey. All along the road there was evidence of human habitation. Driveways led off to unseen houses and cats sat on top of gateposts, but people were strangely absent. The privacy and seclusion offered by these woods is obviously the attraction. A series of signs placed along the side of the road warned trespassers of unspecified consequences. These signs gave way to one that advertised an establishment for young people. Was this the unspecified consequence?

The road along the shore slipped into that familiar pattern of headland followed by bay. I tried hard to build up enough momentum to carry me up the next rise but somehow the hill I had to climb was always bigger than the one just descended. Sod's Law. However, the last vestiges of my earlier grumpiness were dissipated in the continuous green corridor.

I found the scenery very similar to that to be found on the western seaboard of Canada where the trees come right down to the water's edge with lots of little rocky inlets and islets peppering the shore. The hamlet of Salen only added to this impression and it wouldn't surprise me if this is what some people had in mind when they built their wooden chalets. I scanned the bay for a seaplane, as it would have completed the scene.

I thought perhaps I might have some company for my final day. Two cyclists prepared to leave the campsite at Resipole just as I was about to. They were the first cyclists I had encountered since returning to the mainland. Unfortunately they had targets to meet. They synchronised their cycle computers and set off without me.

Maybe it was just as well I was on my own for I stopped half an hour later in the little mining village of Strontian. Strontian is up there with the likes of Berkeley, California, and France as it also has an element named after it. The radioactive element, Strontium, was discovered here by Humphry Davy and is used in fireworks to produce lilac flames, so it isn't exactly a valuable commodity.

The village, with its leafy village green, has a very English air, indeed so much so that the hamlet up the hill was called Scotstown to counteract this very impression. Strenuous efforts have been made to spark some life and commerce into this moribund Highland village. As a result it is a well-appointed little place and a good choice for a meal stop or an overnight.

Inspecting the map I noticed very steep climbs between me and any mine workings, so I decided to enquire at the tourist information if there was anything up there worth seeing – after all, an element was discovered there. The assistant agreed there were mines in the area but if it was aggregate I was after then I should speak to the local quarrier. I had just thought there might be some attempt to exploit a link with the element that the village provided with a moniker.

Beyond Strontian the hills are awesomely bare and I shivered at the thought of losing the comfort of the Oakwoods. I was sorry to be leaving Loch Sunart behind, not only because I would miss its soothing beauty but also because the road turned viciously uphill. I could have avoided the incline by continuing straight on just beyond Strontian, taking a longer route via Glensanda, but I opted for the shorter, hillier option.

I am sure that either the earth was tilting on its axis away from me or some tectonic activity was growing the hill as I climbed. Twice it beat me and I got off and pushed – or rather fell off. The speedometer read 4 mph when I was cycling and 3.5 mph when I was walking so there wasn't much in it. If a car passed I pretended to be looking for a fault.

The high land was bereft of landmarks, save for a road junction. A signpost gave distances to places that were probably no more than a building or two. It was one of the rare occasions on the whole trip when I couldn't see the sea as I was surrounded by low rolling hills.

A long satisfying descent along the pleasantly wooded River Aline deposited me at Loch Aline. Without breaking I rolled straight onto the waiting ferry. The door closed immediately behind me, the way Batman's cave does when he returns from a mission. I had brought my trip unconsciously to an end and all that remained was the short cycle to Craignure for the return ferry to Oban.

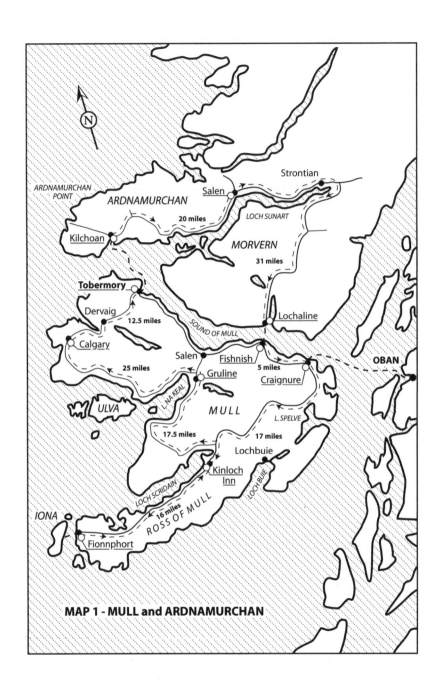

MAP 1 - MULL and ARDNAMURCHAN

Distance: 160 miles

Maps: OS *Landranger* Series (1:50,000), sheets 40, 47, 48, 49, 50. OS *Road Map 2: Western Scotland and Western Isles.*

Banks/Cashpoints: Tobermory, Mull. Credit Card acceptance is patchy so it's best to carry cash and chequebook. Cashback at Spar supermarkets.

Cycle Repair: Oban Cycles, 29 Lochside Street, Oban (01631 566 996); On Yer Bike, Salen (01680 812 337), 2.5 miles detour from Gruline, Loch na Keal; Brown's, 21 Main Street, Tobermory (01688 302 020).

General Stores: Craignure, Kinloch, Bunessan, Fionnphort, Iona, Salen (Mull), Dervaig, Tobermory, Salen (mainland), Strontian, Lochaline.

Traffic: Traffic is mainly light on all roads on Mull and Ardnamurchan. Roads are busiest around the departure/arrival times of ferries. The Craignure to Iona road is probably the busiest, especially in August.

GETTING THERE

Train: Glasgow Queen Street Station to Oban. Journey time is three hours. Each train typically carries six bicycles. Spaces are normally in high demand.

Ferry: Calmac Island Hopscotch. Tickets 6 and 21 cover all ferries en route except the Iona Ferry. Oban to Craignure, Mull – typically 6 ferries per day; journey time is 45 minutes.

ACCOMMODATION

Oban (01631–)

Hotels and B&Bs: Caledonian Hotel, Station Square (–563133); Greencourt Guest House, Benvoulin Lane (–563987); Highcliff Guest House, Glencruithin Road (–565809); Hawthornbank, Dalriach Road (–562401).

Hostels: Oban SYHA, Esplanade (–562025); Jeremy Inglis, 21 Airds

Crescent (–565065); Oban Backpackers, Breadalbane Street (–562107); Waterfront Lodge, 1 Victoria Crescent, Corran Esplanade (–565605).

Campsite: Oban Divers Caravan Park, Glenshellach Road, Oban, one-and-a-half miles from Oban (–562755).

ROUTE INFORMATION

CRAIGNURE TO PENNYGHAEL (17 MILES)

From ferry turn left following A849 out of Craignure. Follow the A849 all the way to Pennyghael.

Terrain: Short steep hill out of Craignure. Level for a time before climbing moderately over Glen More. Long descent to Pennyghael.

Detours: Loch Buie. Turn left six miles out of Craignure signed Loch Buie, 8 miles. Ruined Moy Castle, standing stones, sandy bay, unofficial campsite, post office.

ACCOMMODATION

Craignure (01680–)

Hotels and B&Bs: Craignure Inn (–812305); Chronicle (–812145); Dee-Em (–812440).

Camping: Sheiling Holidays Campsite, 800 metres from the pier (–812496).

Pennyghael (01681–)

Hotels: Kinloch Hotel (–704204); Pennyghael Hotel (–704288).

WATCH OUT FOR!

Torosay Castle. Victorian house and Japanese Garden reached by narrow gauge railway from Craignure.

Duart Castle. Seat of the Clan MacLean, local history and MacLean family history. Turn left one mile from Craignure and then follow road for one-and-a-half miles.

Dugald MacPhail Monument. Monument to local bard. Above turning for Loch Buie.

PENNYGHAEL TO FIONNPHORT AND IONA (16 MILES)

Continue to follow A849 west.

Ferry: Fionnphort, Mull, to Iona – regular ferries from 08:45 until 18:15. Journey time: 15 minutes.

Terrain: Road repeatedly rises and falls. Short and steep at times.

ACCOMMODATION
Bunessan (01681–)
Hotels and B&Bs: Argyll Arms Hotel (–700240); Mrs Helen Leplar (–700471).
Fionnphort (01681–)
Hotels and B&Bs: John Nodding's Seaview (–700235); Achaban House (–700649); Staffa House (–700677).
Camping: Fidden – one mile south of Fionnphort.
Iona (01681–)
Hotels and B&Bs: Argyll Hotel (–700334); Martyrs' Bay (–700357); Bishop's House (–700800).
Hostels: Iona Hostel (–700781).
Camping: Wild camping is tolerated but ask permission first.

WATCH OUT FOR!
Cairn to Mary MacDonald, composer of 'Child in a Manger'. Just as you enter Bunessan.
The Ross of Mull Historical Museum, Bunessan. A small museum that specialises in local genealogy.
The Columba Centre, Fionnphort. Museum dedicated to the life and work of Columba.
Erraid. Tidal island one-and-a-half miles south of Fionnphort, features in Robert Louis Stevenson's *Kidnapped*. Visitors and guests welcomed by the Findhorn Foundation.
On Iona there is the ruined nunnery and the abbey itself.
Staffa and Fingal's Cave tours run from Iona (freephone 0800 783 8470).

PENNYGHAEL TO GRULINE (17.5 MILES)
Take left onto the B8035 at the head of Loch Scridain.

Terrain: long moderate climb followed by exhilarating downhill to Loch na Keal. Very easy cycling to Gruline.

ACCOMMODATION
Gruline (01680–)
Hotels and B&Bs: Gruline Home Farm (–300581); Barn Cottages and Stables (–300451); (at Salen, two-and-a-half mile detour from Gruline) Aros View (–300372); Dunvegan Cottage (–300387); Duntulm (–300513).
Camping: Basic campsite at Killiechronan.

WATCH OUT FOR!
NTS site at Burg. Turn left, signposted for car park at Tioran. Features such as caves and fossilised trees can only be visited on foot.
MacQuarrie Mausoleum. Signposted in Gruline. Burial place of the 'Father of Australia'.

GRULINE TO CALGARY (25 MILES)

At junction take B8073 for Ulva Ferry and follow B8073 up Mull's west coast.

Terrain: Gentle to begin with. Short moderate climb at end of Loch. Fast descent past turning for Ulva Ferry. Undulates for five miles which is followed by a long climb – very steep in places. Fast descent to Calgary.

ACCOMMODATION

Hotels and B&Bs: Calgary Hotel (01688 400 256)
Camping: Small unofficial campsite at Calgary Bay. Wild camping is tolerated on Ulva; be prepared for the midges though.

WATCH OUT FOR!

Turn left at school for Ulva Ferry, signposted. Small ferry takes you over to Ulva. On Ulva there is a tearoom and a visitor centre that concentrates on the island's flora, fauna and heritage. Sheila's Cottage is a restored thatched cottage which tells more of Ulva's history. All included in the ferry ticket.

Staffa Visit. Boats leave from Ulva Ferry for Staffa and Fingal's Cave. Turus Mara run tours daily (freephone 0800 85 87 86). Tickets can also be purchased on the pier at Oban.

Eas Fors Waterfall plunging into the sea two miles beyond Ulva Ferry; take extreme care.

Kilninian Church, on the downhill beyond Torloisk, has a carved Celtic Cross in the vestry.

CALGARY TO TOBERMORY (12.5 MILES)

From Calgary Bay continue to follow the B8073 through Dervaig and all the way into Tobermory. At roundabout turn left for Tobermory.

Terrain: Relatively short steep climb away from Calgary then easy into Dervaig. Between Dervaig and Tobermory there are two long climbs to be overcome but these are fairly well graded. The descents are steep with some difficult corners.

ACCOMMODATION

Dervaig (01688–)
Hotels and B&Bs: Bellachroy Hotel (–400296); Inishkea (–400296); Mrs B. Robertson (–400239).
Tobermory (01688–)
Hotels and B&Bs: Mishnish Hotel, Main Street (–302009); Tobermory Hotel, Main Street (–302044); Failte, Main Street (–302495); Ivybank, Argyll Terrace (–302250).
Hostels: Tobermory SYHA, Main Street (–302481).

Camping: Newdale, on the road from Dervaig one-and-a-half miles from Tobermory.

WATCH OUT FOR!

Old Byre Heritage Centre. Tearoom and Scottish ephemera gift shop. Film show provides a very good overview of Mull.

Mull Little Theatre, Dervaig. Impressive range of performances and is also the world's smallest professional theatre.

Kilmore Parish Church with its pencil shaped steeple.

Isle of Mull Distillery, Tobermory. Guided tours and tastings from Easter to October (01688 302 645).

Isle of Mull Museum, Main Street, Tobermory, will fill you in on Boswell and Johnson's visit to Mull and Mull's many shipwrecks.

TOBERMORY TO KILCHOAN TO SALEN (20 MILES)

Ferry: Tobermory, Mull to Kilchoan, Ardnamurchan – six or seven ferries daily. Journey time is 35 minutes.

From Mingarry pier follow short road to junction, turn right and follow the B8007 all the way to Salen.

Terrain: Climb in three stages, moderate mostly from Kilchoan, followed by a very long downhill. From then on the road undulates, with some short but stiff ascents. Away from the lochside the country is desolate.

Detour: Ardnamurchan Point – the most westerly point on the British Mainland – can be reached by following the road west through Kilchoan. The journey of seven miles, one way, is, to say the least, tough going. At the point there is a lighthouse with an associated tearoom and visitor centre. There is also a whale watching platform.

ACCOMMODATION

Kilchoan (01972–)

Hotels and B&Bs: Sonachan Hotel (three miles west of Kilchoan) (–510211); Dorlinn House (–510209); Kilchoan Hotel (–510200).

Camping: Sonachan Hotel and the Kilchoan Hotel allow camping. There are showers available at the community centre at the pier for £1.

Glenborrodale (13 miles from Kilchoan)

Hotels and B&Bs: Mrs E.B. Kershaw, Cala Darach (01972 500204).

Salen (01967–)

Hotels and B&Bs: Salen Inn (–431661); Duncraig House (–431326).

Camping: Resipole Caravan Park, one mile from Salen on the way to Strontian (–431235).

WATCH OUT FOR!

Camus nan Geall, eight miles from Kilchoan, is a beautiful bay way below the road. Descend to view chambered cairns and ruined houses.

Glenmore Natural History Centre – ten miles from Kilchoan – will tell you everything you need to know about Ardnamurchan's flora, fauna and geology; there is also a tearoom and bookshop.

SALEN TO LOCHALINE (31 MILES)

At junction with A861 at the Salen Inn, turn right and continue to follow lochside. One-and-a-half miles out of Strontian turn right onto A884, follow A884 all the way to Lochaline. Alternatively you could continue on the A861 at the end of Loch Sunart for another six miles, turning right onto B8043. Follow the B8043 for a further 13 miles to the junction with A884 turn left for Lochaline – this is longer but it means gentler climbs.

Terrain: Fairly easy going to the head of Loch Sunart and for the short distance along the opposite shore. The climb away from Loch Sunart is long and tough. You retain high ground for a while before a long descent. Hill eventually peters out with just a couple of small climbs before entering Lochaline on the downhill.

ACCOMMODATION

Strontian (01967–)
Hotels and B&Bs: The Strontian Hotel (–402029); Ben View Hotel (–402333); Craig-na-Shee (–402051).
Lochaline (01967–)
Hotels and B&Bs: Lochaline Hotel (–421657).
Hostels: Dive Centre (–421627).

FISHNISH TO CRAIGNURE (5 MILES)

Ferry: Lochaline, Ardgour to Fishnish, Mull – frequent ferries daily. Journey time is 15 minutes.

A884 continues a short distance away from the pier to a junction with the A849 turn left for Craignure.

Terrain: Climb to junction. Level or slightly downhill into Craignure.

2

SHORTBREAD
PERTHSHIRE IN THE FALL

Tension and excitement – in that order – were working away inside me. Tension because I feared that this trip would not live up to my expectations and excitement because I hoped it would. Autumn didn't know it but it just had to have arrived: I was here to immerse myself in the colours and scents of the season and nothing less would do.

Perthshire is tree-county and it has a tree pedigree. It has old trees, tall trees and fat trees including the superlative in each of these categories, and essentially it has lots of them, especially of the deciduous variety.

Hugh, my companion for a couple of days at least, cleared inches of fallen chestnut leaves from the bench on which he was going to prepare lunch. I didn't see the need to carry all of the paraphernalia necessary to make impromptu refreshment possible but Hugh insisted and he was rather heroically carrying the lot. Now, amongst the almost-buried headstones of Tibbermore churchyard, I was most appreciative. I scuffed through great drifts of chestnut leaves with a mug of tea in hand, uncovering carving of supreme quality and the double-barrelled names of those of breeding. Crests and titles were carefully chiselled to ensure distinctions of class survived after death.

If I were to associate adjectives with Perthshire, they would be 'aloof' and 'quality'. Our starting point of Perth has always had a high opinion of itself. An ancient stalwart of sandstone edifices and locus for deeds of great gravitas, kings were crowned at nearby Scone; and in St John's Kirk, John

Knox sermonised on idolatry and incited a wave of riotous vandalism on Scotland's churches and abbeys. Today Perth is where you'd come to buy a posh car – and there are plenty of them in and out of the showrooms – therefore it was with some relief that we left Perth for its hinterland.

The chestnut trees that had deposited their leaves on the churchyard were looking awfully bare. Had I mistimed it? Was I too late? Hugh had no such worries and set out to provide a running commentary of our journey. Perthshire embodies the popular image of Scotland: castles, fearsome clans, ruthless chiefs, outlaws, whisky, mountains, moor, lochs and glens. Perthshire has it all. With so much material on offer many a scribbler has burst into romantic verse and the Perthshire effect worked its magic on Hugh. He lifted each hand in turn from his bike, gesturing to the surrounding scene of 'yonder hills' and 'bonnie braes'. In truth it was a murky day; scrawny hedges kept us from fallow fields and the hills were invisible.

The road wound back and forth and rose up and down enough to keep us interested and keep Hugh poetic. Substantial well-kept homes lined the way and gave Hugh the idea of knocking on doors to ask to see around for the purposes of research. Cycling 'through the keyhole' was not what I had in mind.

The tea was having its usual effect on Hugh and it was with unseemly haste that we made our way into Crieff. Abandoned by Hugh in the town square, a tableau attached to the outside wall of the Drummond Arms caught my attention. The scene depicted is the final meeting of Bonnie Prince Charlie's war council, the fire is roaring and the light is low. I couldn't wait to go inside and put my ear to the wall to strain for the raised voice of Lord George Murray that would have been absorbed into the walls with the rising smoke. He would have been shouting down the Young Pretender's sycophantic advisers, Sheridan and O'Sullivan, the two Irish 'idiots' who persuaded the prince to fight it out on Culloden Moor.

A yell shook me from my trance: 'Ah'm no' payin' 30p for a pee!' With that Hugh mounted his bike and shot off downhill, no doubt in search of cheaper facilities. There was nothing else for it but to follow. In the past I have spent most of a day searching for a companion searching for me.

Crieff struck me as a bustling little town with much to commend it. Indeed it has always been busy. Up until the nineteenth century it was busy with cows on their annual holiday from the Highlands – well that's what they told them anyway, when really they were on their way to the market at Falkirk. It looks like a well-established market town, though most of the buildings date from the nineteenth century, the Drummond Arms included, as the town was razed to the ground after the Jacobite rebellion.

Having retrieved Hugh from the entirely wrong direction, I set off with him on the back road to Comrie. Every local we asked of the road's whereabouts denied its existence and pointed us to the A85, which is probably why the road was so peaceful. It was obvious really, right, just over the Earn.

Things were looking up. The murk cleared to reveal a sky of deep blue and the mountains stood out, while a windsock collapsed lazily against its staff. In contrast to the churchyard at Tibbermore the trees surrounding Crieff were still in full leaf but there was just a hint of autumn – a hopeful sign.

Ahead spurs of land grew out of rocky hillsides to interlock in the glen, no doubt pushing the road and the river this way and that. It was a scene redolent of the classic landscapes that hang in city art galleries. All that was missing was a well-placed stag.

It wasn't the accepted Monarch of the Glen that was apparent as we approached Comrie. An old gentleman, sensing our curiosity, informed us that the monument that sat on top of the high island outcrop was to Lord Melville, chief minister in Scotland under William Pitt the Younger and regarded as the 'uncrowned King of Scotland'. It was apparently erected by the staff that loved him. Aye! I can just see them handing over part of their wages to the man paying their wages. The old gentleman went on to point out other landmarks, notably Ben-y-hone, describing it as the highest mountain in the area. He seemed to express genuine disbelief when we both said that we had climbed it. It surprised us to hear it described in such a way when there are many higher hills only a few miles away but out of sight, but then they would be none of his concern.

You could be forgiven for thinking that the town of Comrie was a solid and sturdy place. The two spires that reach into the sky from the flood plain of the River Earn would certainly indicate that Comrie folk are at least solid God-fearing citizens. Instead, however, Comrie is known as the 'Shakey Toun'. Why? Well Comrie at one time experienced more earth tremors than anywhere else in the British Isles. The Comrie Pioneers, as they were called, notably Peter McFarlane the postmaster, set about measuring the quakes; that's when the post office really did provide a service!

The ivy-clad Royal Hotel could, I suppose, market itself as the ultimate honeymoon destination with that genuine earth-moving experience to get your marriage off on the right foot. Although, looking at Comrie, that would be far too tacky and gimmicky a marketing campaign. It is a sober little place of family businesses set in sandstone frontages. The exception is a traditional ironmongers and general store (next to the Royal Hotel) which occupies a Charles Rennie Mackintosh building built in the early twentieth century.

Nearby is Cultybraggan, a former PoW Camp. Housing 4,000 fanatical

Nazis it was the second most important camp in the UK. It may have been a deliberate ploy to set the camp in the wooded hills that surround Comrie to remind the Germans of Bavaria's Black Forest and to deter them from escaping. I certainly wouldn't have been digging any tunnels back to the front.

Just out of Comrie, there was no doubting that it was autumn. Russets, auburns, golds, reds and browns, it was a veritable colour chart of the season. My tyres made a pleasant wisping sound as they travelled over wet leaves tattooed to the road. Wisp, wisp, wisp. Branches hung low over us and the tarmac was red with fallen sycamore leaves then gold with birch leaves and always fringed with a thin layer of larch needles. It was 360 degrees of colour. The smell of decay was pervasive but was peculiarly invigorating, along with the wafts of wood smoke that percolated the trees, as the big houses were made habitable for the mid-term holiday.

Our journey with autumn continued all along the south side of Loch Earn. Only when the road climbed at the western end of the loch did we leave the woods behind to look down on Edinample Castle and Lochearnhead. The castle is a fairytale edifice of pepper-pot turrets and perfectly whitewashed walls but it was no fairy that built it. Black Duncan Campbell built it to protect his developing Breadalbane Empire, obtained of course by dubious means. For instance, he attempted to poison his cousin, the earl of Argyll, and was implicated in a couple of murders at least but he kept in with the king so he had nothing to fear. Incidentally he also had a reputation as a great conservator and tree planter.

From above Edinample we could see all the way up Glen Ogle, which until recently was impassable to the sane life-loving cyclist, because the A85 is narrow, twisting and busy in this section. Fortunately SUSTRANS have constructed a cycle path using the track bed of the old Glasgow to Oban line. We could see the line of the path but not the way up to it.

We had to ask a couple of local lads in Lochearnhead the way. They pointed to an anonymous and unsigned lane by the side of the church. The incline started off OK but, although the upper reaches were coated in beautiful black tarmac, it became pathological. It was at least half a mile of near vertical cycling.

It was worth it. The cycle up Glen Ogle was smooth and traffic free. The best description of gliding silently and unhindered high above the haulage on the A85 is to think of it as an out-of-body experience. Real life was down on the twisted A85 and only the crunching gear changes made it to our ears as the lorries coughed their way up the hill.

The sky was greying and the light was fading fast but there was no need to worry as the cycle path carried us all the way to Killin. Once we had left the railway path, the ride into Killin could only be described as the nearest thing to skiing on a bike. Fast bends and blind crests swept us effortlessly to within earshot of the roaring Falls of Dochart at the very heart of Killin.

The darkening skies didn't bring the promised rain. Hugh prepared a satisfying meal, which we ate, al fresco, by torchlight in the public park. Local kids obviously thought this too odd and too scary, so there weren't the expected shouts of derision. Before the trip Hugh and I came to a compromise: I got my way on staying in the B&B and he got his way with the eating arrangements. Still, it was a reluctant and protesting Hugh that stayed indoors that night.

Breakfast is the best bit about staying in a B&B. I am sure it was a Frenchman who once said that the only way to avoid starving in Britain was to eat breakfast three times a day. There was, however, no chance of me starving on just the one. Outside the rain was hammering down, inside limitless toast was being served and Hugh was passing over his bacon and sausage. Oh, how I admire self-control in another!

When it came to setting off, the rain was still beating down. The postman was hunched over with his hand pulling at his ineffective hood, people ran like hell between car and shop and back again, the street lights were still on and chimney smoke filled the street, being driven down by the heavy rain – several compelling reasons for sitting it out with tea and toast.

I was not as well equipped for the rain as Hugh because I had decided that I wasn't going to do rain. Hugh had waterproof trousers and things to put over his shoes, whereas I only had a supposedly waterproof jacket – but then I had bought it abroad. Hugh, ever cheery – well, he had every reason to be – coaxed me on.

The day's eastern destination would be reached by first of all going west and so it was first left up Glen Lochay as we left Killin. The glen is signposted as a dead-end and a look at any map will seem to confirm this, but it ain't. There was a road built to service the hydro schemes that also happens to link this glen with Glen Lyon.

Glen Lochay doesn't seem to know it but first impressions count. Firstly, there is a power station, which although built of local stone still jars, with its '60s architecture that doesn't belong anywhere. Then there is the forest of steel grey transformers and electrical doo-daas. Keep the faith, for it doesn't last long and it is soon forgotten.

If the rain was getting me down it was transforming the River Lochay into a state of ecstatic exuberance. Ferocious doesn't even begin to convey the white water thundering over its cataracts. Despite the rain's best efforts, the flames of autumn colour were licking up the hillside from a green leafy heart. Every layer of the season was in evidence. On the highest slopes the trees were bare and already in their winter trance, but by the banks of the River Lochay summer was just about holding on.

Fortunately, the wind was blowing from the east and gently assisting us with the slowly climbing road; also the dead-end thing is still a bit of a secret so you are unlikely to meet much traffic. All in all, I didn't feel too bad; well, as long as Hugh wasn't telling me how dry he was.

If you find yourself at the end of the road you've gone too far. It may be that you pretended not to see the road rising to your right or dismissed it, saying, 'It can't possibly be that way!' I'm afraid it is. It is a huge climb over the Lairig nan Lunn (Pass of Staves). There should be a sign at the bottom saying 'Feel Free to Curse'. For a road that isn't really there, it's well surfaced if not well graded.

Hugh disappeared into the mist and left me to my own thoughts. One distraction was the Tour de France-style daubings on the road, such as, 'Gregor is a God'. Poor Gregor would have to climb this hill and try to remain composed and on the bike at all times; mere mortals should feel free to get off and push.

Suddenly gravity let go of me and my legs stopped hurting – I was at the top. The top may have taken a while to reach but my bike was now like one of those toy cars powered by a tightly wound elastic band and almost 30 miles of momentum-powered cycling lay ahead. The other benefit of coming this way is that it lets you enjoy just about every inch of Glen Lyon and, believe me, by the time you get to the end you'll be looking for more.

The downhill was as exhilarating as the uphill was uncomfortable. Initially it was more of a plummet than a controlled descent. An anchor to throw out or a parachute might have helped arrest my descent. Spray enveloped me so that the road became a black blur; in my ears everything was a whoosh, so much so that I was unaware that there was a Land Rover on my tail the whole way down. The driver stopped beside us on the bridge over the Lyon at Pubil and he assured me that I hadn't held him up.

In a break with tradition, it is Glen Lyon's 'West End' that has the fearsome reputation for hardmen and big dogs. According to the Gaelic poet Ossian, the legendary hardman Fian or Fingal and his 9,000 warriors lived in Glen Lyon and he tethered his hunting dogs of mythical size and ferocity to a stone that has been identified as one at Cashlie, a short distance further on from Pubil. Out of Fingal legend emerges the Campbell Clan as the descendents of the beautiful and heroic Diarmid. The Campbells of Glen Lyon are probably the most infamous of that notorious clan.

To begin with, Glen Lyon is awesomely desolate and the peaks that shape this end of the glen all top 3,000 ft so that you have to cock your head right back to catch a glimpse of their summits.

Slowly, the golden glow of birch trees and the promise of shelter came closer. Meggernie Castle, perfectly framed and kept private by surrounding trees, is perhaps one of Perthshire's most strikingly beautiful scenes. So reminiscent is the scene of Bavaria that it could be the seat of a crusading Teutonic knight. It was however the home of Mad Colin Campbell and later his great-grandson Robert Campbell. Mad Colin summarily executed 30 cattle reivers. He shot the leader and hung the rest from the trees that line the drive. He took the law into his own hands because those in Edinburgh dismissed his pleas for justice. His great-grandson, Robert, earned himself a notoriety that persists to this day. He was the Captain under whose command the Massacre of Glencoe was executed. Some say he was a convenient scapegoat in no position to refuse to carry out the order. Others detest him and the whole Campbell Clan for the treacherous deed of murdering the MacDonalds of Glencoe in their beds.

Fortunately for the cyclist, Glen Lyon remains relatively unexplored by the passing motorised tourist. Apart from being downhill, west to east that is, the road is little more than a pleasant lane. For the cyclist, it's as effortless as one of those moving pavements you get in airports and aquaria and we slid along under the protective canopy of trees, beyond which can be glimpsed the vast open hillsides of some of Scotland's highest mountains. It is a canopy of trees that also shelters the elusive red squirrel, which I have seen frequently on better days. Optimistically I decided that I had heard the throttled croak of the capercaillie and I can only hope that I will see one some day. I was happy in the knowledge that the birds that flitted before me could be crossbills, a species unique to Scotland's ancient forests, and that there may have been a pine martin sitting on a bough watching me pass.

Civilisation presents itself in the form of a tearoom-cum-post office and an art gallery at Bridge of Balgie. Hugh spied the picnic benches and he motioned to set up his mobile kitchen. I, however, through chattering teeth, insisted as firmly as I could and splodged in through the door of the tearoom. I changed into dry clothes and absorbed all the heat that the tearoom and a bowl of soup had to offer. We sat for as long as I could get away with. I sipped slowly on a cup of tea while watching for a break in the weather. Occasionally I had to glower at every soggy tourist who looked hopefully at our table, for we were clearly finished. Uncannily, just as my squat was becoming unsustainable, the rain stopped and the sky brightened. Topped up with warmth and my morale boosted by dry clothes I was ready to enjoy Glen Lyon.

The River Lyon was transformed. Instead of cold and grey it looked cool and blue in the sunlight. The sun's heat penetrated the foliage, and steam rose from every surface, lifting the must of mouldering leaves with it. Annoyingly, the road was submersed in deep pools of rainwater. It was almost impossible to get through without pedalling or overbalancing. I was now getting wet from the bottom up.

Fortingall is the full stop on wild Glen Lyon and marks a return to genteel Perthshire – and it doesn't get anymore genteel than Fortingall. Conspicuously pretty, it is chocolate box meets shortbread tin or Miss Marple meets Dr Finlay. Immaculately thatched cottages sit in splendid country gardens. Craw stepped gables merge with the sublime curves of the thatched roofs.

Hugh declared the wooden bus shelter cosy and proceeded to brew-up and cook his favourite concoction of Christmas Pudding and custard cooked in the same pan. It is a mushy mess but it imparts all the warmth and comfort of a big woolly blanket.

Again with mug in hand I peered in through the windows of the Fortingall Hotel, which is the kind of place to draw up to in a red roadster or an old Jag. The fact that it was closed was all the justification that Hugh needed for bringing his stove and I had to agree.

Fortingall has two very special claims to fame. Firstly, the oldest living thing, possibly in the world, but definitely in Europe, grows in the form of a Yew Tree within the churchyard. At over 3,000 years of age it was old by the time the Romans got here. Secondly, Pontius Pilate may have been born beneath its very branches. Pontius Pilate's father was a Roman emissary dispatched to guarantee peace with the Picts around 10 BC. Would his pregnant wife have ventured with him? Of course, she needn't have been aware she was pregnant when she left Rome, for it would have been an epic journey. Unlikely as it sounds, the legend persists. There is no doubting that Fortingall is a choice place to live and the remains of many people surround the hamlet.

Handsome homes, buildings and hedgerows burgeoning with sloe berries line the way into Aberfeldy. We crossed the Tay into Aberfeldy on General Wade's celebrated bridge. Dorothy Wordsworth didn't think much of it, probably because you can't see the river for its high sides. By the Tay is the memorial to the Black Watch, that most elite of British Army regiments, and, appropriately, the town in which the regiment first came together is orderly and regimented – even the Tay flows straighter. We chose a B&B in a street of houses standing to attention. There wasn't even so much as a bump in the continuous façade or roofline.

We were lucky to be allowed to leave the B&B after Hugh refused the fry up. This is obviously unheard of in the B&B world. I tried several times to offer him a way out of the situation but he didn't seem to get my drift. I would have eaten it.

A thick fog had settled on the town overnight. In addition I had a slightly thick head after a night with the Aberfeldy Folk Club in the basement of the Crown Hotel. Hugh and I parted company, with him disappearing to the south and me to the north. The fog at least removed the need to look back and wave.

The sun promised to break through and bring the unnaturally still landscape to life. Red rowanberries acted like cat's-eyes, showing the edges of the road. I was retracing yesterday's route into Aberfeldy for five miles so it isn't as if I hadn't seen it all before. Somehow, however, I hadn't quite noticed what was around me. I now knew that demons and dragons lived in the high wooded bluffs above Weem, but today was not the day for demon or dragon spotting. Perhaps they were watching me.

Who was watching out for me? The fog was dense and muffled the sound of approaching vehicles, making it difficult for me to detect where they were coming from. Only a donkey could be heard persistently ee-awing in the gloom.

Beyond Coshieville and the turning for Glen Lyon the road slowly climbed and to my left a deep birch-filled gorge was developing. The birches are something of a feature in this part of the world. Robert Burns even composed a poem entitled 'The Birks of Aberfeldy'. The birch, to be blunt, is a puny tree and stature eludes it. In a group, especially when wearing its autumn strip, the birch is magnificent. The gentle shake of a breeze blowing through the branches of a birch tree is one of the most therapeutic sounds I know. The golden birch leaves by the roadside shone through the fog, dancing like fireflies in the light wind.

I emerged from the fog, reached the top shortly afterwards and turned downhill. The road I was now on was signed as unsuitable for lorries and cars towing caravans. However, there was nothing untoward about the road that skirts the beautifully conical Schiehallion. Snow poles suggest a seasonal problem, but the expected descent takes a long time to get going, indeed the road even goes back up. Why no lorries and caravans then? Well, because there's a sting in the tail, that's why. It was all I could do to keep my speed down to make it round the hairpin bends and avoid the toiling mobile bank.

Exquisite holiday homes and hunting lodges dot the lochside and the woodland. At best there is a part-time role for this area as a playground for rich leisure seekers – a Perthshire version of Martha's Vineyard, perhaps, only the big houses are surrounded by high stone walls rather than white picket fences. Fewer people are living here every year and now the area around Loch Rannoch is seriously underpopulated. Only the presence of a boarding school on the lochside makes the population credible.

When folk did live here in bigger numbers they fought with each other. The whole area around Loch Rannoch was a fermenting cauldron of bitter clan squabbles and skirmishes. Information boards all around the loch put each clan in its place like scout troops at a jamboree. There were the McGregors, the Camerons, the MacDougalls and the Stewarts, to name but a few. Although the Jacobite cause united them, they all paid dearly for their involvement in the months after Culloden. Redcoats were stationed among them in the barracks at Georgetown at the head of the loch to hunt down any returning warriors.

The cloud remained low, pushed down by the cold sinking air. It was still cold but not as cold as it had been in the fog. The road at least was completely level so I tried to keep my speed up to keep the cold out. It seemed to be working, for I was warm everywhere except for my toes, which were inside shoes still damp from the previous day's downpour. I tried to avoid looking out over the steel grey loch as it was interfering with warm thoughts. Instead I concentrated on the ever-present and much warmer colours of autumn.

The road comes to a dead end at Rannoch Station, a station that is 19 miles from Kinloch Rannoch, the community that it ostensibly serves. Many tourists come this far before they realise that Sir Harry Lauder's 'The Road to the Isles' can go 'By Tummel and Loch Rannoch' but cannot go any further than Rannoch Station. Sir Harry forgot to mention in the song the 12-mile gap. A far-from-easy walk across the desolate Rannoch Moor is required to reach the road up the west coast, which if you hitch, I suppose, will get you to the isles. It is worth bearing in mind before you set off across the Rannoch Moor that the only way they could get the railway line across the moor was to float it on a bed of brush.

Rannoch Station is a wonderful survivor from a less utilitarian age of rail travel and built in the style of a Swiss Chalet. Apparently the railway company even went as far as importing the construction materials from Switzerland. People come from all over to photograph the station signs, the architecture, the ironwork on the bridge; to marvel at the isolation and drink tea in the tearoom that admittedly tries to be evocative. I was so grateful for the mug of tea from the station tearoom, especially as I knew that had I been a day later it would have been closed for the season.

I had hoped to stay at either of the two hostels at Corrour – the next stop up the line. One had closed inexplicably and the other was not answering its phone so I thought it unwise to get the train up the line to a station with no other means of access on the off-chance that it was open. Reluctantly, I decided to head back east along the northern shore of Loch Rannoch to Kinloch Rannoch.

By the time I reached Kinloch Rannoch I had clocked up 60 miles and it was now that I was really starting to miss Hugh and his mobile kitchen. The only place to eat was the rather formal-looking Dunalastair Hotel. The hotel, along with church, both in grey granite, form a little village square that gives the village more civic stature than it deserves. The many weekend guests that pulled up in their large countrified vehicles suggested to me that tweed was *de rigeur* whereas Lycra was not.

I chickened out of dinner in the Dunalastair and headed for the Spar shop instead. Dinner consisted of marshmallowy snowballs and a hot soggy sausage roll washed down with milk and chocolate éclairs. Accommodation was the next problem. I hate to be constrained by booking in advance but there are only three B&Bs in Kinloch Rannoch. Only the one furthest away had any vacancies. When I arrived, there was still just enough light to cycle by.

With every mile towards Pitlochry some of the wild and untamed beauty of Perthshire's interior seeped away. Picnic benches with barbecue pits, caravan sites, visitor centres, nature trails and viewpoints sanitise the wild and point out the beauty for those who cannot see it for themselves.

When I reached Pitlochry I was firmly back in comfortable and genteel Perthshire. Pitlochry is unapologetically a tourist town selling Scottish trumpery by the ton to coachloads of mainly elderly tourists. The truth is, I didn't object to the change and, besides, the autumn display was at its most wonderful by the banks of the River Garry. The canopy of brown, red, yellow and gold was complete in every direction.

I didn't want to shop so I ate and drank. I felt as though I deserved to, mainly in a cosy little hostelry a mile out of Pitlochry known as the Moulin Inn. It is especially at this time of year that you can really appreciate an inn like the Moulin with its log fires and atmospheric low and smoky light.

The next morning I cycled onto Dunkeld, which is more the thinking man's tourist town, but with just as many ways to spend money as in Pitlochry, although you might get something just a little more distinctive.

From Dunkeld I watched closely to see if Birnam Wood was about to repeat its move to High Dunsinane but it didn't. Therefore, in the absence of an inauspicious occurrence, I overcame the temptation to call it quits early and catch the train back to Perth and cycled on to close the circle.

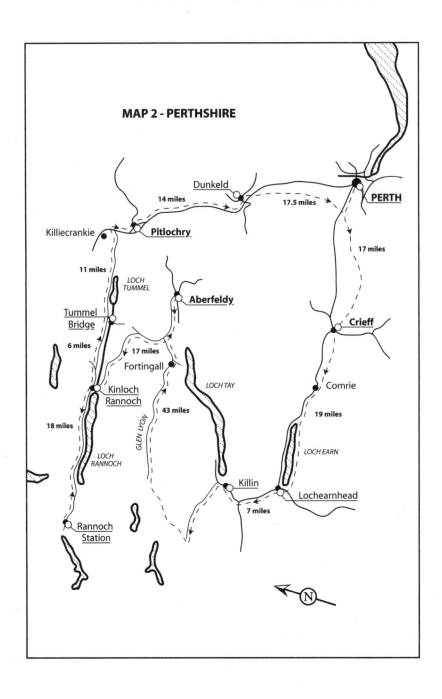

MAP 2 - PERTHSHIRE

Dunkeld

14 miles

17.5 miles

PERTH

Killiecrankie

Pitlochry

17 miles

11 miles

LOCH TUMMEL

Aberfeldy

Tummel Bridge

Crieff

6 miles

17 miles

Fortingall

LOCH TAY

Comrie

Kinloch Rannoch

GLEN LYON

43 miles

19 miles

18 miles

LOCH RANNOCH

LOCH EARN

Killin

Lochearnhead

Rannoch Station

7 miles

N

PERTHSHIRE: ESSENTIALS

Distance: 200 miles

Maps: OS *Landranger* series (1:50,000), sheets 58, 57, 42, 52. OS *Road Map 1: Northern Scotland* and *Road Map 3: Southern Scotland*.

Banks/Cashpoints: Perth, Crieff, Killin, Aberfeldy, Pitlochry, Dunkeld.

Cycle Repair: J.M. Richards, 44 George Street, Perth (01738 62 68 60); R.S. Finnie, Leadenflower Road, Crieff (01764 652 559); Escape Route, 8 West Moulin Road, Pitlochry (01796 473 859).

General Stores: Perth, Crieff, Comrie, Killin, Aberfeldy, Kinloch Rannoch, Pitlochry, Dunkeld.

Traffic: The roads in general are very quiet. From Tibbermore to Crieff you may experience slightly more traffic. In and around Perth expect busy roads; there is an intermittent cycle lane on the way out of Perth but it tends to be blocked by parked cars. Pitlochry will also be busier. Cycle paths bypass the A85 from Lochearnhead to Killin and the A9 to Dunkeld.

GETTING THERE

Train: Regular train service from Glasgow Queen Street and Edinburgh Waverly to Perth. Typically there is space for two bikes on each train. As these services continue to Inverness and Aberdeen they tend to be very busy, especially around commuter times. Journey time for Glasgow/Edinburgh to Perth is around one hour.

ROUTE INFORMATION

PERTH TO CRIEFF (17 MILES)

From Perth Railway Station. Turn left out of the station car park and after a short distance turn left again into St Andrews' Street. Follow Inner Ring Road to the right until it becomes Caledonia Road. At traffic lights at Waverly Hotel go straight over. At next set of traffic lights go straight on. At the roundabout turn right.

At next set of traffic lights turn left for Crieff A85. Follow Barrack Street to a roundabout and turn left for Crieff A85, also signed as Inverness Bankfoot Cycle Route. At each of the following roundabouts and one set of traffic lights go straight through. Go uphill past Perth College and eventually Tesco and out of Perth.

Continue past Perth Mart and once in West Huntingtower take the next left for Tibbermore and Madderty. Follow a minor road through Tibbermore and Balgowan all the way into Crieff. At T-junction in Crieff turn right onto the A85 and follow for short distance into Crieff Town Centre.

Terrain: Mostly level. Only real climb in Perth.

ACCOMMODATION

Perth (01783–)

Hotels and B&Bs: Kinnaird House, 5 Marshall Place (–628021); Park Lane Guest House, 17 Marshall Place (–637218); Station Hotel (–624141).

Camping: Cleve Caravan Park, Glasgow Road (–639521).

Crieff (01764–)

Hotels and B&Bs: Ardo House, 29–31 Burrell Street (–652825); The Comely Bank, 32 Burrell Street (–653409); Galvemore House, Galvemore Street (–655721).

Camping: Crieff Holiday Village, Turretbank (–653513).

WATCH OUT FOR!

Huntingtower Castle. The twin towers of the castle are obvious to the right of the A85 as you leave Perth. James VI was kidnapped and held here for ten months by the Earl of Ruthven in 1582.

Glenturret Distillery, Crieff (01764 656565). Scotland's oldest distillery, can be reached by following Milnab Street from Comrie Road and then following Turretbank Road across the A85. The distillery is about one-and-a-half miles from the town centre.

CRIEFF TO LOCHEARNHEAD (19 MILES)

From Crieff town centre follow signs downhill for Stirling A822. At T-junction at the bottom of the hill turn left, signed Stirling A822. Cross River Earn on substantial humpbacked bridge and turn right as soon you have crossed the bridge onto Strowan Road; follow road all the way into Comrie. Cross Earn once again and at T-junction opposite the Royal Hotel turn left onto A85, Dunira Street. Follow A85 out of Comrie. Just out of Comrie turn left over humpbacked bridge and once over bridge turn right. Follow this road to junction with A85. Turn left onto A85 and follow for about two miles. Just before entering St Fillans turn left onto South Loch Earn Road. Follow road all the way to Lochearnhead. Turn right onto A84 for short distance into village.

*Terrain:*Easy cycling in the main as far as St Fillans. Road along south side of Loch Earn undulates and is steep in places. Road climbs high towards head of loch behind Edinample. Downhill into Lochearnhead.

ACCOMMODATION
Comrie (01764–)
Hotels and B&Bs: The Royal Hotel, Melville Square (–679200); Mrs King, Vean House, Barrack Road (–670869).
Camping: West Lodge Caravan Park (–670354).
St Fillans (01764–)
Hotels and B&Bs: Mrs Ross, Earngrove Cottage (–685224); Achray Cottage (–685383); Achray House Hotel (–685231).
Lochearnhead (01567–)
Hotels and B&Bs: Lochearnhead Hotel (–830229).

WATCH OUT FOR!
Earthquake House, Comrie. Not open to the public but earthquakes are still measured here, information boards explain. For Earthquake House take the left fork once over the old bridge at Ross.

Brough and MacPherson Ironmongers, Comrie – Charles Rennie Macintosh building opposite the Royal Hotel.

LOCHEARNHEAD TO KILLIN (7 MILES) – COMPLETELY OFF-ROAD

Having turned right onto A84, after 400 yards turn left onto narrow lane, unsigned, at Scottish Episcopal Church. Follow lane which becomes a cycle path steeply uphill. You soon attain the level of the old track bed of the Oban line, now a cycle path. Follow National Cycle Network signs all the way to Killin. Emerge in Killin at the Clachaig Hotel. Cross narrow stone bridge into Killin.

Terrain: The climb up to join the cycle path is very tough indeed and you will probably have to get off and walk. Once on the cycle path it is level until you cross over the A85, from then on it is an exhilarating downhill into Killin.

ACCOMMODATION
Killin (01567–)
Hotels and B&Bs: Breadalbane House, Main Street (–820134); Fairview House, Main Street (–820667); Dall Lodge Hotel (–820217).
Hostels: Killin SYHA (–820546).

WATCH OUT FOR!
The Falls of Dochart are best viewed from the old bridge over the River Dochart in Killin.

Clan MacNab Burial Ground is on an island in the Dochart, access from bridge (key required).

Breadalbane Folklore Centre. On the far side of the bridge over the Dochart. Has St Fillan's (1,300 years old) healing stones on display.

Finlanrig Castle. Seventeenth-century ruin by Loch Tay, complete with beheading pit.

KILLIN TO ABERFELDY (43 MILES)
Continue downhill on Killin's main street. Proceed to leave Killin and just after Killin Youth Hostel turn left – signed for Moirlanich Longhouse (NTS). After a short distance turn left at T-junction. Follow Glen Lochay for six miles. Just before road runs out take easy-to-miss right uphill. If you end up in the car park you've missed it. Follow this road steeply uphill; and then downhill into Glen Lyon. Follow the whole length of Glen Lyon to Fortingall. A couple of miles beyond Fortingall at junction with B846 turn right. Follow B846 through Weem and over Wade's Bridge into Aberfeldy.

Terrain: For the length of Glen Lochay the road gently rises. It is a challenging and sustained climb over into Glen Lyon. It is, however, worth it for it is more or less downhill all the way to Aberfeldy.

ACCOMMODATION
Invervar, Fortingall and Coshieville (01887–)
Hotels and B&Bs: Invervar Lodge (–877206); Fortingall Hotel (–830367);

Fendoch, Fortingall (–830322); Coshieville Inn (–830319).
Aberfeldy (01887–)
Hotels and B&Bs: Balnearn House, Crieff Road (–820431); Ardtornish, Kenmore Street (–820629); Tigh'n Eilean (–820109).
Camping: Aberfeldy Caravan Park (–820662).

WATCH OUT FOR!

Moirlanich Longhouse (NTS). A rare example of the Scottish Longhouse by the roadside near the turn into Glen Lochay, signposted.

The Dog Stane. A two-foot high stone by the roadside near Cashlie where the mythical Fian is said to have tethered his staghounds.

Fortingall Church. Inside the church is St Adamnan's Bell. St Adamnan was St Columba's biographer and Abbot at Iona.

Fortingall Yew. The oldest living thing in Europe and possibly on Earth is adjacent to the church at Fortingall.

Carn na Marbh (Mound of the Dead), Fortingall, in the field opposite the church is a mound where plague victims were brought in the fourteenth century.

Menzies Castle (01887 820 982). Sixteenth-century 'Z'-plan castle. Open daily April to mid-October.

Old Church at Weem. Mausoleum of the Clan Menzies.

Wade's Bridge. The bridge across the Tay into Aberfeldy built in 1733 and designed by architect William Adam.

Black Watch Memorial, Aberfeldy. Marks the spot by the Tay where the famous regiment was first assembled.

Aberfeldy Water Mill (01887 820 803). See how oatmeal was milled in the nineteenth century, open daily Easter to mid-October.

Aberfeldy Distillery (01887 822 000). Free guided tours Monday–Friday.

ABERFELDY TO KINLOCH RANNOCH (17 MILES)

Leave Aberfeldy by way of Wade's Bridge and retrace the route through Weem but continue past the turning for Glen Lyon. Follow B846 to the top of the hill. Just beyond the high point take the left, signed Schiehallion Road – unsuitable for lorries and caravans. Follow minor road via the Braes of Foss to Kinloch Rannoch.

Terrain: First five miles are level then it is moderately uphill for about three miles. Trend from then on is downhill although there is the occasional rise. Beyond the Braes of Foss the road is steeply downhill with hairpin bends. Once on the valley floor it is level into Kinloch Rannoch.

ACCOMMODATION
Kinloch Rannoch (01882–)
Hotels and B&Bs: The Dunalastair Hotel (–632323); Rannoch House (–632407).

WATCH OUT FOR!
A cairn and plaque at Braes of Foss Car Park commemorates the surveys on Schiehallion that led to the first determination of Newton's Gravitational Constant in 1744.

KINLOCH RANNOCH TO RANNOCH STATION (18 MILES)
Leave Kinloch Rannoch by the way you entered. Once over the bridge take right and then right again. Follow road along south side of Loch Rannoch to Bridge of Gaur. At T-junction with B846 turn left. Follow to road end at Rannoch Station.

Terrain: Level almost the whole length of the loch. There is a small climb towards the end of the loch. It is level or gently uphill out to the station.

ACCOMMODATION
Rannoch Station
Hotels and B&Bs: Moor of Rannoch Hotel (01882 633 238).

WATCH OUT FOR!
The Clans of Rannoch Trail. Eight information panels around Loch Rannoch.
　　Rannoch Station. Isolated station that is evocative of the golden age of rail. There is a tearoom at the station.

RANNOCH STATION TO TUMMEL BRIDGE (24 MILES)
Follow B846 through Kinloch Rannoch all the way to Tummel Bridge.

Terrain: Mostly level until Dunalastair, where there is a short but very stiff climb.

ACCOMMODATION
Killichonan and Dunalastair (01882–)
Hotels and B&Bs: Talladh-a-Bheithe, on the north side of Loch Rannoch, six miles west of Kinloch Rannoch (–633203); Mr. Wilson, Garden Cottage, Dunalastair (–632434).

Tummel Bridge (01882–)
Hotels and B&Bs: Dalriach House (–634333); Mrs Ellis, Bermuda (–634277).

TUMMEL BRIDGE TO PITLOCHRY (11 MILES)

At Tummel Bridge turn left onto the B8019 signed Queen's View and Pitlochry. Follow B8019 for about ten miles to T-junction and turn right signed as B8019 Pitlochry 2 miles. Follow road under A9 and into Pitlochry.

Terrain: Road from Tummel Bridge involves constant ascent and descent. All are short and never more than moderate.

ACCOMMODATION
Strathtummel
Hotels and B&Bs: The Tummel Inn (01882 634 272).
Pitlochry (01796–)
Hotels and B&Bs: Fishers Hotel, 75–79 Atholl Road (–472000); The Poplars, 2 Lower Oakfield Road (–472129); Port-na-Craig Inn (–472777); Arrandale House, Knockfarrie Road (–472897); The Well House, 11 Toberargan Road (–472239).
Hostels: Pitlochry SYHA, Knockard Road (–472308); Pitlochry Backpackers Hotel, 134 Atholl Road (–470044).
Camping: Milton of Fonab (–472882).

WATCH OUT FOR!
Queen's View, Loch Tummel. Good view over wooded Loch Tummel associated with Queen Victoria. Visitor centre and café.

Pass of Killiecrankie and Soldier's Leap (NTS). Turn left at junction with B8079, signposted. Visitor centre contains natural history displays and features displays on the battle of 1689 at which the Jacobites defeated the government troops.

Pitlochry Power Station (01882 634 709). Exhibition, visitor centre and salmon ladder. Open daily late March to late October.

PITLOCHRY TO DUNKELD (14 MILES)

Head south on Pitlochry Main Street and once under the railway line turn right over the Alder Bridge and then turn left following NCN 7 for Logierait (4).

After steep descent into Logierait then turn left signed NCN 77. Cross the Tay, the railway line and the A9 and then take cycle path which leaves road on the bend to the right. Follow cycle path parallel with A9. Eventually you join a minor road signed for Blairgowrie.

Follow minor road to T-junction with A923. Turn right into Dunkeld.

Terrain: A few short ups and downs at first. Once on the cycle path it is easy going all the way to Dunkeld.

ACCOMMODATION

Dunkeld (01350–)

Hotels and B&Bs: Royal Dunkeld Hotel, Atholl Street (–727322); The Bridge, Bridge Street (–727068); Byways, Perth Road (–727452).

Camping: Inver Mill (–727477).

Birnam

Hotels and B&Bs: Waterbury, Murthly Terrace (01350 727 324).

WATCH OUT FOR!

Dunfallandy Stone (HS). Pictish carved stone to the right of the minor road about 200 yards beyond the A9.

Dowally Craft Centre and Café.

Dunkeld Cathedral (HS). Ruin of twelfth-century cathedral by the banks of the Tay.

Ell Shop (NTS) original 'Ell' measure on display.

The Little Houses (NTS). Twenty or so early eighteenth-century whitewashed houses owned by the NTS that give Dunkeld its particular look.

Loch of the Lowes. Scottish Wildlife Trust Reserve, two miles north-east of Dunkeld on the A923. From April to August, nesting Ospreys are the star attraction.

DUNKELD TO PERTH (17.5 MILES)

Dunkeld and Birnam Station may be a better place to stop and catch the train rather than cycling into Perth. From Dunkeld cross the Tay on Telford's fine bridge and then turn left for Birnam, Beatrix Potter Centre and Birnam Wood. Follow the cycle path signs up steps to railway station, across car park and then alongside the A9 and on to junction with B876 for Bankfoot. Join B876 and follow to Bankfoot. Just as you leave Bankfoot take right for Moneydie, Pitcairngreen and Almondbank. At each set of crossroads go straight on following the road all the way to Pitcairngreen. At Pitcairngreen turn left for Almondbank and Perth. Follow road round to the right past the village green and the hotel. Descend into Almondbank across a narrow bridge and follow road through Almondbank to T-junction with A85. Turn left for Perth. Follow A85 into Perth. From Huntingtower Castle onwards retrace outward route.

There is a pavement that runs along the A85 which you may feel happier pushing your bike along into Perth. There is also a cycle route which enables you to skip the section of the A85 to Huntingtower Castle.

It is, however, not well signposted and very muddy in places. Basically you turn left onto College Mill Road before crossing the narrow bridge at Almondbank; this leads you over a footbridge past a MoD establishment and onto a muddy lane and into a housing estate from where you go to the left to emerge onto the A85 at the castle.

Terrain: Road crosses undulating countryside. Some of the climbs are stiff.

ACCOMMODATION
Bankfoot
Hotels and B&Bs: Kayrene, Cairneyhill Road (01738 787 338).

WATCH OUT FOR!
Beatrix Potter Exhibition, Birnam (01350 727 272). Beatrix Potter holidayed in this part of the world and wrote the *Peter Rabbit* stories while she was here.

Perthshire Visitor Centre and Macbeth Experience, Bankfoot. Exploits the links between Shakespeare's play and the locality. The exhibition tries to show the real Macbeth.

3

THE ENGLISH
EAST LOTHIAN AND SCOTTISH BORDERS

A wet and windy winter had suddenly come to an end and the final days of March truly resembled spring, so I took my cue and set off from Edinburgh on a tour of the Scottish border country. By mid-morning I had reached the East Lothian coast and was enjoying a gentle introduction to the new cycling season. My legs very much appreciated the level terrain and the gentle wind at my back, but my bum was struggling to find a comfortable fit. Hmm . . . perhaps the saddle had shrunk!

The sun hadn't been shining that long, a few hours in fact, but it had already affected some people in the head. A group of misguided unfortunates were now making their way across the road before me to the beach, showing far too much winter-white flesh and clutching cool boxes, deck chairs, bats and balls, barbecues and other beach paraphernalia. Scots – I knew for sure they were Scots – feel that they have to enjoy the sun while they can and sometimes behave irrationally. However, the air was filled with the heady scents of salt water and pine and so evocative was it of childhood holidays that I nearly dismounted and joined the madness.

Golfers were also out in force, enjoying the first rays of spring, and I could hear the thwack of golf clubs from behind the pine trees that secure the precious links.

Occasionally I caught glimpses of golfers in their sensible woolly jumpers and I am in no doubt that it is this superior thermostatic control that leads these people, and not the premature sunbathers, to be the wielders of power and influence as well as of their clubs.

There are few places as well suited to golf as East Lothian and some of the oldest and finest courses in the world are to be found along the coast. The sandy machairs may provide the playing surface but it is East Lothian's already genteel tenor that puts the ball in the hole for these, the poshest of golfers.

I had made good progress since leaving Edinburgh behind. I skipped effortlessly through Musselburgh and Prestonpans, the venue for an early victory for the Jacobites in 1745. The charming little fishing port of Port Seton with its red pan-tiled cottages and picturesque harbour deserved more time but the easy cycling was addictive and it was too early to stop and eat.

At Longniddry I headed inland for Haddington, swapping sandy beaches for ploughed fields and dank cuttings as I was following a disused railway line. The engineers that laid these old railways didn't foresee their use by scenery-seeking cycle tourists. Out in the open I was travelling across a giant chessboard of fields of freshly tilled rusty red earth and of deep green grass. The red earth has inevitably led to comparisons with Tuscany and I feel these are valid. East Lothian may not be known for the finest of wines and olive oils but there is a long tradition of good local ales, honeys and jams and a general association with the finer things in life.

The cycle path dropped me on the outskirts of Haddington. On the way in I passed an old gentleman in tweed riding a sit-up-and-beg roadster, stone villas with golden gravel drives, preposterously large cars and a hotel that announces itself simply as Brown's; no doubt they are betting that the riff-raff will never work out that it's really a hotel.

Apart from posh hotels, Haddington is full of assertive buildings and the favoured style is Georgian, but it still sits on a medieval plan of burghage plots. The pends and closes that lead off the broad high street hold onto their medieval atmosphere and are worth a wander. Unusually for provincial Scotland, it is a town in good health with lots of little shops selling luxury goods catering in particular for the country set.

Haddington is frequently accused of doing too good an impression of England and nowhere more so than by the riverbank. The riverbank was perfectly calm, artists were set up under trees burgeoning with blossom, there were people enjoying an al fresco lunch in a riverside pub and ducks paddled themselves stationary against the Tyne. The critics, I believe are confusing Englishness with how any of the human race behaves in drier weather, but the critic might fire back, 'Ahh, but they've had plenty of practise!'

In an episode that became known as the 'Rough Wooing', that old romantic Henry VIII sent an army north to take the infant Mary Queen of

Scots south to marry his son Edward. The Scots and the French, who had already come to an arrangement regarding the infant queen, met the English army at Haddington and stopped them in their tracks. The English were holed up for 18 months in Haddington and when they left many questions were asked of the townspeople.

The idle pleasures on the riverbank were being enjoyed within yards of the church where George Wishart and later John Knox first preached the Reformation and just maybe it's Knox's disapproving Calivinism that draws the perceived distinction between dour Scottishness and more carefree and guilt-free Englishness.

The church in question is St Mary's or 'The Lamp of the Lothians'. It would seem to have always been in a state of recovery and it has been in the way of every force invading Scotland, as this was the most comfortable route for English armies. Edward III destroyed the first one in his 'Burnt Candlemas' and it wasn't until the 1970s that the damage inflicted during the 'Rough Wooing' was undone.

The East Lothian countryside is nowhere to be without a map. From the old signposts there appears to be a dozen different ways of reaching your destination and many more ways of not. Somehow I'd managed to lose my map. It was probably shaken from my handlebar bag when I was cycling over the cobbled Nungate Bridge in Haddington.

Fortunately, Gifford was easy to find. What was not so easy was resisting the temptation of a second lunch or even a third. I had no idea really if lunch at the Goblin Ha' or the Tweedale Arms would be any good – they just looked the kind of places to spend a long beer-soaked lunchtime.

For the first time I was having to put a bit of effort into my cycling but I wasn't far out of Gifford when the road chose its level in the Lammermuir Hills and, for a while anyway, it stuck with it.

Gifford was pretty and had life. With its wide main street, an old Dutch-style church, a village square, a village green, good pubs and restaurants, it has a tick in every box for the tourist looking for a quaint village. So, encouraged by Gifford, I descended from the levelish main road to Garvald.

Garvald should be a dull place, so low in a wooded valley, but the red pan-tiled roofs of the hugger mugger cottages radiate up at you. The village was silent but for a calling wood pigeon. The exotically named Papana Water is crossed via a little stone hump-backed bridge and each cottage boasts of a previous purpose – 'Old Schoolhouse' or the 'Old Bakehouse'. I didn't encounter a soul as I pedalled along its narrow and contorted streets and out the other side on an insanely steep hill.

Villages and hamlets in the Lammermuirs pop up as regularly as watchtowers along a wall and create the feeling of comfortable progress.

Each village is roofed in the regulation red pan tiles and built of sandstone, but each has its own quaint touch. Stenton has an old tron that was once used for weighing sheep, the remant of a truly ancient church now inhabited by pigeons, houses with that very peculiar Scottish characteristic of the outside staircase and a covered well. Innerwick is a classic farming community. It was particularly pleasing that they are quaint in a Scottish way and not merely an attempt at copying England's chocolate-box look as is the case elsewhere.

The latter part of the day's journey required me to work even harder. A steep descent sent me into a ford with a *weee* and out the other side with a shudder and an, 'Oh shit', as I struggled to control the bike on the unseen cobbled surface. The way up on the other side was essentially a pony track with tarmac slapped on it, so with all momentum lost there was nothing for it but to walk. Even bigger climbs followed, especially the one from Spott over to Innerwick.

I was very tired and very cold in the haar that was rolling in off the North Sea by the time I reached Cockburnspath and it was very dark. I have always relied on serendipity when it comes to accommodation. I hate booking ahead in case I change my mind. Until this occasion I have always managed to find somewhere but not this time. I was forced to walk, after contracting four punctures, ten miles in the dark to Dunbar. The experience means I definitely book ahead wherever I think accommodation will be scarce.

By the next morning my spirits were lifting. The weather was clearer, if a little colder, the wind was with me and spring had clearly sprung. Lambs raced over to stick their heads through the now blossoming hedgerows of hawthorn and stare inquisitively until their mothers escorted them away with a scold.

The Lammermuirs are not so high as to preclude agriculture on their very tops, rather ploughed fields made the rounded summits bald and then they dropped off the sides into unseen wooded dells. As a physical barrier the Lammermuirs are easily overcome. The roads don't necessarily follow the line of least resistance, however, and I braced myself for the long climb over Dunglass Common.

As I climbed, there were more changes than I expected. I could see more Lammermuirs in the west which were higher, wilder and more heathery. Spring was no longer and the sheep were clearly pregnant rather than the concerned mothers of lower down. The unfenced road was rough and thick with mud.

As I approached the hilltop farm, in what would appear to be an unsustainably remote location, I triggered a cacophony of panic. Hens stopped pecking the ground and took off for their coop, a pregnant ewe scaled a stone dyke and small children dropped their bikes and ran for the house, probably to tell their Pa of the stranger riding into town. Fortunately, a fast but far from smooth downhill carried me quickly away from any precipitate action on Pa's part.

A great big Highland coo just about did for me though. It was standing exactly where it shouldn't be. I braked but slithered close enough for intimate relations and to be able to see through its glaikit fringe into its doleful eyes. I only just managed to get out of the way of its flicking horns. I was, however, saved by a car horn which frightened the animal back into the field; thankfully it wasn't Pa who was driving.

I was now in the wooded Valley of the Monynut and its steep and enclosing slopes bore all the scars of winter. The gnarled and stunted trees were not yet in leaf but encrusted with lichens, and their broken boughs and branches littered the road and hillsides. The innocuous looking Monynut Water had obviously been wreaking havoc, judging by the piles of gravel and sand that lay across the road.

I could afford to absent-mindedly wander behind the debris and the potholes because once again I had this scruffy little glen to myself. Isolated, secluded and on the road to nowhere may have been the reasons why a wife of an earl of Dunbar founded a priory at Abbey St Bathans, at the confluence of the Monynut and the Whiteadder, for Cistercian nuns in the twelfth century. Unfortunately the priory found its way onto the itinerary for advancing armies and each time one passed through they would have to swear allegiance to one king or another. The soldiers that passed through during the 'Rough Wooing' erased it from the landscape.

The Riverside Café/Restaurant, it doesn't say which, at Abbey St Bathan's had a guard duck – or was it a goose on patrol? Anyway, it was big and came at me with its mouth menacingly open, a clever ploy perhaps to get the swithering customer to dash for cover in the café. To avoid a repetition I tried ordering duck but had to make do with tea and scones and then run the gauntlet on the way out.

I soon emerged out of the trees and the valley onto the surface again of sun-bathed green fields. I was warm, the road was smooth and there was no livestock at liberty.

My fast exit from the Lammermuirs was as dramatic as the change in scenery. Ahead of me lay the highly ordered landscape of the Merse. Rich in alluvial deposits this is prime farming country and the large mansion houses are testimony as to how rich.

Manderston near Duns is perhaps the finest Edwardian House in the country but visiting is limited to summer Sundays and Thursdays. It would appear that every day is Sunday in Duns; it was barely awake when I passed through.

The dull light of impending rain was not showing off the Merse at its best. In the summer sun and when the huge industrial-scale fields are filled with swaying crops it is a golden landscape, and I suppose golden in respect of the ample rewards returned. It is no small thing that Scotland has managed to hold onto this rich and fertile land so close to the border.

My hopeful memory that the Merse was flat was plain wrong. It is akin to crossing a swollen sea. Waves of land had to be climbed with a short reprieve before the next one, thwarting my attempts to gain speed and beat the approaching rain. Finally I got to a point from where it was downhill all the way to the Tweed and on into England at Coldstream over an impressive bridge which I daresay would be worth fighting over, should the English ever fancy a rematch.

The differences between Scotland and England are immediately apparent. The hotel in Cornhill-on-Tweed is mock Tudor in style and the notice at the church of St Helens makes no reference to a denomination, a distinction that has to be made in Scotland, and it asks you to contact the vicar at his vicarage rather than the minister at his manse.

Before disappearing into the Cheviot Hills I resolved to fight the strengthening easterly and pay my respects at Flodden Field. In 1513 10,000 Scots lost their lives in battle with the English. The battle was there for the Scots to win but the opportunities were missed. Their greater numbers and strong position were not capitalised on and the Scots suffered a most ignominious defeat in which King James IV lost his life along with most of his nobles. For the Scots it was a classic case of seizing defeat from the jaws of victory, a scenario that fans of the national football team are all too familiar with.

It was a battle that Scotland didn't need to fight. Neither Scotland's interests nor independence were at stake, there was no occupying force to be ejected and it came at a time when Scotland had never had it so good and its king had never been more popular with his people.

I felt no sense of poignancy on the battlefield but in the church of St Paul's, just a few hundred yards from the memorial, there survives an arch through which the body of James IV, wrapped in his standard, would have been carried and laid on the altar. Here I felt a sudden connection with the events of 500 years ago. Inside at least I could rule out the cold easterly wind as the cause of my shiver.

My race against the rain had left me weary, but at least I'd won. By the time I'd reached the youth hostel at Kirk Yetholm I had developed a perplexing inability to speak. They seemed to know what I wanted and since they'd answered all of my questions without me having to say anything I just nodded and located a bed.

By the next morning I was in a condition to take in my surroundings. The village was uncannily still and empty, for this is the end of England's premier long-distance footpath, the Pennine Way. Its completion is generally celebrated in the mock Tudor Border Hotel, but the night before the bar had only contained a few locals and my fellow hostellers who were walking the St Cuthbert's Way to Lindisfarne.

The Borders has a long tradition of itinerant people. Kirk Yetholm was the home of the Gypsy Kings and the site of their coronations, the last of which was attended by 10,000 people in 1898. The Gypsy Palace, where the coronation took place, still exists as a modest dwelling house. Then there were the travelling minstrels who carried with them the oral legend and lore of the borders and especially of the reivers – the villains and outlaws who exploited the border to evade the law.

To me this tradition of itinerancy is palpable in the Borders. There is an appealing but not overbearing wildness to the hills and they are dotted with sheltered and comfortable corners – perfect for stealth and evasion while at the same time providing safe places to rest up.

As I cycled away from Kirk Yetholm and its twin, Town Yetholm I was completely enveloped by the lime-green Cheviot Hills. The road was as peaceful as it would have been when travel was simpler and slower; the air was filled with the fresh smell of wet grass and the song of a multitude of hedgerow birds; a huge heron flapped up from a marshy loch and sheepdogs were escorting a flock of sheep down a slalom course marked out by clumps of vibrant yellow broom.

As hills the Cheviots defy easy description for there are not many distinctive features. Craggy outcrops are rare and they don't induce awe, although the whole scene would be accepted as the picture of a peaceful rural idyll. The countryside was filled with a spring buzz and I felt guilty about my own meandering purpose – if it could be described as a purpose.

It may appear idyllic and stuck in a pre-war time-warp that is considered by many to have been a golden age of rural living. If, like the gentleman at Haddington, I were to don tweed, and swap my modern bicycle for his roadster, I would be perfectly in tune. We may yearn for a return to simpler times but it would be invariably as the tweedy gentleman farmer and not as the put-upon farm labourer.

The large farm at Cessford dominates the tiny community that is attached to it and the labourers' cottages are easily picked out by their stable-like uniformity. It was the women who paid the rent on these homes with incessant back-breaking labour. Known as *bongdagers*, slaves really, virtually every job that was not mechanised was in their remit, including running the home.

I drifted away from the Cheviots towards Jedburgh along gentle lanes. The swaying treetops implied a strong breeze but the hedges sheltered me. The sun, however, was unimpeded and I grew unseasonably hot, sweaty and thirsty. I certainly would not have been tackling the hill between Crailing and Jedburgh with the one-geared roadster and, if in tweeds, I would almost certainly have expired.

Very considerately, Jedburgh lies in the valley, enabling me to sail into town with the panache of a fit and accomplished cyclist. As I never do history on an empty stomach I called in first at 'Simply Scottish' on the High Street. Lunch was uncharacteristically light as I was already aware of my very steep exit route and thought it best not to over indulge.

Jedburgh is the site of one of the great border abbeys. Jedburgh Abbey was in constant danger, being so close to the border, and the community of monks certainly endured many attacks. The monks that founded these abbeys enjoyed royal patronage and they probably had their pick of the whole country and accordingly picked the best available. They recognised in the Borders that compelling mix of fertile river valleys, ample game and good grazing, not to mention that this side of Scotland is appreciably drier.

I have avoided mentioning Sir Walter Scott up until now, for no other reason than he has too much to say about the Borders and evidence of his presence is ubiquitous. He is everywhere, a ghost at every feast and always pushing his romantic take on things to the forefront of my mind.

Sir Walter was able to pipe the tune of two masters. He reconciled Scottish patriotism with Scotland's place within the Union. He rehabilitated Scotland's history and made it palatable. Anyone who spends time in the Borders will find that the people can quite easily be fervent Scottish patriots and at the same time be relaxed about being British. They vote Liberal Democrat, a party that has consistently offered Scotland a measure of autonomy within Great Britain. In their towns they commemorate the bloody battles with England every year. In Coldstream they ride out to Flodden to pay their respects. In Hawick they remember the events of 1514, the year after Flodden, when a raiding group from Hexham Priory was ambushed by Hawick men; the English came off worst and they lost their banner. Borders folk may not have a good word to say about the English, as is the case in the rest of Scotland, but there are no obvious signs of a desire to change the relationship with England.

Scott, however, would have been the most enthusiastic guide. Perhaps when he heard I was bound for Liddesdale, the heart of reiving country, he would abandon his legal duties at Jedburgh, accompany me on a 'raid', him mounted on a galloway nag – the chosen horse of the reiver. I wouldn't have to strain my neck to converse with him for they weren't very big horses. We would probably agree on ancient resonance of the hamlet of Bedrule and the comfortable beauty of the Valley of the Rule. He would point out the distinctive volcanic cone of Rubers Law and inform me of the Bronze Age people who had a fort on its summit, which the Romans used as a signal station, and the large flat stone that the persecuted Covenanters used as a communion table.

Sir Walter would probably coax me on at the appealing pub at

Bonchester Bridge, eager to record some hitherto unrecorded Ballad recounting an unknown escapade of a border reiver. What would it be this time? A gaol break and a lucky escape from the gallows, revenge meted out to the Warden of the Marches or the death of an evil magician?

We could only speculate as to the difficulty of Mary Queen of Scots' journey from Jedburgh to Hermitage Castle in inclement weather to visit her lover Bothwell, who had been severely injured by Little Jock Elliot, for we were enjoying the early evening of a perfect spring day and the utter peace of a sheltered border lane.

I would maybe ask him about how he came to miscalculate and establish the tartan-clad Highlander as the quintessential Scot and the Highlands as the embodiment of Scotland. This question would probably offend and he would kick on his horse and leave me to struggle alone up the steep hill.

He would, however, wait for me at the summit of the pass, grabbing me by the forearm and warning me what devils the Armstrongs and the Elliots can be. I would pause to look out over the bewildering vastness of the border hills. No hill is a landmark and there are many hidden dells into which an army of thieves and hundreds of head of cattle could disappear without a trace, leaving their pursuers to give up and retreat for fear of ambush.

It would be my turn to be ahead as we descended into Liddesdale. Revelling in the plunging downhill, he would never catch up and instead pull up somewhere for the night and earn his bed and board by reciting ballads from his *Minstrelsy of the Scottish Borders*, for Liddesdale is no place to be out after dark.

The loneliness of the Highlands is disrupted by those searching for loneliness, but most are completely unaware of the lonely dales of the south. This wasn't always the case. The railways opened these valleys up to the excitement of Victorian Britain and judging by the plethora of Victorian architecture they embraced it wholeheartedly. The railways were only to remain for 100 years and the valleys closed up again. The people have to go in search of the outside world but the outside world doesn't often come to them.

There is talk of reopening the Waverley Line that ran from Edinburgh to Carlisle. It would be a stupendous journey and an enormous boost to this part of the world, in addition to allowing cyclists to get here more easily.

I mistimed my arrival in Liddesdale and therefore there was no time to make the detour to Hermitage Castle. I have been before and it is intimidating and would be more so after dark. If you ever want to capture the bloodthirsty times of the reiver then visit Hermitage Castle. It's guaranteed to send a shiver down your spine.

I made it to Newcastleton just the right side of total darkness. Newcastleton is the total antithesis of the anarchy of the reivers. It is a planned village and there isn't a hair out of place. The order may have been an attempt to counteract the disorder for which this valley was renowned. For not even the combined efforts of James IV and Henry VIII could quell the outlaws. I do wonder, though, about the town's unusually aggressive First World War memorial of a soldier thrusting his bayonet forward; perhaps they've never quite got it out of their system.

The steep climb out of Newcastleton is avoidable but the road across the Tarras Moss was recommended to me by the landlady of the B&B. The road, once it had reached its level, was but a paper-cut in a huge desert of dead brown heather. The heat was already shimmering off the tarmac. Consequently the hills were blurred and easily took on the character of dunes. The Tarras Moss was the frequent refuge of pursued Armstrongs hoping to vanish in the expanse. The Morse Code call of the curlew alerted all to my presence.

To Hugh MacDiarmid the Tarras Moss was a 'Bolshevik Bog' and the whole way across I tried to put my finger on what he meant. His admirers must have detected some fondness in his sentiment because on the Moss's very edge they erected a bronze sculpture to his memory. However this was the only thing perplexing me.

As I stood trying to work out the symbolism of the bronze which is in the form of an open book, an American toting a bottle of Coca-cola surprised me.

'You'd have thought they'd supply some sort of explanation,' he complained.

'Maybe you have to work at it.'

'Humph!' With that he returned to his hire car and poured Coke down his front. The bottle obviously lacked instructions.

The descent into Langholm was not a pleasant one. It is extremely steep and twisting and it is imperative you don't overshoot at the bottom onto the A7.

Langholm was the cue to finally turn north and to start making my way back to Edinburgh. In crossing the Tarras Moss I had swapped the Borders for Dumfries and Galloway and Liddesdale for Eskdale.

Eskdale is a classic Border valley of big doughy hills that overlap into each other. All the usual compliments and superlatives apply, however Eskdale and the Ettrick valley are particular favourites of mine. I have cycled them many times and I have to confess that I was secretly looking forward to this part of the journey. I don't really know why, maybe it is that they sum up all that is best about cycling in the Borders.

At some point I passed through what the locals refer to as the 'Gates of Eden', into, presumably, Eden. The hamlet of Bentpath puts in a convincing bid as the capital. Its old sandstone bridge, whitewashed cottages, its church tower and the rolling hills around it compose the perfect picture of a Borders paradise. If Adam and Eve had been cyclists I'm sure they would have foregone the forbidden fruit and stayed.

The hill, however, over to Eskdalemuir spoiled it a bit and I can't imagine conifers being part of God's plan of perfection. The weather station at Eskdalemuir hasn't been sited there to ascertain the weather in paradise but rather the extremes induced by being so far from the sea. However Shangri-la was just around the corner. No, really.

Stupas, flapping prayer flags, head-shaven monks in red robes and a fully fledged Tibetan Monastery are to be found just a mile up the road from Eskdalemuir. The extent of this complex is a testimony to the peace and serenity to be found in Eskdale.

Carpets and big cushions mean a tearoom with a difference and a mug of Himalayan tea refreshed more than my thirst – the general soreness of my legs and bum was slowly dissipated by some secret ingredient. I spent three hours in the monastery tearoom talking with a retired couple called Joan and Dave. Enthusiastic converts to travelling by bike, they were keen to discuss experiences and ideas. In the past five years or so they had cycled across the USA and had visited Cuba and Vietnam.

The vast Craik Forest sits across the watershed between the Esk and the Ettrick. A sign informed me that should I spot a fire I should report my position as OD2. But to whom? I wonder if you can send a postcard saying, 'Greetings from OD2'; Gawd, it's tragic. The inevitable consequence of the sun shining for most of the day on thousands of acres of moisture-laden conifers was an evening mist. The mist found me and clung on, leaching every drop of warmth from my body.

A hundred barking dogs announced my arrival in Ettrick. My pilgrimage to the birthplace of James Hogg (aka the Ettrick Shepherd), author, poet and very good friend of Sir Walter Scott was brief. The achievements of this self-educated man who had worked as a shepherd since the age of six are, to say the least, remarkable. Even John Paul Sartre was behind a revival of interest in his most famous work *Confessions of a Justified Sinner*.

I had hoped to reach the Gordon Arms over in the Yarrow but I was much too cold to pass the Tushielaw Inn. The Inn is redolent of an age of gentlemen motorists. An old AA sign gives the distance to Selkirk and an old rusting petrol pump marks the change from watering horses to replenishing petrol tanks.

I straightened my jacket and flicked the drip from my nose before I entered, fearing if I looked too cold the price would increase. The hotelier, however, abandoned the single-room supplement at the slightest hint from me that I was up to cycling on.

Over a mountainous breakfast I watched a shepherd bring in his flock, a hare preen himself by the river and trout leap. The night before, those patronising the bar dwindled to three: me, a mechanic from Edinburgh who disliked cyclists, and a sheep farmer to whom Sir Walter Scott – and James Hogg – was a style guru. Bushy sideburns and tweed are more common than you'd think.

The conversation centred around matters agricultural: the price of lamb, foot-and-mouth, supermarkets and hunting. The farmer stared forward the whole time, making clipped and precise interjections which were clearly not to be challenged. Indeed, he usually had a violent solution for anything that got in his way, especially protesters. It seemed to me as if he was delivering a *logical* argument line by line without reference to the conversation; he could well have been talking to himself or even to one of his sheep.

The road between the Tushielaw and the Gordon Arms is an old coach road. It is very favourably graded and known as Paddy's Slack. On reaching the Gordon Arms it was a scene reminiscent of numerous road movies – the oblivious traveller peering hopefully into the lifeless motel and the sign squeaking in the wind. If the ballads are to be believed gruesome acts were common by the Yarrow. So I pushed on without delay, although I wouldn't have evaded anyone going uphill at 5 mph.

The climb over from the Yarrow to Traquair meant a return to the Tweed and the realisation that the loop was closing. I filled up my water bottles in St Ronan's Well in Innerleithen but the water didn't seem to have the potency of the Buddhists' Himalayan Tea. The sun burned through the morning cloud and escorted me through the Moorfoot Hills to Edinburgh. Most importantly, I had returned to Edinburgh without ever encountering rain.

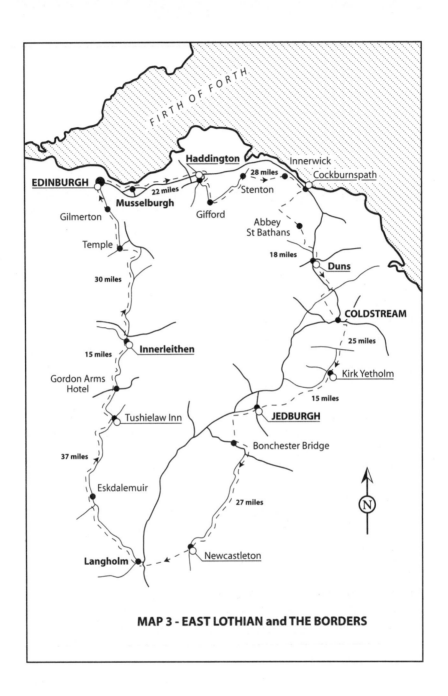

FIRTH OF FORTH

EDINBURGH

Haddington
Innerwick
Cockburnspath
28 miles
Stenton
22 miles
Musselburgh
Gifford

Gilmerton

Temple

Abbey
St Bathans

18 miles
Duns

30 miles

COLDSTREAM

15 miles
Innerleithen
25 miles

Gordon Arms
Hotel
Kirk Yetholm

Tushielaw Inn
15 miles

JEDBURGH

37 miles
Bonchester Bridge

Eskdalemuir
27 miles

Langholm
Newcastleton

N

MAP 3 - EAST LOTHIAN and THE BORDERS

Distance: 236 miles.

Maps: OS *Landranger* series (1:50,000), sheets 66, 67, 73, 74, 75, 79, 80. OS *Road Map 3: Southern Scotland*.

Banks/Cashpoints: Edinburgh, Musselburgh, Haddington, Duns, Coldstream, Jedburgh, Newcastleton (inside PO), Langholm, Innerleithen.

Cycle Repair: MacDonald Cycles, 35 High Street, Musselburgh (0131 665 1777); Bob's Cycle Shop, 126 High Street, Prestonpans (01875 819 072); Cycle Services, 78 High Street, Haddington (01620 826989); P&S Dorricot, 53 High Street, Jedburgh (01835 862 423); Bikesport, Peebles Road, Innerleithen (01896 830 880).

General Stores: You'll have no problem finding a general store except in the Lammermuirs, between Jedburgh and Newcastleton and between Langholm and Innerleithen.

Traffic: Moderate levels of traffic may be experienced on the B1348 from Musselburgh to Longniddry although there are sections of legal pavement cycling, so watch for signs. Also take care for one mile on the A6112 into Duns, on the A698 between Coldstream and Cornhill-on-Tweed and on the very short section of the A7 into Langholm. On the return to Edinburgh you will experience increased levels of traffic once you reach Bonnyrig. However, legal pavement cycling or a cycle lane is generally available. In Edinburgh, cyclists often share the bus lanes – I don't know if this is a good thing but you'll not be alone; there are always plenty of cyclists on the roads in the city.

ROUTE INFORMATION

EDINBURGH TO HADDINGTON (22 MILES)

Alternatively take the train to Musselburgh or Longniddry from Edinburgh Waverley. It is a six- to twenty-minute journey and services are hourly.

Cycle up the ramp out of Waverley Station. Turn left and then turn right at roundabout. At T-junction turn left onto the Mound and follow to crossroads with High Street (Royal Mile). Go straight over High Street. Join cycle lane in Bristo Place and follow to junction with Teviot Place. Turn left into Lothian Street and follow round onto Potterow. Continue past Crichton Street car park. Continue along road that becomes Chapel Street and then Buccleuch Street. Go straight over at traffic lights at crossroads with Melville Drive. Take next left into West Preston Street. Go straight over Newington Road onto East Preston Street. At junction with Dalkeith Road go right and then left between glass offices and Commonwealth Pool, onto Holyrood Park Road. Follow cycle route left into East Parkside then follow signs round to right in new housing development and follow into tunnel. This is the Innocent Railway Cycle Path. Take care on leaving tunnel.

Follow cycle path to Duddingston Road West. Cross road following signs for Bingham and Musselburgh. Follow cycle path to Duddingston Park South. Cross road and rejoin cycle path which continues over to the left. Surface deteriorates. Follow cycle path through underpass across the car-park and over bridge, unfortunately. Ignore signs for NCN 1. Instead go straight over for Brunstane Burn Cycle Path. Follow path to Edinburgh Road (A199) and turn right. Edinburgh Road becomes North High Street and then Bridge Street. Cross River Esk and go over junction into Dalrymple Loan. At the end of Dalrymple Loan turn left into Inveresk Road which becomes Pinkie Road. Follow Pinkie Road to roundabout. Take the exit for Ravenshaugh Road (B1348).

Follow the B1348 for five miles through Prestonpans and Port Seton. Pavement cycling is allowed for much of the way. At junction with A198 turn right and follow to roundabout. Turn left and then after 300 yards turn right for Longniddry–Haddington Railway Path. Go under railway and follow signs for car park. Go through gate to join railway path, not great in places, and follow all the way to Haddington. In Haddington climb to road and turn right and then descend to T-junction. Turn left and follow road into Haddington.

Terrain: Level the whole way. Some of the path surfaces are not great.

ACCOMMODATION

Haddington (01620–)

Hotels and B&Bs: The George Hotel, 91 High Street (–826677); Mrs Cunnigham, 2 Rosehall Place (–825119); Schiehallion, 19 Church Street (–825603).

Camping: Monk's Muir Caravan Park (–822254); on the eastern edge of Haddington by the A1.

WATCH OUT FOR!

Prestongrange Industrial Heritage Museum, Prestonpans (0131 653 2904).

Seton Collegiate Church (HS), Port Seton (01875 813334). Fifteenth-century church.

St Mary's Church, Haddington. Fourteenth-century church and John Knox's own parish church.

Jane Carlyle Museum, 2 Lodge St, Haddington (01620 82738). Childhood home of the wife of Thomas Carlyle.

HADDINGTON TO COCKBURNSPATH (45 MILES)

Leave Haddington by the Nungate Bridge and then turn right at the end of Bridge Street. Climb out of Haddington to junction with B6369. Continue straight on and follow into Gifford. Enter Gifford at Yester Church and leave Gifford by Duns Road on the other side of the church. One mile out of Gifford turn left for Garvald and Stenton, B7360, Hillfoots Trail. Four miles out of Gifford turn right for Stenton, Dunbar and West Barns. Continue through Stenton for Pitcox. At Pitcox, at crossroads go in the direction of Spott and Dunbar (old signpost points the way). A half mile out of Pitcox turn right (unsigned). Remain slow descending through ford. At T-junction beyond ford turn left for Spott.

In Spott turn right uphill for Brunt, Elmcleugh and Woodhall. Once over the top remain slow descending through ford. Climb away from the ford, and turn left before reaching the top. Descend for one-and-a-half miles to T-junction and turn right. Continue to Innerwick.

Beyond Innerwick follow signs for Oldhamstocks. Turn right at T-junction. At next T-junction at sub-station turn right. Follow road to Oldhamstocks and turn left at Oldhamstocks. At Hoprig turn left for Cockburnspath.

Terrain: Life becomes a bit more difficult after Haddington. In the Lammermuirs the hills are short but steep and frequent.

ACCOMMODATION
Gifford (01620–)
Hotels and B&Bs: Goblin Ha', Main Street (–810224); Tweedale Arms, High Street (–810240); Eaglescairne Mains (–810491).
Cockburnspath (01368–)
Hotels and B&Bs: Linhead Farm (–830499); Townhead Farm (–830465).
Camping: Pease Bay Caravan Park, on the coast two miles from Cockburnspath.

WATCH OUT FOR!
Lennoxlove House and Gardens, en route just outside Haddington (01620 823720). Home of the Duke of Hamilton. Death mask of Mary Queen of Scots is on display.

Yester Church, Gifford. Eighteenth-century church in a Dutch style. Parents of John Witherspoon, signatory to the American Declaration of Independence, are buried in the churchyard. Commemorative plaque to Rev. John Witherspoon is set into the Manse wall.

Stenton Wool Stone. Medieval tron for the weighing of wool.

Rood Well. Fourteenth-century well with conical roof by the road as you leave Stenton.

Dunglass Collegiate Church. One mile north of Cockburnspath, a fifteenth-century church with a richly embellished interior.

COCKBURNSPATH TO DUNS (18 MILES)
At the foot of Hoprig Road turn right for Berwick A1 then after a short distance turn right again for Abbey St Bathans and Stockbridge Caravan Park. Continue straight through Ecclaw. Beyond Ecclaw turn right on the bend for Monymusk. Ascend over what's known as Dunglass Common. It is a very fast descent into the Monymusk valley. Follow narrow road to Abbey St Bathans. Continue following this road into more open country for three miles to T-junction with B6355. Turn left for Duns and Preston. Swap the B6355 for the B6365 following signs for Duns. At T-junction with the A6112 turn right and follow into Duns.

Terrain: A long climb to start with but it isn't too steep. The remainder of the route is mostly either level or downhill.

ACCOMMODATION
Duns (01361–)
Hotels and B&Bs: Claymore, 8–10 Murray St (–883880); St Albans, Clouds (–883285); Wellfield House, Preston Road (–883189).

Swinton (01890–)
Hotels and B&Bs: Wheatsheaf Hotel (–860257).

WATCH OUT FOR!
The Jim Clark Room, 44 Newton Street, Duns (01361 883 960). Celebrates the career of the world motor-racing champion.

Manderston House (01361 883 450). The quintessential Edwardian House, two miles to the east of Duns on the A6015. Limited opening times.

DUNS TO KIRK YETHOLM (25 MILES)
Leave Market Square by Easter Street and turn right for Berwick and Chirnside. At roundabout take left for A6015 for Chirnside, Berwick, Eyemouth and Manderston House. Just as you leave Duns turn right for Sinclairshill and Wedderburn Castle. Follow road all the way to Sinclairshill and junction with B6460. Turn left and cycle 100 yards and then turn right. A half mile further on turn left then right and follow road to Swinton. Turn right at church and proceed through Swinton. Beyond village green turn left and then follow road round to the right. After one-and-a-half miles at Swintonmill turn left. Follow long straight road to Coldstream. At Coldstream turn left onto High Street, the A698 and follow out of Coldstream and downhill to bridge over Tweed. Climb into Cornhill-on-Tweed. In Cornhill take the right for Learmouth and Mindrum. Continue straight on at East Learmouth for Mindrum and Yetholm. After two miles take right fork and go straight on at crossroads shortly afterwards and follow the B6041 for Town Yetholm.

Terrain: Very easy going between Duns and Swinton. The road from Swinton to Coldstream has some pronounced undulations. Once beyond the Tweed the cycling is relatively easy to Yetholm.
Detour to Flodden Field: At Learmouth turn left for Branxton and Millfield. After one mile turn left for Flodden Field. Memorial is a couple of hundred yards on the right.

ACCOMMODATION
Coldstream (01890–)
Hotels and B&Bs: Castle Hotel, 11 High Street (–882830); Attadale, 1 Leet Street (–883047); Kengarth, 7 Market Street (–882477).
Cornhill-on-Tweed (01890–)
Hotels and B&Bs: Collingwood Arms Hotel (–882424).
Kirk Yetholm (01573–)
Hotels and B&Bs: Border Hotel, The Green (–420549); Blunty's Mill

(–420288); Valleydene, High Street (–420286); Springvalley, The Green (–420253).
Hostels: SYHA Youth Hostel (–420631).
Town Yetholm (01573–)
Hotels and B&Bs: The Plough Hotel (–420215).

WATCH OUT FOR!

Coldstream Museum. Local history and special section on the Coldstream Guards.

The Hirsel Estate (01890 882 834). Attractive grounds, museums and crafts.

Flodden Field. Site of 1513 battle between the Scots and English – a bad day for the Scots.

The Gypsy Palace, Kirk Yetholm. Now a private residence but once the home of the Gypsy Kings and the place of their coronations. Go uphill across from the Border Hotel.

KIRK YETHOLM TO JEDBURGH (15 MILES)

Follow the B6401 out of Town Yetholm, eventually passing through Morebattle. Two miles beyond Morebattle turn left for Crailinghall and Cessford. At Crailinghall go straight over at crossroads for Jedburgh. Climb steeply and then descend very steeply into Jedburgh. At junction with A68 turn right and then take next left uphill past the abbey.

Terrain: Delightfully easy cycling as far as Crailinghall. There then is a big climb to be tackled before descending very steeply into Jedburgh.

ACCOMMODATION
Morebattle
Hotels and B&Bs: Temple Hall Hotel (01573 440249).
Jedburgh (01835–)
Hotels and B&Bs: Willow Court, The Friars (–864601); Kenmore Bank (–862369); Glenfriars House, The Friars (–862000); The Royal Hotel, Canongate (–863152).
Camping: Elliot Park (–863393).

WATCH OUT FOR!

Cessford Castle. Ruin of fifteenth-century L-plan castle, home to the reiving family Ker.

Jedburgh Abbey (HS) (01835 863 925). A majestic ruin of the abbey founded in 1138, an excellent visitor centre which has the priceless Jedburgh comb on display.

Jedburgh Castle Jail Museum, Castlegate (01835 864 750). History of Jedburgh.

Mary Queen of Scots Visitor Centre (01835 863 331). The ill-fated queen's story.

JEDBURGH TO NEWCASTLETON (27 MILES)

Climb (10 per cent) out of Jedburgh on the Castlegate in the direction of the town's golf course. Once over the top of the hill and on the downhill turn left for Bedrule and Chesters. Follow signs for Chesters. At next T-junction with B6357 turn right. Follow the B6357 round to the right at Hallrule. Do not go straight on for Chesters. Follow B6357 to T-junction with A6088. Turn left for Bonchester Bridge. Turn right at the Horse and Hound. Go round to the right at phone box and climb to B6357. Turn right and follow road all the way to Newcastleton.

ACCOMMODATION

Bonchester Bridge (01430–)

Hotels and B&Bs: Horse and Hound Inn (–860643); Nether Swanshiel, Hobkirk (–860636).

Newcastleton (013873–)

Hotels and B&Bs: Woodside, North Hermitage Street (–75431); Liddesdale Hotel (–375255).

WATCH OUT FOR!

The Hermitage Castle (HS) (01387 376 222). An eerie and imposing ruin which dates back to the fourteenth century. A couple of miles off-route but worth the detour. Turn right for Steele Road.

Liddesdale Heritage Centre, Newcastleton. Local history and genealogy.

NEWCASTLETON TO TUSHIELAW (39 MILES)

From Douglas Square turn right into Langholm Street and climb steeply out of Newcastleton. Follow road over to T-junction with A7. Turn left onto A7 and follow for a short distance into Langholm.

Leave Langholm by turning right off the A7 onto the B7068, Thomas Telford Road for Eskdalemuir and the Samye Ling Tibetan Monastery. After a short distance take up the B709 and follow for about 28 miles to the Tushielaw Inn.

Terrain: This section has a steep climb out of Newcastleton but once out of the way there is only one other short climb before descending steeply into Langholm. It is a very long but mostly gentle climb to Eskdalemuir followed by another to the Tushielaw.

ACCOMMODATION
Langholm (013873–)
Hotels and B&Bs: The Reivers Rest, 81 High Street (–81343); Mrs Geddes, Esk Brae (–80376); Border House, 28 High Street (–80377); Crown Hotel, High Street (–80247); Burnfoot House, Westerkirk (–70611).
Camping: Ewes Water CCP, Milntown (–80386).
Eskdalemuir (013873–)
Hotels and B&Bs: Hart Manor (–73217).
Samye Ling Tibetan Monastery: The monastery accepts guests on a full-board basis (–73232). It is essential to book in advance. Accommodation is a dormitory or a twin room. Plentiful vegetarian food. Guests are asked to work two hours a day in addition to the room charges (single: £27, twin £42, dorm £16). Camping is also available (£13). Online booking at www.samyeling.org
Tushielaw (01750–)
Hotels and B&Bs: Tushielaw Inn (–82232).
Camping: Angecroft CP (–62251); Honey Cottage CP (–62246).

WATCH OUT FOR!
Clan Armstrong Museum, Langholm. Armstrong memorabilia and archives.
    Telford Memorial, Bentpath. Plaque to local lad Thomas Telford, the famous civil engineer.
    Samye Ling Tibetan Monastery, Eskdalemuir. A wonderful atmosphere surrounds this incredible complex. Accommodation, café and shop.
    James Hogg Memorial, Ettrick. Statue at the birthplace of James Hogg, poet, author of *The Confessions of a Justified Sinner* and friend to Sir Walter Scott.

TUSHIELAW INN TO INNERLEITHEN (15 MILES)
From the Inn continue north for a half mile and then turn left, still the B709, and follow to the Gordon Arms. Go straight over the A708 at the Gordon Arms and continue following the B709 over to Traquair. Continue through Traquair, ignoring the B7062 unless you want to visit Traquair House. Follow road round to the left and cross the Tweed and enter Innerleithen. At T-junction with the A72 turn right onto High Street.

Terrain: Two well-graded climbs over two passes as pleasant as going uphill gets.

ACCOMMODATION
Traquair (01869–)
Hotels and B&Bs: The Old Schoolhouse (–830425); Quair View (–830506).
Innerleithen (01869–)
Hotels and B&Bs: Caddon View, 14 Pirn Road (–830208); Traquair Arms, Traquair Road (–830229).

WATCH OUT FOR!
Gordon Arms. The inn where Sir Walter Scott and James Hogg met for the last time.

Traquair House, Traquair (01896 830 323). Follow signs for the oldest inhabited house in Scotland, brewery and Bear Gates unopened since the failure of the 1745 rebellion.

St Ronan's Well Interpretative Centre, Wells Brae, Innerleithen. Sample health-giving waters from nineteenth-century spa.

Robert Smails Printing Works (NTS), High Street, Innerleithen (01896 830 206). See how printing was done at the beginning of the twentieth century.

INNERLEITHEN TO EDINBURGH (30 MILES)
Leave High Street by turning left into Leithen Road, just beyond Robert Smail's Printing Works. Leave Innerleithen on Leithen Road, B709. Follow road through golf course and climb steadily through the Moorfoot Hills. Keep left at the right turn for Heriot.

About 15 miles from Innerleithen take the left for Middleton. At Middleton turn left at crossroads and continue past next turning for Outerston, Yorkston and Temple.

At next T-junction (opposite impressive gates) with B6372 turn left for Temple and Penicuik. Follow the road to the right for Carrington. Once over the bridge take the right for Carrington. In Carrington follow road round to the right and follow signs for Cockpen and Dalkeith out of the hamlet. Follow road all the way to junction with the B704. Turn left and proceed to roundabout.

At roundabout take the exit for Edinburgh, Galashiels and Hawick. At roundabout with A7 go straight over. Enter Dalkeith and Eskbank. At roundabout take third exit for Edinburgh B6392.

At next roundabout take left signed Edinburgh City bypass. Follow RR (green/red) signs. At next roundabout take the exit for Gilmerton. At

Gilmerton follow RR signs through both roundabouts (legal pavement use). Do not go onto the bypass.

Go straight over at next roundabout onto Drum Street. Go straight through at traffic lights and after about 100 yards join the cycle lane. Follow Gilmerton Road through traffic lights at Kingston Avenue. At T-junction with Liberton Road turn right. Join cycle lane/bus lane. Leave Liberton Road by going round to the left onto Craigmillar Park. Re-join cycle-lane/bus-lane. Keep going straight on all the way to T-junction with Princes Street. Turn left onto Princes Street. Beyond Princes Mall turn left and then left again into Waverley Station.

Terrain: Long slow but moderate climb through the Moorfoot Hills. After fast downhill to Middleton there are lots of ups and downs. Once in Edinburgh it is more or less level.

4

HOSPITALITY SUTHERLAND

Lairg has the feel of a place where you'd come to sell your fur, service your vices, stock-up on supplies and leave. The look is of a functional modern village built quickly between winters, hanging loosely together along the side of Loch Shin.

No matter where you are headed in Sutherland the chances are you'll end up in Lairg. I didn't ride into town on one of the five roads that come together here; I arrived by train from Glasgow via Inverness, a journey that seemed to be timed to allow for the knitting of one jumper.

An extra jumper would have been appreciated, for despite it being 1 May it was very cold and it would require more than dancing round the maypole to reawaken my dormant fertility. Indeed, had I been made of brass there would have been a need for surgery. Low cloud was trying valiantly to lift itself higher into the sky but it just sank further after every vain attempt. Loch Shin was slate grey and such a reservoir of cold discouraging sentiment.

I doubted the sanity of setting out under such an inauspicious sky and undertook to find a breakfast of sufficient size as to sustain me over the 47 empty miles to the north-west coast. There is nothing I fear more than hunger.

After a good breakfast I indulged in the activity of reluctance. I checked the brakes, the tyres, various nuts, zeroed the trip on my odometer and had my water bottles refilled. I pored over the map without really taking anything in. After all, in the whole day I would be required to turn left twice and right once and my destinations would be the only places on the signposts.

An encouraging fanfare of birdsong announced my eventual departure from Lairg. The cycling was surprisingly easy and I quickly slipped into an efficient rhythm and became mesmerised by the rapidly changing odometer. The terrain was failing to challenge or inspire. I was only vaguely aware of sheep grazing on coarse grass and their monotonous baaing. In every direction heather slowly rose to some unseen and ill-defined high point.

A wind picked up and pushed a gentle finger into my ribs as if to say, 'Whoa there, slow down, take it all in. Enjoy!'

'What?' I shouted.

Then, to make the point, the wind lifted the cover of cloud to unveil the snow-capped peaks of Ben More Assynt and Conival on the far side of Loch Shin.

'Oh, that!' It was a convincing snow covering for so late in the season and the peaks looked good against the patch of deep blue sky – they weren't so much white fangs, more a full-set. Ben Hee was next; lower, it was merely dusted suggesting it had been snowing recently.

The strengthening wind was having no impact on the ground. There were no trees to bend or swish or grass to ripple through, just motionless dead and wiry heather. No more than a faintly mouldy smell reached my nostrils. Unfairly, I put it down as a landscape bereft of stimulation and returned to my dwam.

The wind's temper grew, pushing me down into a hunch over the handlebars; the sky grew menacingly dark and the inevitable followed. The rain hammered down with fury.

Thank God for telephone boxes! Until someone develops a mobile phone that comes with a pop-up umbrella facility I will favour the stout red public variety. I occupied myself by phoning friends and family and drew up a list of suggestions to make phone boxes more comfortable. As the rain fell so heavily as to obscure the view through the glass I now thought my earlier reluctance justified. Being ill-prepared for a trip such as this would not pose any serious danger but the discomfort would be huge.

Cheery waves from the post bus, which incidentally had its headlights on, lifted my spirits as I ventured from my shelter. Almost exactly 20 years ago legendary travel writer Paul Theroux revelled in the post bus journey from Lairg to Durness. He observed that it was the postman – who was really the milkman – the paperboy – a concerned friend – and bus driver – who made life bearable and possible in such desolation.

If the Royal Mail has to make the transformation from national institution to commercial company then such a service will have to have a price and the failure to come to a sensible price will mean that it will probably be scrapped as uneconomic. Genuine concern will be replaced with corporate smiles and platitudes and the post will be delivered with a chin up and a 'You have a nice day now'.

An abandoned roofless cottage sits at the foot of the waterfalls draining the hillside on the far side of Loch Merkland, a reminder of what happens when there are those who decide that life here is not in the commercial interest. Theroux's account would hardly need revising to reflect the current experience but in 20 years will the road even be maintained?

Much changed in the descent from Loch Merkland to Loch More. The sun was shining strongly, birch trees hissed in a gentle breeze and mountains burst from the moor, shedding heather and peat as they rose to rocky peaks.

Arkle at 787 metres is not especially high but is most impressive and every bit the mountain. Its seemingly impregnable ramparts of grey Lewissian Gneiss is among the oldest rock in the world. It is fitting that such an old mountain should have such a distinguished grey head. Unfortunately, with age comes decrepitude. Arkle's unprotected slopes are splintering in the extremes of cold, wet and warm. Great fans of scree give the clearest indication that this, like all mountains, is on its way back to moor again.

Beyond Loch More I encountered a man propped against the parapet of a bridge. I commented to him on the improving weather but it was as if I had drawn attention to his idleness and he jumped to his feet and went off to join the industrious buzz centred on a group of houses slightly further on.

This was Achfary, HQ of the Duke of Westminster's Sutherland estate. One group of men were repairing a covered gateway, like the ones at the entrance to Anglican churches with great blocks of fresh green oak. There was an inscription in the green oak which mirrored the sentiments of a plaque on the wall opposite. Both remembered with fondness the Second Duke of Westminster and his contribution to life here. That was, building houses, improving the fishing and such like. They're a good sort, the British aristocracy.

No one paid me any attention, they were much too busy. I sat on a rock and watched them work and took in the view. Maybe it is appropriate that such an awesome landscape should be owned by such a wealthy man, as the price tag on as fine an example of a U-shaped valley as this would surely have to be high. As would the cost of an extremely old mountain such as Arkle, and as Loch More is particularly deep and beautiful it would have to be priced even higher.

The activity suggested an imminent visit by His Grace so I waited around to try and catch a whiff of stinkin' rich. Nothing happened so I moved on in case I was asked to make a contribution.

The venerable old Laxford Bridge straddles the River Laxford at the instant it enters the sea. The sea was blue and sparkling in the sun, the bridge was framed by vibrant yellow broom and the stone was warm to the touch when I stopped to peer into the gentle rapids for migrating salmon; the river takes its name from *lax*, the Norse for salmon.

Low-lying coastal land stretches out of the shadow of the mountains and into the sun. The mountains act as moisture magnets and the locals claim that it is dry out on these peninsulas more often than is popularly believed.

The many rocky surfaces poking through the grass give the countryside the acoustics of a cathedral. I could hear two disgruntled fishermen cursing their luck with pin-sharp clarity even though they were many hundreds of yards away. I stopped to watch their ungainly stumble back to their car. Their obvious difficulty would have been no less had they been crossing a landscape of icy seracs and crevasses. Expletives rang in the air as they disappeared off each rocky crest into another dip, usually by slipping on the wet grass, trying desperately not to use their rods as walking poles.

The early geologists dispatched to Assynt to unravel the conundrum of the area's complex geology complained that the terrain they came to study 'severely taxed their physical stamina'. They were sent to try and explain why older rock lay over young rock; their explanation is beyond the scope of this book but basically the mountains are upside down, chronologically speaking.

Easyish cycling, a favourable wind and a terse warning from my host for that evening that were I to be late for dinner I would have to starve, meant that I was well ahead of schedule by the time I reached Rhiconich.

An old Glasgow street preacher, complete with sandwich-board of doom and a regularly thumped bible, would holler, 'There is the short broad path to hell and there is the long narrow path to heaven!' Well I have found it: the long narrow path to heaven, that is. Once I had conquered the steep climb away from Rhiconich, the road that stretched before me was certainly narrow and appeared to be of infinite length as it disappeared to a point in the distance. The snag was that it was downhill and I don't think the Glasgow preacher would have had anything quite so easy in mind. We'd certainly agree on its heavenly potential.

The morning sun was gaining in strength but the air was still free of obscuring haze. Three mountains to my right – Arkle, Foinaven and Cranstackie – were vivid in this limpid atmosphere. This has to be one of the finest mountain views in Scotland. Their rise is rapid, their outline rocky and each peak stood separately.

Tiny is how the isolated croft at the foot of Cranstackie looks in such a magisterial landscape. If it weren't for its whitewashed walls I'd fancy it would easily be lost even to a long-standing resident.

Just as I was approaching a very satisfying top speed of 35 mph on a road which was straight enough and empty enough for me to take in the view as well, I spotted a well with the customary plaque attached heralding yet another improvement for Sutherland. It can't be the well, for fresh water is something Sutherland is never likely to be without. The 'improvement' was the road. OK, I can go along with that but there was the implication that the simple folk of Sutherland would not have been able to build one for themselves had the need arisen. The inhumanity of the Clearances is frequently justified by the claim that their life was improved immeasurably by the 'improvements' that followed.

I stopped to refresh my water bottles and was joined by two other cyclists who were on their way up. They congratulated me and themselves at the same time on our choice of route. It turned out that we had common acquaintances but not common goals. These guys were averaging over 100 miles in a day and on the look out for big hills to climb.

I told them of my intention to stop at Durness and to visit Cape Wrath. They somehow got the idea that I intended to cycle the 24 miles out and back. On the map there are more arrows, which indicate steep inclines, than I have ever seen on any one stretch of road, and in their view this probably makes cycling the road irresistible – but not for me. Only one of them had successfully made the trip out to the Cape and only then after several attempts.

After exchanging best wishes I continued my descent at the same speed as they continued their ascent, but then I'm more than muscle, I'm a connoisseur. The road along with the rapidly descending River Dionard soon runs into the sand. The great expanses of sand of the Kyle of Durness that greet the river trying to make its way out to sea rob it of its sense of purpose, sending it this way and that.

On the far side of the Kyle is the road to Cape Wrath, which sounds at least as scary as Cape Horn, even if 'Wrath' is merely from 'Twarth' the Norse for turning point. It probably is scarier because NATO uses it as a live firing range. Wherever there is peace you can rely on the military to declare war on it.

The road can only be reached by a small passenger ferry. A minibus meets the ferry to drive visitors out to the Cape – the most north-westerly point on the British Mainland. For cyclists who rise to the challenge and cycle out to the lighthouse there is the Cape Wrath Fellowship, administered by the CTC, who will provide a badge and certificate to those who provide suitable proof and the required amount of money.

NATO, the weather or the tide could mean the trip out to the Cape may be impossible but none seemed to hold as I turned off the road for Keoldale and the slipway. No, I was to be denied because Celtic and Rangers were playing in the Scottish Cup final. Phooey!

I was not the only one to be unimpressed. One couple decided to vent their disappointment on every institution they could think of – from the tourist board, as this was no way to run a bank holiday weekend, to the Department of Transport for not having built a bridge. Apparently they spent the whole morning looking for a bridge and hence missed the only ferry of the day. I did try phoning in advance but my calls were never answered. For me the dilemma was: should I stay put and try again in the morning or push on. I decided to let Durness decide.

Durness, scattered over two headlands separated by Sango Bay, so obviously lives with the sea but has no harbour. The sea was not the reason for living here, rather it was limestone. The underlying limestone means calcareous soils and swards of green grass rather than soggy black peat and wiry heather. The green grass was also the reason why people were to be cleared from the land, but a riot led by the women of the district saw off an attempt to drive them away. Durness was too remote for the government to assist the landowner by deploying troops so they managed to stay put for another year.

Durness looked happy in the sun and I decided to stay. The campsite on its cliff-top didn't look so preposterous in such fine weather. The whole coastline was one of high forbidding cliffs and even in the sandy bays the crashing Atlantic rollers struggled to find their way ashore through rocky defences. I became quite entranced by the huge waves rippling along a wall of rock that runs out to sea at right angles to the tide; each wave leaves a wet imprint behind, the start of the slow process of etching the ripple into the rock.

I drifted, not down to the beaches but west again to the Balnakeil Craft Village. A little colony of artists have colonised a disused early warning station, a hangover from the Cold War. It was one of the places from which the infamous four-minute warning could have emanated.

Each flat-roofed hut is a separate artistic enterprise. Wandering from one outlet to another I found that it was not difficult to establish the source of their inspiration. For what you see on the outside all around, you see on the inside. It is earthy art of pottery fungi and glazed rock for sale at prices that would lead the Duke of Westminster to believe he is sitting on an estate of infinite value.

The good weather continued into the next day. A thin veil of mist hung around the cliffs and sea stacks as the ocean continued its onslaught. It was a perfect Sunday morning and without a thought for my plans to visit the Cape I turned downhill from the Youth Hostel, over the huge cavern of Smoo Cave which lies directly beneath the road and out of Durness. The sky was already deep blue and although it was invigoratingly cool there was the promise of warmth in the air.

Each chip of granite set in the road was a jewel in the sunlight, people were waving from the doors of their cottages and I was feeling so comfortable that I had the breath to whistle and even sing. The road east twisted round delectable sandy bays which I felt obligated to sample in true tourist tradition but managed to resist. The golden sands meet the dark blue water to give the coast a regal trim.

As I spun easily round to Loch Eriboll the pleasure only increased. Foinaven, Arkle and Cranstackie, from this perspective, were a crowded range of peaks at the head of the loch, their ridges on this side accentuated by slivers of snow. The glen that lead into them looked little visited. Hanging onto a remnant of ancient forest it had a prehistoric quality. If I were looking for woolly mammoths, I'd check there first.

People weren't cleared to make way for sheep – I think it possible that they were cleared because the aristocracy believed that the simple folk of Sutherland couldn't possibly cope with such awesome beauty and had to be moved away lest they go mad.

The seamen of the Second World War would not have agreed that it was the beauty of the place that would drive a person mad but rather its hopeless isolation. Loch Eriboll was a safe assembly point for ships before they made the dash across the Atlantic and ironically the surrender point for the German U-boat fleet. The sailors nicknamed it 'Loch 'Orrible' but then they had the gloom of war bearing down on them and maybe even some rain.

Of course, had the weather been bad and progress not so easy then I might not have been so enthusiastic. However, I have been here in bad weather and the landscape is still dramatic and a little threatening and the 25 miles to Tongue do seem endless. Whereas today 25 miles is not enough and had there been a bridge back across to the start I would have gladly gone round and round. Well, if there had been a bridge *and* somewhere to get a bite to eat.

The east side of the loch needs a little more work than the west side. The climbs and descents introduce tiny nuances and unseen tucks to the lochside that throw up little novelties such as a copse of broad-leaved trees or clumps of vibrant broom reeking of vanilla. One small cove with its colourful little cottage on the shore almost persuaded me that I could give everything up and settle here.

A helluva pull away from Loch Eriboll introduced a measure of reality. The sweat stung my eyes and the warm water in my bottles failed to quench my thirst but complaints on a day such as this would have been churlish. It was so still that Ben Hope, a simple and elegant mountain, was perfectly reflected in Loch Hope at its foot.

The descent to Loch Hope was marred by the ascent looming ahead. It was signed as 15 per cent and climbed to over 700 ft from sea level. The route along the north coast from now on was tough with several ups and downs before the gentler Flow Country. You can opt out of the hill on the first bend by taking the turning for Altnaharra and Lairg, although this would short circuit the whole route; it's something worth bearing in mind.

Historically, the lines of communication followed the straths north and there was no real need to cross the high ground between them. However the Clearances moved the people from the fertile straths out onto the rocky coastline, thereby necessitating coastal roads. Thus the Clearances effectively turned the county inside out.

The familiar outline of a roofless building, which apparently had been built as an inn, was waiting for me at the highest point of the road. Its isolation against the backdrop of Ben Hope makes it photogenic and its singular presence gives scale to the empty moor. On the gable there was yet another plaque praising the Marquis of Stafford, later to become 1st Duke of Sutherland, for once again initiating the building of the road. I wonder who initiated and paid for these plaques?

My momentum would have carried me all the way across the causeway over the Kyle of Tongue to Tongue if it hadn't been for the strong wind blowing up the kyle. Tongue was tantalisingly close but I struggled as if I was cycling in the surrounding sand rather than on the causeway. The whole time I was overlooked by the ideally placed Castle Bharraich on a spur above the kyle and backed up by the imposing Ben Loyal.

There was a choice of hotels for lunch in Tongue. I chose the Tongue Hotel over the Ben Loyal Hotel for no other reason than it had its doors open wide. However the Tongue Hotel was designed with colder weather in mind with its heavy wood and pictures of the hunt, and cosiness seems to be the desired effect to chase the chill of whatever hunt from your bones.

It happened twice in Durness and now in Tongue: the minute I mentioned I was bound for Bettyhill, faces crumpled and a variation of the same warning followed. 'Oh they're a hard lot in Bettyhill.' 'Ah wouldnae be stayin' in Bettyhill.' 'There's a lot a hard drinkin' goin' on in Bettyhill.' I had forgotten the Durness warnings but hearing them again gave greater credence to them.

At first I went as fast as I could so as to have time to push on to Melvich but this wasn't a day for rushing. A good lunch had removed my hungry impatience and I settled down to a pleasant unrushed pace. It seemed more likely that I would fall short of Bettyhill.

Soon the kyle was far below. From above, the Rabbit Islands do indeed look like big green rabbits and it was on one of these islands that a ship, the *Hazard,* was deliberately run aground while being pursued by the

Royal Navy. On board was French gold to help pay for the Jacobite Rebellion of 1745. The crew were apprehended and all but two chests of the gold confiscated. The missing two were supposedly dumped in Loch Hakel (south end of the Kyle of Tongue) and as yet have not been recovered.

H. V. Morton, the motorists' travel writer, said there would be a change at Tongue. He was travelling in the opposite direction to me but, still, there should be a change and there was. There was none of the sterility of the high moor between Eriboll and Tongue. Communities seemed stronger and there was hardly a missing roof. People were taking advantage of a warm afternoon to plough and plant.

I decided to stick to my original plan and stay in Bettyhill but time my arrival for as late as possible. I detoured from the main road, taking the turning for Skerray. I soon found myself in a valley that I knew to be close to the sea but the sea was locked from my view by small but steep hills.

Skerray is a traditional community. Colourful little salmon boats sat on piles at each croft awaiting a new coat of paint, peat was piled by doorways, old dogs sniffed at my panniers, an old RAC sign pointed out a telephone box; the shop and post office had a thatched roof. Occasionally there was someone out cleaning what looked like the first generation of tractors and they were all of this vintage, though, judging by the small areas that were ploughed, their lives have not been too taxing. Skerray's graveyard, overlooking Torrisdale Bay, documented the plight of its people. Whole families lost at sea in stricken emigrant ships, disease, war, drowning and misadventure in the colonies, the after-effects of the Clearances.

Another climb took me over the final headland and into Strathnaver. The contrast with the rest of Sutherland was dramatic. When I first ventured from Lairg I wondered what it was that made people want to stay but, of course, that was the type of land they were cleared to. The fertility of Strathnaver is undeniable; it's a veritable jungle and it was in Strathnaver that the ugliest scenes of the Clearances were witnessed.

Bettyhill, where many of the evictees ended up, is right on the limit of the land, to underline the point that their presence was only grudgingly accommodated. Bettyhill must have been painfully close to their former homes.

It was 1 p.m. the next day before I set off from the Farr Bay Inn in Bettyhill. I spent most of the morning lying out on the sand dunes immediately behind the inn hoping the gentle sound of waves would ease the pain in my head. All night all the locals felt it their responsibility to buy me a drink. Each time they presented themselves at the bar they would add, '. . . and whatever Paul's having.' It was not long before there was a backlog of seven pints, which it was only good manners to consume. I did try to intervene and prevent an order going through; the reply, however, was indignant, 'And what'll be wrong with my money?'

They regaled me with stories of poaching, infidelity and brushes with the law. We discussed whether the statue of the Duke of Sutherland above Golspie should be blown up in the manner of a fallen Communist leader and why I happened to be passing through. Jim MacLeod the proprietor told them I was from the Inland Revenue but still they bought me drink. We did discuss their reputation for hard drinking – the men couldn't understand such a slur but the women nodded in resigned agreement.

A gravestone near the entrance to the Strathnaver Museum reads: 'Born – New Zealand. Died – London. Buried Here.' It is indicative of the sense of humour of the Bettyhill folk but also their need to migrate in order to find stable employment. It turned out that most of my generous hosts were only home from London for the holiday weekend.

The road from Bettyhill to Melvich followed much the same pattern as the road from Eriboll to Bettyhill, up and down with by now tedious regularity. Orkney, John O'Groats and the Old Man of Hoy all came into view at some point on the road between Bettyhill and Melvich but it was the green pasture of Caithness ahead that caused me a feeling of disquiet, even more so the sight of the nuclear reprocessing plant at Dounreay. I suppose I wasn't ready to give up the unique Sutherland landscape for something so familiar.

I'd intended lunching at the Melvich Hotel as Edwin Muir had done. He had found it particularly favourable for its lack of dead animals on the walls but I feared the consumption of alcohol might be as compulsory in Melvich as it was in Bettyhill.

I picnicked by the roadside and contemplated my day's destination of the Garvault Inn. The people I spoke to in Bettyhill were emphatic that I should not stay at the Garvault. Away from the coasts the hotels are the only destinations. They exist in splendid or perhaps overwhelming isolation largely to service anglers. The Garvault Inn claims to be the most remote establishment on the British Isles and from its position on the map this seemed likely.

I set off anyway up Strath Halladale thinking I might stay at the Forsinard Hotel only 14 miles away rather than the Garvault which was 30 miles inland. The moment I set off I encountered two End to Enders on the penultimate leg of their journey to John O'Groats. They had stayed the night at the Forsinard Hotel and they had been told not to stay at the Garvault. They didn't really know why and I told them that the people in Bettyhill didn't really offer a reason either.

Away from the coast the air was stationary and the heat sapping. The road though was only gently rising. There was no dominant feature on the skyline, only acres of commercial forestry or bare gently rising slopes of yellowy grass.

A corrugated-iron church by the roadside and the hot silence created the eerie atmosphere of an abandoned mission in some war-torn colony. This is the Flow Country, once the place to plant tax-evading commercial forestry until the RSPB stepped in and reminded everyone that it was also a unique habitat of worldwide significance. Some would even go as far as saying that as an outstanding ecosystem the Flow Country is on a par with the Amazon rainforest. The slick exhibition in the RSPB Visitor Centre at Forsinard Station tries very hard to get across the extent of the diversity of plant, animal and bird-life that the Flow supports.

At Kinbrace I became self-consciously aware of my lonely isolation to the extent that I began to doubt if I really was alone. It was little things like sounds I couldn't attribute to anything and a feeling of being watched. I would stop and look all around but there would be nothing, and I mean nothing, as the whole area is indescribably vast. The mountains that drew me west and along the north coast were like the stumpy rim of a long extinct volcano, placing me at the centre of its enormous crater.

As the road went up and down – but mainly up – I caught glimpses of the Garvault Inn. I couldn't form any kind of opinion from where I was except that it looked very small and there was no other building. I was sure now that I was being followed; by who or what I had no idea – though my imagination favoured a what. Loch Ness may be so deep as to hide a monster, the Flow is certainly big enough to be the home of a great big slavering beast.

The turn off for the Garvault presented itself but I lost sight of the hotel altogether. I tried to think of someone who definitely knew I was here but I couldn't think of anyone except my wife, who only has a vague idea of where I am at the best of times. I could have stayed at the Forsinard but it was twice the price and didn't have the title of Britain's remotest hotel.

The bark of a dog caused my body to spasm. He was slavering but he was more Labrador than beast. The hotel, a cobbled collection of extensions to an old core was not exactly braw. Inside the hotel looked tired; let's say it wasn't a deliberate attempt at retro.

The lady of the house showed me to my room with the words, 'You'll be in the spooky room.'

'You mean there is only the one?'

It didn't feel particularly spooky but once I had come to bed after having spent as long as was polite in the bar I discovered the door didn't lock. Once I was safely ensconced in my bed, which faced the door, I settled down to identify the source and an explanation for every pop, creak, footstep, tap, rattle, hum and scrape, when the bloody door popped open.

I now had a view of a darkened corridor with doors suspiciously ajar. The owners had looked and behaved normally enough. I stared and stared into the gloom trying to detect the merest hint of a presence. Gingerly I made my way to the door to close it over and then fumbled with the lock, but to no avail.

I swapped beds, for no other reason than to be further away from the door, you understand, and to give myself a sporting chance. Every 30 minutes, pop, the door would swing open and bang against the wardrobe. The next time it happened I remembered about the wardrobe. I should have checked inside and the top. For the next hour I practised reaching for the bedside light, switching it on and pointing it at the door Gary Cooper style. By 3 a.m. I was really quite good at it.

Over breakfast I lied about having slept well, which must have been apparent because I was asked several times. Breakfast was huge and I was sent on my way with a much-needed baseball cap to keep off the unexpected sun and good recommendations for every hotel in the area that I might want to stay at. The Hendersons were very kind hosts and it seems that their hotel has a bit of a cult following. You have to do it – it's an experience.

It was another incredibly bright day, which I don't suppose suited the fishermen and women on the Naver. Looking up and down the river from Syre I could see several groups evenly spaced along the banks and their very big posh cars parked on the road. The Naver is one of Scotland's premier salmon rivers. It is a river with a very even temperament, the rapids are gentle and the banks are straight. In fact you could believe it was designed for the purpose.

Conifer forest detracts slightly from the appeal of the Naver at Syre but it is obviously a spot where people once thrived. Strathnaver men grew to over 6 ft tall and were welcome recruits in any army, and it has been established that people have lived here for several millennia. Syre is to the Clearances as Tolpuddle is to the struggle for workers' rights. The most defining moments of the policy of forced clearances took place here, not least due to the fact that Patrick Sellar, a name Sutherland folk can hardly bring themselves to mention, lived here.

Sellar was a man who used whatever means necessary to get the job done and probably coined the phrase 'ruthless efficiency'. He was resident at the time Donald MacLeod recalls in his polemic *Gloomy Memories*: the dogs barking, women and children screaming, 300 roofs burning and the beasts in a state of distress. Boats in Torrisdale Bay reported difficulty in finding their way through the palls of smoke for at least three days afterwards.

Sellar was eventually arrested and tried for culpable homicide in Thurso but he was acquitted. Donald Macleod, for his troubles, was evicted again from Thurso and banished from the estate. However, the trial did put the policy of clearing people from the land high on the political agenda and the Crofters Act of 1886 resulted. The act was too late for Sutherland, though, and the damage had been done. If I were to be honest – and the three cyclists I met by Loch Naver were – we were all here for the emptiness.

It had all seemed too easy when I reached Lairg once again. The final miles passed without me really noticing and I wished I had savoured them. It could have been very different had the weather been bad but them's the breaks.

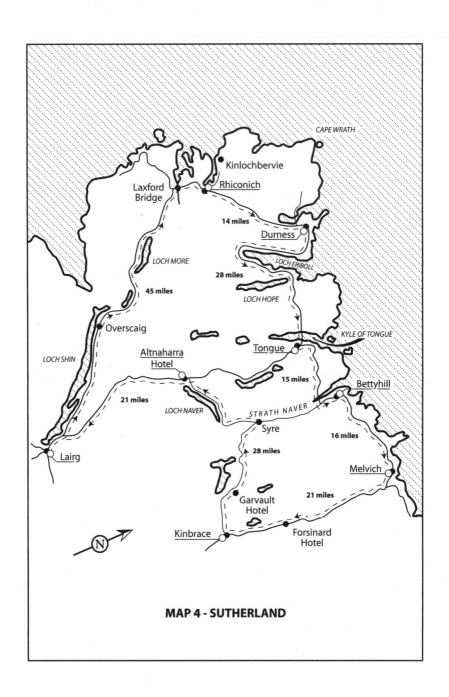

CAPE WRATH

Kinlochbervie

Laxford Bridge

Rhiconich

14 miles

Durness

LOCH ERIBOLL

LOCH MORE

28 miles

45 miles

LOCH HOPE

Overscaig

KYLE OF TONGUE

Tongue

LOCH SHIN

Altnaharra Hotel

15 miles

Bettyhill

21 miles

LOCH NAVER

STRATH NAVER

Lairg

Syre

16 miles

28 miles

Melvich

Garvault Hotel

21 miles

N

Kinbrace

Forsinard Hotel

MAP 4 - SUTHERLAND

SUTHERLAND: ESSENTIALS

Distance: 185 miles

Maps: OS *Landranger* series (1:50,000), sheets 9, 10, 15, 16, 17. OS *Road Map 1: Northern Scotland*.

Banks/Cashpoints: Durness, Tongue and Bettyhill.

Cycle Repair: There are none available en route. The nearest cycle shops are in Thurso.

General Stores: Lairg, Inshegra, Durness, Tongue, Melvich. There are no shops between Melvich and the return to Lairg.

Traffic: You will experience some traffic on the coastal roads and virtually none on the interior roads; on the whole very quiet.

GETTING THERE

Train: Glasgow Queen Street Station or Edinburgh Waverley to Inverness. Change at Inverness for Lairg. Typically two bikes per train. Advance booking of spaces is essential. Journey times: Glasgow/Edinburgh to Inverness is 3 hours 30 minutes; Inverness to Lairg is 1 hour 40 minutes. You should allow a whole day for travel to and from Lairg.

ROUTE INFORMATION

LAIRG TO RHICONICH (45 MILES)
Leave Lairg on the A836 and follow for four miles. Turn left onto A838 for Scourie, Kinlochbervie (45) and Durness (55). Follow the A838 for 37

miles to Laxford Bridge. Turn right at Laxford Bridge for Kinlochbervie (9) and Durness (19) and Rhiconich (5).

Terrain: Level or gently rising for most of the 45 miles. Only two short steep hills.

ACCOMMODATION
Lairg (01549–)
Hotels and B&Bs: The Nip Inn (–402953); Park House (–402208).
Hostels: Carbisdale Castle SYHA, seven miles to the south of Lairg. Leave train at Culrain (request stop) (–421232).
Camping: Dunroamin' Caravan and Camping Park (–402447)
Rhiconich, Inshegra and Kinlochbervie (01971–)
Hotels and B&Bs: Rhiconich Hotel (–521224). Old School House, Inshegra (three miles off route towards Kinlochbervie) (–521383).

WATCH OUT FOR!
Ferrycroft Countryside Centre, Lairg. Travel Information Centre, walks, archaeology and local and natural history.

RHICONICH TO DURNESS (14 MILES)
Continue to follow the A838 north from Rhiconich for Durness (14) and Tongue (44).

Terrain: Steep climb away from Rhiconich. Short descent followed by moderate climb. Long fast downhill follows but there is a small rise into Durness.
Detour: Three miles short of Durness take the left-hand turn signed Keoldale ¼ mile for the ferry to Cape Wrath. It is a challenging 22-mile round trip to the Cape Wrath Lighthouse and Clo Mor cliffs. There is a minibus if you don't fancy cycling. Ferry: Mr J. Morrison (01971 511376). Minibus (May–Sept.): Mrs I. Mackay (01971 511287). Cape Wrath Fellowship – more detailed information from the CTC who, if you send a cheque and some proof that you cycled there and back, will send you a badge and a certificate. More details at www.ctc.org.

ACCOMMODATION
Durness (01971–)
Hotels and B&Bs: Cape Wrath Hotel (Keoldale Ferry) (–511212); Puffin Cottage (–511208); Parkhill Hotel (–511202); Mr Martin Mackay, Glengolly (–511255).
Hostels: Durness SYHA (May–Sept) (–511244); The Lazy Crofter Bunkhouse (–511209/511366).
Camping: Sango Sands (–511262).

WATCH OUT FOR!
Balnakeil Craft Village. One mile to the west of Durness, signposted from the village. The village's Loch Croispol Bookshop and Restaurant is a pleasant place to lunch.

Balnakeil Church and Churchyard, *circa* 1619 – contains graves of murderer Domhnuall MacMhurchadh and monument to the Gaelic poet Robb Donn.

Smoo Cave. Largest sea cave in Britain. There are boat trips into the inner caves.

DURNESS TO TONGUE (28 MILES)

Turn right to follow A838 east through Durness. The A838 continues around Loch Eriboll and then over the Moine to Tongue.

Terrain: Starts off easily enough but there are two significant climbs in quick succession. There is a steep climb away from Loch Eriboll and another away from Loch Hope.

Detours: Talmine and Melness (six-mile round trip) – old salmon fishing and crofting communities. Turn left just before crossing the causeway over the Kyle of Tongue.

Kyle of Tongue – rather than cross the causeway to Tongue you can round the end of the Kyle following the old road off to the right on the downhill to the causeway. This detour will add about seven miles and is challenging in places.

ACCOMMODATION
Tongue (01847–)
Hotels and B&Bs: The Ben Loyal Hotel (–611216); The Tongue Hotel (–611206); Rhian Cottage (–611257); Woodend (–611216).
Hostels: Tongue SYHA (–611301).
Camping: Kincraig (–611218).
Talmine (01847–)
Hotels and B&Bs: Cloisters (–601286).
Camping: Talmine Camping (–601225).

WATCH OUT FOR!
Varick Castle. Ruin of eleventh-century Norse stronghold overlooking the Kyle of Tongue.

TONGUE TO BETTYHILL VIA SKERRAY (15 MILES)

Follow round to the left at the Tongue Hotel and uphill out of Tongue, continue past turning for Lairg A836, instead join the A836 and follow it east for Bettyhill and Thurso. Four miles out of Tongue take the minor road to the left for detour via Skerray. Emerge to re-join the A836 at the Borgie Hotel and turn left for Bettyhill (6).

Terrain: There is a moderate climb out of Tongue. From then on it is fairly gentle until you return to the main road at Borgie where there is a moderate climb over into Strathnaver.

ACCOMMODATION
Borgie (01641–)
Hotels and B&Bs: Borgie Lodge Hotel (–521332).
Bettyhill (01641–)
Hotels and B&Bs: The Farr Bay Inn (–521230); Bettyhill Hotel (–521332); Shenley (–521421); Bruachmhor (–521265).

WATCH OUT FOR!
Jimson's Centre, Skerray (01641 521445). Renovated thatched cottages housing a post office, craft shop, Skerray studio, garden centre and museum.
Strathnaver Museum, Bettyhill. Focuses on the Clearances and prehistory.

BETTYHILL TO MELVICH (16 MILES)

Follow the A836 east through Bettyhill to Melvich.

Terrain: Several up and downs between Bettyhill and Melvich, the first of which is the steepest.

ACCOMMODATION
Melvich (01641–)
Hotels and B&Bs: Melvich Hotel (–531206); Mrs Joan Ritchie (–531262); The Sheiling (–531256).
Camping: Halladale Inn Caravan Park (–531282).

MELVICH TO KINBRACE (21 MILES)

Leave Melvich on the A836. One mile out of Melvich turn right for the A897 for Kinbrace and Forsinard RSPB Wetland.

Terrain: Very gently rising road all the way to Kinbrace; very pleasant, in fact.

ACCOMMODATION
Forsinard (01641–)
Hotels and B&Bs: Forsinard Hotel (–571221); Station Cottage (–571262).

WATCH OUT FOR!
Forsinard RSPB Nature Reserve Visitor Centre (01641 571225). An exhibition on the Flow Country and the abundance of bird life and wildlife that lives in it is housed in the old railway station buildings.

KINBRACE TO ALTNAHARRA (28 MILES)
At station take the right, B871, for Syre (16) and Altnaharra (27). At T-junction at Syre turn left for the B873 for Altnaharra (11) and Lairg (27).

Terrain: Nothing more than moderate uphills that don't last especially long; in the main the cycling is relaxed.

ACCOMMODATION
Garvault
Hotels and B&Bs: Garvault Hotel, seven miles beyond Kinbrace, (01431 831224).
Altnaharra
Hotels and B&Bs: Altnaharra Inn (01549 411222)

WATCH OUT FOR!
Rosal Clearance Village. Turn left just before you cross the Naver at Syre and follow signs. There is a trail that explains the events that took place throughout Strathnaver during the Clearances.

ALTNAHARRA TO LAIRG (21 MILES)
At T-junction with A836 turn left and follow the A836 all the way to Lairg.

Terrain: Climbs moderately at first followed by a long downhill and then level into Lairg from highpoint.

ACCOMMODATION
Crask
Hotels and B&Bs: Crask Inn (nine miles south of Altnaharra) (01549 411241).

5

THE GAELS
THE WESTERN ISLES

'Four boats, two trains and two buses' was how we sold a cycle holiday to our two daughters Beth, five, and Claire, three. They were clearly impressed, as they went off to pack their things there and then.

Over the next few weeks we whittled down their list of essential items to a shared pack of pens, two colouring-in books and a pack of *Teletubbie* Snap Cards with the promise of purchasing a kite and a bucket and spade as soon as we arrived. We answered all their questions and at the same time encouraged a little anticipation.

'Are the boats big boats?'

'Oh yes!'

'Will we be staying a tent?'

'Yes.'

'Will we see dolphins?'

'Hopefully!'

That was the winner. They danced around chanting, 'We're going to see dolphins.'

Twelve hours after leaving Glasgow's Queen Street Station we sailed out of the swollen Minch and into the waters sheltered by the outstretched arms of Barra and Vatersay.

I tried various strategies to distract them from their disappointment that five hours in a ferry didn't yield a single dolphin sighting. I tried to turn our ferry into a Viking longship or a Hebridean galley but they were beyond the limits of their inexperienced imaginations, as was a lug-sailed herring wherry but they loved the sound of that, prompting them to spin round, arms out, and recite, 'Herring wherry, herring wherry, herring wherry . . .' ad nauseam.

Kisimul Castle, sitting on its own little island in the bay, was next to grab their attention.

'Is there a queen?'

'And a princess?'

'No, I don't think so!'

'Humff!'

With no princesses and no dolphins Barra was not going to be an automatic hit. Although the chiefs of the Clan MacNeil, who occupied the castle, used to send a minion onto the battlements to declare, 'The MacNeil having dined, all the other princes of the world may now eat.'

The pomposity of such a declaration suggests that Barra has always been fairly detached. Colonel Gordon of Cluny, the island's most infamous owner, thought the island an excellent place to send all of Britain's crooks and criminals so he offered it to the Crown as a penal colony and set about clearing all the innocent inhabitants from the island. Now the perverse logic that says you banish people from an island, so as you can banish people to an island, so that innocent and guilty are treated alike, displays the more sinister form of detachment from reality that the people of these islands and most of the rest of Highland Scotland have had to endure for generations. Incidentally, the Crown refused his offer but sent him an emigrant ship anyway to get rid of the infernal folk.

On the car deck waiting for the bow doors to open were at least 100 other cyclists. Some were easily identified as such by their Lycra shorts, luminescent jackets, permanently affixed helmets, shoes that clacked with every step, aerodynamic eyewear and a tendency to spontaneous stretching exercises.

There were others who for all the world looked like motorists – calm and casual – and it wasn't until they lifted their bike to disembark that they gave themselves away. Then there was us, unmistakably cyclists but different from all the others. I was pulling Claire behind me in a trailer along with most of our camping equipment and Beth was attached to my wife Catherine's bike on a trailer bike. This meant that Beth could assist her mother by pedalling and, rather ironically, limited the amount of luggage they could carry.

Immediately we swapped sea legs for cycling legs and set off up the short steep hill into the village. As a hundred or so cyclists made their way ashore, rather than us leaving a Calmac Ferry, the scene could instead have been home time at some Beijing factory – an impressive and encouraging sight.

Catherine never quite found her sea legs so Beth joined Claire in her trailer for the short journey out of the village past Kisimul Castle and out to a headland camping spot. There are no official campsites on Barra but I would've only used one if it had been here, overlooking the bay sheltered by the hills of Barra and Vatersay.

It was a very auspicious start. The sky was cloudless save for wisps hanging round the summit of Heaval as if it were a dormant volcano sending out a reminder of its volatility. Kisimul Castle glowed pink in the setting sun, then dwindled to a silhouette before vanishing altogether in the black night.

Rain always sounds heavier in a tent. The taut nylon exaggerates the pitter-patter into an emphatic drumbeat but when it sounds like the timpani section beating out the *1812* Overture you know that it really is heavy. Despite the previous evening's glorious sunset it was a manky Sunday morning.

We tolerated the tent being used as a bouncy castle, we fed the children and ourselves unhealthy amounts of stodgy comfort food, played endless games of Snap and I Spy but there is only so much confinement a three-year-old and a five-year-old can take. By early afternoon they were both higher than a waitress in a Dutch café. Mercifully the rain stopped.

Three seals playing in the bay amused Beth and Claire while we broke camp and packed. Within half-an-hour of the rain abating we were off.

The light under the grey sky was not very flattering. It emphasised that Barra, along with most of the rest of Highland Scotland, is painted with few colours. The grey sky was mirrored in the grey sea and Castlebay would not require camouflage were we to be at war.

In Castlebay people provide the colour and they were absent from the scene. The night before, the whole island seemed to be packed into Castlebay's two bars. There is probably a specific Celtic gene that triggers a need to drink large quantities of whisky and have a raucous good time.

We left Castlebay to tackle the island in a clockwise direction, which meant a smaller hill to begin with and a big change in outlook right away. Climbing the hill, it felt as though I had dropped anchor in the bay and had only now drifted to the full extent of the chain, although by the time I had reached the top and was filling my lungs with Atlantic air I had forgotten the struggle.

The downhill and the strong south-westerly kicking in behind us had the girls whooping and hollering. Beth was screaming, 'We're beating you!' while Claire rocked back and forward in her trailer to stimulate more speed and yelled, 'Faster Daddy! Faster!' At 15 mph we could run out of road in less than an hour.

We were zipping along, hundreds of birds were singing together and the ocean was breaking hard on the beaches. The machair was ablaze with the colour of thousands of flowering daisies and buttercups. The beaches were busy with people, walking off hangovers, perhaps, in the bracing wind.

The adrenaline pumping through our bodies was partly due to the speed, partly to do with the drama of the setting and partly due to the fact that our venture was working. The only downside was that Seal Bay was predictably without seals.

In no time at all we were turning north off the main round island road for Eoligarry. We chose to camp on the machair that fringes Barra's beach airport. The airport is Barra's premier idiosyncrasy. I don't know what I imagined but running onto the beach runway was rather like jumping into a swimming pool with no water in it. Your legs buckle when they don't sink, as expected, into the soft sand, rather like when you're expecting one more step on a flight of stairs. It was brick-hard cockle-shell sand.

The airport terminal was instantly recognisable to the girls as one from their Lego kits at home, complete with dinky fire engines. We wandered over for a close-up look at a small plane heavily weighed down with rocks on ropes and wedged in the sand that had a damaged propeller, tail and windscreen. This more than made up for the lack of seals in Seal Bay.

We woke the next morning to a deep blue sky. The sun was warming and the wind still blew strongly from the south-west. As long as it stayed there we would be fine. Still ensconced in our sleeping bags we watched while a tiny little speck in the east became a tiny little plane on the beach. In the end it was the everydayness of the operation that was remarkable. The plane returned to the sky with as little fuss as it had landed.

The ferry between the north end of Barra and Eriskay was an intimate journey through droves of little islands and skerries. The ferry resembled the amphibious landing craft that the marines use and sitting as low in the water it provided a perfect opportunity for dolphin spotting. This time the girls, sensing that my disappointment was growing, spotted them for me. 'Look there's one there.' 'And there, Daddy.' It's funny, I thought it unethical to kid them on.

To me the ferry sums up Hebridean life – you live with geographical limitations and you work round about them. The ferry slows things down and keeps things just slightly out of your control. No matter how hassled your journey, here is a need to stop and do nothing more than take in the view.

It was a partial reunion of the cyclists who had sailed over from Oban. We discussed panniers, good spots to camp and the big hill on Eriskay. For someone towing a trailer filled with a heavy child and camping equipment there was a tendency to dwell on this information. Rather than looking forward to Eriskay as the island of *Whisky Galore* or as the most romantic island in the Hebrides, I was thinking of it as the island with the big hill.

Some people pushed their bikes off the ferry, up the slipway and then kept pushing up the hill. I'd found it wasn't especially easy to push the bike and trailer so I gave cycling up the hill a go. Finding a steady but slow rhythm, I made it all the way to the top, although Catherine and Beth working as a team made it look quite easy.

From the top of the hill looking down on the village, 'The Colourful Island' seems a convincing epithet. The cottages and the island's prominent church are whitewashed. Many roofs are in either bright blue or red. On the downhill a statue of Our Lady was striking in blue and white, adding another spot of colour to the rough green hillsides.

The island is probably all the more colourful for the events of 1941 when the SS *Politician* ran aground with a cargo of bicycle parts and 240,000 bottles of whisky. The islanders' selfless efforts to rescue the whisky from a watery grave were immortalised and romanticised in Compton MacKenzie's book *Whisky Galore* and later by the Ealing film of the same name. In real life, however, the Inland Revenue had some of the islanders prosecuted and imprisoned for theft.

The island also happens to be famous for its own unique breed of pony, as well as Gaelic's most romantic love song, 'The Eriskay Love Lilt', and it was on Eriskay that Bonnie Prince Charlie first placed his feet on Scottish soil in 1745. For an island considered too barren even for sheep it has fared well.

Had another whisky-laden ship run aground? For we found Eriskay was closed and deserted. Complaints of hunger drove us on, over the causeway to South Uist. Had there been a ferry we could have had a long, hungry wait. The new causeway was long enough and exposed enough to the sea to maintain the feeling of leaving an island.

For a time the road was into the west. Cycling into the wind was tough and the road was close enough to the ocean to feel the spray on our faces and the salt on our lips. When we turned north the wind was once again at our backs and pushing us along like the cycling equivalent of the jet-stream. Indeed, there was no need to pedal.

The road on South Uist sticks to the low-lying land on the west. The road is not flat, rather it has a melodious quality. The melody has a very gentle tempo and it was easy on the breath; it was lulling and hypnotic. The girls were strangely compliant and silent as we glided along. To the Australian Aboriginals the landscape is full of song and it is the song that describes their world. Well, like the Aboriginals, I think I can almost hear the song this landscape is singing.

The South Uist folk no doubt know the song by heart. I imagine there will be a beautiful Gaelic air that will perfectly describe the look and the mood of this landscape. Despite the contrasts between the pure white sand dunes, the vivid green machair, the tousled heather, sticky black peat and grey rock of the moor, the lie of the land is harmonious and flowing. From the beach to the hills the land rises without an eye-offending judder.

It was especially to South Uist that the folklorists and ethnologists flocked to record the stories and songs that the storytellers and bards kept in their heads, before these people died and these tales were lost.

On any map, the Outer Hebrides look hopelessly vulnerable on the edge of the overwhelming Atlantic Ocean. The hills on the east give South Uist substance but even the land seems to be composed of a high proportion of water. Reedy lochs lap against the road and we had to avert our eyes from the glare of the reflected sun.

There are many communities signposted Cille Pheadair or Smeircleit but they don't really come to any defining point. Instead, they straggle into each other. The scattered crofts give the feeling of space counteracting the slightly clustering claustrophobia of Eriskay. Dalabrog (or Daliburgh) is the nearest South Uist gets to an island capital. Among its civic amenities is the Co-operative supermarket housed in a large windowless shed that can only be entered via a narrow doorway.

The supermarket was well stocked and the prices didn't seem to be out of line with the mainland. The assistants were likely to be the only people we'd meet so I quizzed them on what was up ahead, where the next supermarket was and whether they could suggest a picnic space. Every question was answered thoroughly, even if they had to go and ask someone else. They even let the girls use the staff toilets and refilled our water bottles.

It was too windy for the suggested picnic site on the machair so we continued north to find a more sheltered spot. It wasn't looking at all promising. We'd travelled four miles with the girls complaining more loudly with every mile. We were all in need of lunch but a picnic can only be enjoyed in the right spot. It was then that the right spot presented itself: the birthplace of Flora MacDonald – the woman whose bravery enabled Bonnie Prince Charlie to escape to France.

Behind the low wall, which is all that remains of Flora's birthplace, was a perfect spot for a picnic. With our backs against the warm stone obelisk we continued to enjoy the sun out of the wind. We dined and then snoozed like vagrants, while the girls went off and had 'adventures'.

It was four before we set off again and then stopped after five hundred yards at the roadside museum. At the museum an elderly lady became very intrigued by our mode of transport, 'New Age, is that what it is?' I'd never considered our approach to be anything other than a good way to travel. I suppose the freedom that it bestows and the environmental aspect are New Age ideals so I was happy to be considered from the New Age. It might also explain the look of disdain that we got from some motorists.

'Some folk just come over on the ferry to Loch Boisdale and then drive up to Lochmaddy and get a ferry back off again. How can they see anything or speak to anyone at that speed? Slow's the way to do it.' She added to her approval with a squeeze on the forearm but wanted to see Claire actually in the trailer in order to complete the picture and pass on her experience, knowing she had seen it with her own eyes.

At an abandoned post office we turned off the main road and cycled in among the scattered crofts of Bornish. Old sheep dogs came over for a sniff, chickens scuttled from the road, women gathered in washing, while others added blocks of peat to beehive-shaped piles, boys played football on what looked impossible gardens of rocks and hollows and a man stood in a field and sharpened a scythe. Some would wave or shout a greeting, while others would just stop and stare.

The road felt very low, lower even than sea level. Behind the dunes the air was still, warm and heavy with the smell of peat smoke. Claire lay back in her trailer stripped to the waist, with her bare feet hanging out of the front.

The hills of South Uist – Hecla, Beinn Mhor and Beinn Corradail – are a graceful threesome. All of similar height, each peak sweeps into the next. I knew that a carefully chosen campsite would mean a view of both the ocean and the hills to the east. Rather than return to the main road to proceed to Howmore, we pushed our bikes along a sandy track over a rickety bridge across the smooth machair and as high up the dunes as we could manage.

We pitched our tent on the very lip of the dune, about 15 ft above the beach. The hills were in full view, as was the ocean. The beach at Howmore didn't disappoint. The sand was white and soft – almost snow like.

Tent up, we all tumbled down the dune and walked along the beach barefoot kicking up water. There were many carcasses of underwater mines from the Second World War washed up on the beach, most half-submersed in sand. However, the army fire rockets along this coast so there can be things found on the beach that are not necessarily harmless.

That night, sitting in the tent doorway, I watched the sunset and its reflection on the hills. Green became gold then warm pink. Out at sea the sky grew ominously dark, rain clouds were sailing in with a rainbow as the figurehead at its prow. Suddenly the exposed dune didn't seem such a good idea. The rain battered through, buffeting the tent, although not managing to wake the girls. Not even when the elusive corncrake resumed its post storm croaking did anyone stir.

An information board I had read by the roadside, amongst other things, suggested a trip to a fish farm. Fish farms are as ubiquitous as lochs and about as interesting as car parks. To try this hard to find something tangible for the tourist to visit and witness is to miss the point. The pleasures in the Outer Hebrides are the glory of the flowering machairs, the ever-present birdsong and the constantly changing light. The relaxed attitude to wild camping means that the camping cycle tourist can stop almost spontaneously and enjoy a particularly good spot for any or all of the above.

The next morning more rain looked a definite possibility. The wind was stronger but still from the south-west. The hills were obscured by low cloud and the colours were muted. A short push over machair brought us to the hamlet at Howmore with its white church and thatched cottages.

The church is unusual for the island in that it belongs to the Church of Scotland. South Uist, like Barra and Eriskay, is Roman Catholic. The full force of the Reformation was never felt in the Uists. One landowner tried to beat them into Protestantism but a devotion to St Barr survived and the Catholic Church found it easy to re-establish itself once things had calmed down.

The church overlooks the site of five ruined medieval chapels. Howmore would have been an important ecclesiastical hub in its day. The cottages that still stand, known as black houses, are thatched. The youth hostel is one such building. Run by the Gatliff Hebridean Hostels Trust it provides cosy and atmospheric accommodation. The hostels are unmanned, have no telephone, you cannot book and you pay by way of an honesty box.

Around the hostel is what is left of the medieval community. We spent time wandering the evocative muddy lanes between the chapel, the tumbledown homes and the bog irises, stopping to read the gravestones that are placed to take advantage of spots in which the soil is deep enough for a burial.

It was a cool day and the wind had worked itself into a gale. The bare-topped girls of the day before were now wrapped in fleeces and cagoules. Cyclists who had already made the trip north and were making their way south again were struggling severely in the wind and could only manage pained smiles.

At the top of what would be a tiny 60-ft rise elsewhere, we could see the next three days' cycling open up below us. Our eyes easily overlooked flat Benbecula in the foreground to Eaval on North Uist and beyond to where the cloud clung to the hills of Harris. To our right was the stone grey statue of Our Lady. The statue was erected at the same time as the army opened their rocket range, almost as a charm against any mishaps on the part of the army. The square grey concrete boxes of the army installations blended into the hillside surprisingly well; only their outline and the radar paraphernalia gave them away.

The causeway across expansive Loch Bi gave us false hope that we'd crossed over to Benbecula, although that causeway wasn't much further on. The wind funnelled between the large boulder shoulders of the causeway and shoved us onto Benbecula. The crossing was tidal before the war and apparently many people and horses died when they lost their way and were enveloped by quicksands.

More and more we had to pull over for convoys of army jeeps. The presence of the army changes the atmosphere for the worse for a time, although they were always very polite and patient on the roads.

As our motivation was low and heavy rain seemed imminent, we stopped at the only campsite on the southern isles at Lionacleit. The campsite was drab and orderly compared with camping on the dunes. Moreover, there was no view of the sea. There was, however, another reason for stopping – a much needed wash. Next door to the campsite is the high school and at 4 p.m. the school's swimming pool is turned over to the community and passers-by like us, which is just as well, for the campsite had a problem with hot water.

Once I had found a way through the dunes to the rear of the campsite I found the beach. It had been there all along. Yet again the girls conked out early leaving me to walk the beach alone. Otters played in a pool and the light indulged in another sunset variation. A thin layer of cloud diffused the fading and cooling sunlight so that the white sand turned a deep and bloody purple and the trapped pools of green sea water were emptied, to be replaced by a pink potion.

The next day was a day for a waulking song rather than a motivating melody. Just as the women chanted repetitively to maintain the rhythm and relieve the tedium of waulking the cloth – beating the tweed on a table to preshrink it – so too did we have to maintain a steady rhythm to counteract the resistance of the wind which had moved round to the north-east.

The campsite owner had sent the girls on their way with a variety of treats and given me an impromptu lesson in Gaelic pronunciation as I tried to tell him of our day's route. The girls were quiet and both in the trailer while we struggled through the army town of Balivanich with its anywhere architecture and fast-food outlets.

The causeway ricochets off Grimsay on its way over to North Uist. It was not built even with today's relatively light traffic in mind. The road is effectively a trench and once a section is embarked upon there is no turning back or pulling over which meant that drivers had to be very patient behind us and ahead of us.

Temple Trinity was our chosen ruin for lunch. There are many 'Teampulls' marked on the map but only the 'Teampull Trionaid' at Cairnis is highlighted in blue as a site of note. A sign points it out but you have to work out your own way through two gates, two fields and find a path

Mull's dramatic west coast road. The Mitford's island of Inchkenneth can be seen in Loch na Keal (Chapter 1).

Waiting for the tiny Ulva Ferry (Chapter 1).

Preparing lunch in
the churchyard at
Tibbermore
(Chapter 2).

Cycling in autumnal
Glen Lyon (Chapter 2).

Arriving at the Samye
Ling Tibetan Monastery,
Eskdalemuir (Chapter 3).

The imposing Hermitage
Castle, the scene of many
a bloody act (Chapter 3).

Looking back east towards Arkle and Ben
Stack from Kinlochbervie (Chapter 4).

'The long narrow road to
heaven.' On the road to
Durness with Foinaven in
the background
(Chapter 4).

Cycling through the ancient village of Tobha Mhor (Howmore) on South Uist (Chapter 5).

Mother and child pausing for a breath on the west side of Barra (Chapter 5).

Enjoying an ice cream from the Cream of Galloway (Chapter 6).

Kirkcudbright's
impressive Georgian
High Street (Chapter 6).

The old iron railway bridge over the River Spey, now part of
the Aberdeen to Inverness Cycle Route (Chapter 7).

On the beach at Whiting Bay, Arran and the Holy Isle (Chapter 8).

Surveying the Aberdeenshire
Coast at Slains Castle,
Cruden Bay (Chapter 9).

Dining at sunset, Gardenstown (Chapter 9).

through the irises. Built as a monastery in the thirteenth century, some claim it as Scotland's oldest university, attracting such luminaries as the theologian and opponent of St Thomas Aquinas, Duns Scotus. In the orgy of destruction that was the Reformation, the building was ransacked and its priceless books and artwork burned or thrown in the sea. The monastery was also the scene of the slaughter of the MacLeods at the hands of the MacDonalds.

On top of a grassy knoll not far from the sea shore its tumbledown walls and sinking gravestones are grass grown and precarious. The girls recognised it as the perfect place for a pirate to bury his treasure and set about searching for it. Our pirates became explorers who got frequently lost in the irises and had to abandon expeditions to have their laces tied or their nose wiped. They became completely immersed in their game and, in Claire's case, also in mud.

'Help! Help! I'm stuck!'

'Why did you go that way?'

'Cause the map said so!'

'What map?'

'This map,' said Claire, holding out empty hands.

There were those who predicted the nightmare of bored and belligerent children staging a mutiny. Fortunately it never transpired; in fact I've never known them so contented.

Keen to change our perspective we abandoned the road that goes clockwise round North Uist to go inland and follow the 'Community Road' across North Uist's empty interior. It is known as the Community Road because it was built to provide employment during the potato famine and the workers were paid with food. It was the first time we hadn't followed the coast in almost a week. The road climbs probably more than any other but home-time traffic meant the coast road was busier than we'd been used to and a series of blind summits meant a lot of stopping.

The climb can't have been that strenuous, for we kept well ahead of a tractor all the way to the top. The descent was a rare hurl and a welcome break from pedalling slowly into the wind. Lapwing and plover flew about our heads, piping us safely through their territory.

That night we camped on the edge of an expanse of sand known as the Valley Strand. There is no view out to the open sea as the way is blocked by the tidal island of Vallay. The large derelict Edwardian house on the island was a spooky presence on the horizon when the sun went down. As we were facing north there was no spectacular sunset but the night by the strand was distinguished as a hot and sultry one and by the sight of our first corncrake.

Their numbers must be recovering, for their grating croak echoes throughout every night. However, I didn't feel that my Hebridean experience would be complete until I'd seen one. Catherine and the girls didn't share my delight as they thought it a scrawny brown bird, which in fact it is.

It was on North Uist that we had most contact with the islanders. People would get out of their cars and stop for a blether or come away from their front door and down to the road to chat. It seemed to me that the North Uist folk were the most content, although we hadn't yet met the people of Berneray.

For the first time since we had arrived on the islands we had a fixed idea of where we wanted to be by the end of the day. Up until now we had just stopped at the best possible place or when we thought the girls would tolerate no more. We wanted to be on Berneray and Berneray is as far as you can go on the southern isles.

From the high point of the minor road between the A855 and Port nan Long you look out over the Sound of Harris and a myriad of islands and skerries. To the east the sea looked so sheltered and still that it had the character of a body of inland water. To the north, as well as Berneray, there are the islands of Pabbay and Boreray. They were once all connected by sand banks that people would use to walk between them. Pabbay and Boreray are no longer inhabited and in Pabbay's case it is said that the population was broken up because of its illicit whisky distilling.

I know that a sunny day can flatter to deceive, so when we arrived on Berneray and looked over the bay I knew that I'd have to add the caveat, 'It's not always like this.' Boats with brightly coloured hulls bobbed in the harbour, a couple of fishermen unloaded lobster pots onto the quayside and luminous nets were already spread on the shore to dry.

On the far side of the bay the whitewashed wall of the youth hostel shone in the sun. To reach it we had to follow the road for as far as it goes and then follow a grassy track over the machair to a headland that overlooks the Sound of Harris – a beach of silver sand and a turquoise sea. To compare it with the Caribbean would be to flatter the Caribbean.

The hostel may be white but it is a black house. The black house was the traditional Hebridean home and built in such a way as to withstand the elements. Basic characteristics are a double wall with the turf and thatched roof sitting on the inner wall so that there are no eaves for the wind to tug at. A group of black houses have been redeployed as a youth hostel, again run by the Gatliff Trust.

One of the houses was being re-roofed when we arrived. Huge squares of turf were layered on the roof so that it resembled a bread and butter pudding. On top of the turf dried and pressed maram grass cut from the dunes was laid.

We spent three hot days on Berneray doing little more than cycling to the shop for ice cream or even lunch. Indeed, it became so hot that we even paddled in the crystal clear sea. Everywhere we went we were asked to tell the story of our trip and where home was. The girls were happy to stay by the hostel and receive the attention of fellow hostellers. Climbing in and out the kitchen window with the hostel cat kept them amused for hours.

The furthest we cycled was the couple of miles over to the dunes and the beach on the west of the island. We picked our way through the flower-matted machair where even orchids were commonplace. The beach was as beautiful as the rest but it was the view over the Sound of Harris to the hills of Harris that set it apart. It is a world-class view, yet it is a view that still has the threat of destruction hanging over it. An aggregate company have plans to quarry a whole mountain away. Shame!

That night we returned to the west side of the island for a concert in the community hall. The concert was given by students of the Gaelic Music College on Benbecula. The concert demonstrated that Gaelic is more than the language of signposts. The language and the music are not optional extras for these people or even an occasional novelty.

Again, no one was prepared to let us or any of the other visitors sit next to them and not find out who they were and why they were there. 'Oh, I saw you out on the road the other day' was the usual opening line.

The songs sung in Gaelic were slow and intimate, just as our journey had been. Berneray was a high point of the trip and I have never left a place with such a longing to return. As the infamously noisy ferry chugged over the Sound of Harris from Berneray there was a very real sense that the holiday was over. The weather had returned to grey and cool and by the time we'd reached Harris, Catherine had decided she and the girls would take the bus to Stornoway. Bus drivers on the Western Isles are happy to take bikes in the luggage compartments.

The driver informed me that it was 57 miles to Stornoway but not to worry – Lewis was flat so I only had Harris to worry about. I decided to go via the ancient church at Rodal increasing the mileage to nearly 70 miles.

I chose the gentler west coast route to Tarbert from Leverburgh. Every cyclist I had spoken to had raved about the beaches on Harris's west coast. First up is Scarista which appears like a great big golden tooth in the green hills with the sea but a blue haze in the distance. Not much further on is Luskentyre. It doesn't disappoint. It sits in the corner of Loch Siar, a mountain-sheltered loch of the most complex geography. White water seems to break everywhere, a sign that even the tide is confused.

Crowds were gathered on the shore not to photograph the mountains that plunge into the sea but Taransay, the island of BBC *Castaway* fame – you can catch a boat over for a closer look.

Harris is unmistakably Scotland but it looks as if it has been squeezed. The hills are steeper and closer together. However, the landscape that surrounds the climb from Luskentyre is not of this world. As I climbed, the hillsides became entirely of rock. Shattered rock was everywhere. The sun, which by now had returned, bounced off it with an unforgiving intensity.

This hill would definitely have been the end of the road for the girls, although we could have cycled all together as far as Luskentyre and then caught the bus to Stornoway. Unfortunately it was Saturday and there would be no buses on a Sunday which would mean two days at Luskentyre and carrying two days' food. Nothing opens and nothing moves on a Sunday on Harris or Lewis, or on North Uist for that matter.

A sign placed regularly by the side of the road at the golf course says: 'Strictly no golf on a Sunday!' There seems to be a note of panic in this sign. I felt irritated by this challenge to civil liberties and frustrated at the thought of a day lost. On the other hand it is good that people do stop and rest. I suppose that in this age if you showed the slightest sign of compromise it would be lost for everyone.

The Harris landscape certainly didn't compromise. I was totally unprepared for the sight of the huge climb over the pass just to the east of Clisham, the highest mountain in the Western Isles. I regretted instantly the fish and chips I had just eaten in Tarbert. At first I thought it was a lost cause but I did at least manage to keep ahead of a Volkswagen Camper Van. Thankfully the conditions were perfect. There was very little wind and the evening air was cool.

Perhaps the week on the low-lying Uists had distorted my sense of scale but these mountains felt huge and the rocky outcrops overbearing. On the descent I crossed over onto Lewis and it appeared that Harris had had the same effect on the bus driver who told me that Lewis was flat. Lewis is anything but flat. The road just rolled into one dip after another.

To explore Lewis properly would have involved at least another week of cycling up each of the island's roads. Each road runs to a dead end so it means going back the way you came – something I usually avoid. I would, however, make an exception for Lewis.

It was ten at night when I reached Stornoway and there was still plenty of light left in the day. The town was as raucous as Castlebay had been the previous Saturday. The only difference was that at midnight the Stornoway revellers would be stopped in their tracks, which is probably just as well for their abused livers.

Sunday was very wet. It is the slowest day I have spent anywhere without even so much as a paper to read. For the time being, that's the way they want it. The cracks are starting to appear and there is the same pressure to change many other aspects of the way of life in the Hebrides. I would dearly like to return and find what's left of the Hebridean way of life, still intact.

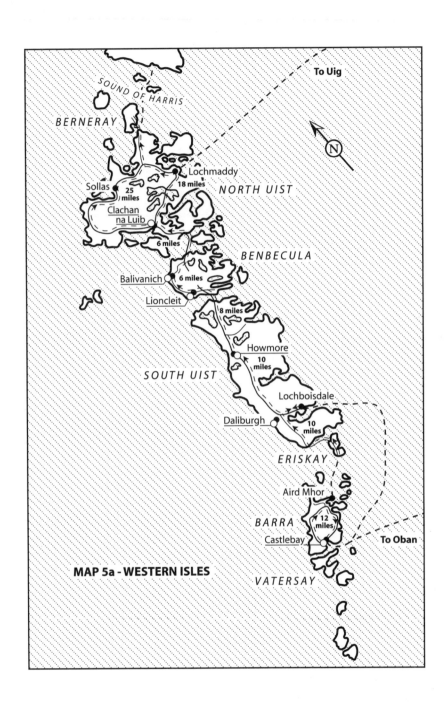

To Uig

SOUND OF HARRIS

BERNERAY

Lochmaddy

Sollas

25 miles

18 miles

NORTH UIST

Clachan na Luib

6 miles

BENBECULA

Balivanich

6 miles

Lioncleit

8 miles

Howmore

10 miles

SOUTH UIST

Lochboisdale

Daliburgh

10 miles

ERISKAY

Aird Mhor

BARRA

12 miles

Castlebay

To Oban

MAP 5a - WESTERN ISLES

VATERSAY

N

THE WESTERN ISLES: ESSENTIALS

Distance: Barra to Stornoway – in the region of 150 miles depending on the route taken.

Maps: OS *Road Map 2: Western Scotland and the Western Isles*. OS *Landranger* series (1:50,000), *Barra and the Uists*, sheets 32, 22, 18; *Harris and Lewis* 8, 14, 22.

Banks/Cashpoints: Cash can be obtained from Co-op Supermarkets as cashback. Banks in Lochboisdale (South Uist), Balivanich (Benbecula), Lochmaddy (North Uist), Tarbert (Harris) and Stornoway (Lewis).

Cycle Repair: Rothan Cycles, Howmore, South Uist (01870 620 283); Alex Dan's Cycle Centre, 67 Kenneth Street, Stornoway (01851 704 025).

General Stores: Castlebay, Eriskay, Daliburgh, Howmore, Lionacleit, Balivanich, Clachan na Luib, Sollas, Berneray, Lochmaddy, Leverburgh, Tarbert, Balallan, Stornoway.

Traffic: Traffic is always light by mainland standards but generally you will be using the only roads available so always expect traffic. The busiest times are early morning, early evening and around the time of ferry arrivals/departures.

GETTING THERE

Train: Glasgow Queen Street Station to Oban. Each train typically carries six bicycles. Spaces are normally in high demand. The 08:12 from Queen Street is the only train that will get you to Oban in time for the ferry the same day. Journey time is three hours.

Ferry: Oban to Castlebay, Barra and Lochboisdale, South Uist – one ferry daily July and August, otherwise ferries every day except Tuesday and

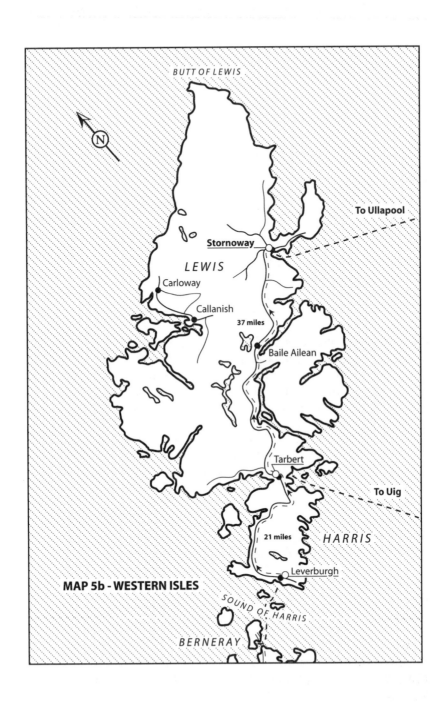

BUTT OF LEWIS

N

To Ullapool

Stornoway

LEWIS

Carloway

Callanish

37 miles

Baile Ailean

Tarbert

To Uig

21 miles

HARRIS

Leverburgh

MAP 5b - WESTERN ISLES

SOUND OF HARRIS

BERNERAY

Sunday. Journey time is six hours to Barra and seven hours to Lochboisdale.

GETTING BACK

Option 1: Cycle the southern islands and return to Lochboisdale by bus or cycle for the ferry back to Oban.

Option 2: Cycle to Lochmaddy, North Uist, and cross to Uig, Skye, and cycle the 50 miles to Kyle of Lochalsh for the train to Inverness and onwards to Glasgow and Edinburgh. Public transport on Skye will not convey bicycles. Purchase Island Hopscotch 20.

Option 3: As option 2, only cycle the 59 miles to Armadale for the ferry to Mallaig and then catch the train to Fort William and then for Glasgow. Purchase Island Hopscotch 15.

Option 4: From North Uist cross to Harris and cycle as far as Tarbert for the ferry to Uig, Skye, and then follow either option 2 or 3. Purchase Island Hopscotch 23.

Option 5: Cycle all the way to Stornoway, Lewis, and take the ferry to Ullapool. Nearest train station is Garve, 32 miles from Ullapool, however there is public transport to Garve or Inverness, although Inverness is the simplest. Tim Dearman Coaches run a once-daily service from Ullapool to Inverness. Bicycles are carried if space permits and at the driver's discretion; contact them on 01349 883585 or at tim.dearman@timdearmancoaches.co.uk. You can charter a bus from Scotpackers Hostel, Ullapool that can carry six to seven passengers and their bikes. Ullapool to Inverness Railway Station: £70. Contact Richard Lindsay on 01854 613126 or at r.lindsay@btinternet.com. Purchase Island Hopscotch 8.

ACCOMMODATION
For Oban see Mull and Ardnamurchan Essentials

ROUTE INFORMATION

BARRA: ROUND ISLAND, DISTANCE (12 MILES); CASTLEBAY TO ARDMHOR FERRY (8 MILES); CASTLEBAY TO VATERSAY (5 MILES)

Terrain: There are climbs out of Castlebay in both directions, the biggest one in the anti-clockwise direction. The road to Vatersay is a steep uphill followed by a steep downhill. Otherwise the cycling is gentle.

ACCOMMODATION
Castlebay (01871–)
Hotels and B&Bs: Castlebay Hotel (–810223); Craigard Hotel (–810200); Mrs Flora Clelland, 47 Glen (–810438); Tigh na Mara (–810304).
Hostels: Dunard Hostel (–810443).
Camping: There is no campsite. Ask at the tourist info or a crofter for permission to camp. There are public toilets on the piers at Castlebay and Eoligarry. Water is usually available nearby.
Elsewhere
Hotels and B&Bs: Isle of Barra Hotel, Tangasale Beach (–810383); Ocean View, Borve (–810590); Geardhmor, Craigston (–810668); Northbay House, Northbay (–890225).

WATCH OUT FOR!
Kisimul Castle (HS), Castlebay (01871 810 313). A small boat conveys visitors to the island fastness.

Barra Heritage and Cultural Centre (01871 810 413). Local history and exhibitions, craft shop and café.

An Dubharaigh and Dun Bharpa. Museum and chambered cairn. On the west side of the island turn off at Craigton/Baile na Creige. The museum sits high on the hillside and involves about one mile of walking.

Cille Bharra. North of the island on the road to Eoligarry, site of the St Barr's seventh-century monastic community, contains replica of runic stone, grave of Compton Mackenzie in the graveyard.

Cockle Strand. Island's beach airport. Landing/take-off times available locally.

Annie Jane Memorial, Vatersay. Marks the mass grave of the 350 souls who perished on their way to Canada.

Catalina, Vatersay – wreckage of a WWII flying boat on the hill above the road round the bay.

ERISKAY, SOUTH UIST AND BENBECULA: ERISKAY TO DALIBURGH (10 MILES); DALIBURGH TO HOWMORE (10 MILES); HOWMORE TO LIONACLEIT (8 MILES); LIONACLEIT TO BALIVANICH (6 MILES)

Ferries: Aird Mhor, Barra to Eriskay – small ferry operates a daily service; contact Faire on 01851 701 702 for details and booking. Castlebay, Barra, to Lochboisdale, South Uist, Calmac – daily sailing July and

August, no service on a Sunday and Tuesday otherwise. This service is included in the Island Hopscotch Service but takes you north of Eriskay.

Terrain: There is a big climb away from the slipway on Eriskay followed by a fast downhill through the village, level or gently undulating from then on.

ACCOMMODATION
Eriskay and South Uist (01878–)
Hotels and B&Bs: Mrs MacInnes, Eriskay (–720232); Polochar Inn, Pol a Charra (–700215); Borrodale Hotel, Dalabrog (–700444); Karingeidha, Dalabrog (–700495); Arnabhal, Milton, Bornish (–710371); Cross Roads, Staoinebrig (01870 620321).
Hostels: Howmore Hostel, no phone and no advanced booking.
Camping: Rough camping is tolerated, ask permission where possible. Next to Howmore Hostel for a small fee.

ACCOMMODATION
Benbecula, Lionacleit (01870–)
Hotels and B&Bs: Dark Island Hotel (–603030); Creagorry Hotel (–602024); Hestimul (–6020033); Bainbhidh (–602532).
Camping: Shellbay Camping Park, Lionacleit (–602447).

WATCH OUT FOR!
Am Politician Pub, Eriskay. Artifacts and whisky from the SS *Politician* on display.

St Michael's Church, Eriskay. Spanish-style church built with bits from various naval vessels.

Flora MacDonald's Birthplace. Signed from the road, ruined settlement of Milton where the heroine was born.

Kildonan Museum. Local history, crafts and tearoom on the right of the main road just beyond Flora's birthplace.

Ormacleit Castle. Ruin of the eighteenth-century home of the chief of Clanranald. Take second left after Kildonan Museum and follow minor roads to Howmore.

Howmore. Restored thatched cottages and ruins of twelfth-century ecclesiastical buildings.

Our Lady of the Isles. Granite statue of Our Lady erected in 1957, good viewpoint.

Museum nan Eilean (01870 602 864). Within Lionacleit Community School. Island Heritage and natural history.

NORTH UIST AND BERNERAY: BALIVANICH, BENBECULA TO CLACHAN NA LUIB NORTH UIST (12 MILES); CLACHAN NA LUIB TO BERNERAY VIA SOLLAS (25 MILES); VIA LOCHMADDY (18 MILES), VIA COMMUNITY ROAD (17.5 MILES)

Terrain: Lots of ups and downs and blind summits especially when heading west from Clachan na Luib, becomes a bit tedious as you can't see very far ahead. The Community Road is a long moderate climb. There is a moderate climb out to Berneray.

ACCOMMODATION
North Uist and Berneray (01876–)

Hotels and B&Bs: Temple View Hotel, Cairinish (–580676); Cairinish Inn (–580673); Lochmaddy Hotel (–500331); Old Shop House, Bayhead (–510395); Lapwings, Bayhead (–510376); Sheillaidh, Sollas (–560332); Corran, Sollas (–560288); Struan House, Sollas (–560234); Burnside Croft, Berneray (–540235).

Hostels: Taigh Mo Shennair, Claddach Baleshare (–580246); Berneray – no phone, no advance bookings; Uist Outdoor Centre, Lochmaddy (–500480).

Camping: Rough camping is tolerated, ask permission where possible. Next to Berneray Hostel for a small fee.

WATCH OUT FOR!
Teampull na Trionaid College of the Holy Trinity. Turn left at Cairinis and walk across field. Thirteenth-century college and monastery associated with Duns Scotus and scene of a bloody slaughter in 1601.

Claddach Kirkibost Centre. Tearoom, e-mail and crafts.

Balranald RSPB Nature Reserve (01876 510 223). Haven for corncrakes, opportunities to watch for seals, porpoises, whales and dolphins.

Uist Animal Visitor Centre and MacAskills Leisure Café, Bayhead (01876 510223). Rare Scottish animals. Good for kids.

Taigh Chearsabhagh Museum, Lochmaddy (01876 500293). Various exhibitions.

HARRIS AND LEWIS: BERNERAY TO LEVERBURGH TO TARBERT (21 MILES)

Ferry: Berneray to Leverburgh – three or four ferries daily except Sunday. Read the timetable carefully for the correct day and time of year. Journey time – 1 hour 10 minutes.

Follow the A859 west out of Leverburgh for Tarbert and Stornoway.

Terrain: Gentle along the coast. When the road leaves the coast it embarks on an epic climb. It is a steep and twisting descent into Tarbert.

ACCOMMODATION
Leverburgh, Rodel and the west coast (01859–)
Hotels and B&Bs: Sorrel Cottage (–520319); Grimisdale (–520461); Caberfeidh House (–520276); Rodel Hotel, Rodel (–520210); Scarista House, Scarista (–550238); Moravia (–550262).
Hostels: An Bothan (–520251).
Camping: Rough camping is tolerated, ask permission where possible. The favoured camping spot is at Luskentyre.
Tarbert (01859–)
Hotels and B&Bs: Hillcrest, Tarbert (–502119); Tigh na Mara, Tarbert (–502270); Harris Hotel, Tarbert (–502154); Allan Cottage, Tarbert (–502146).
Hostels: Rockview Bunkhouse, Tarbert (–502626).

WATCH OUT FOR!
Church of St Clement (HS), Rodel (three miles east of Leverburgh). Sixteenth-century church with an imposing square tower. Contains many fine tombs of the chiefs of the Macleods especially that of Alasdair Crotach (d. 1547).

Seallam Visitor Centre, Northton (Taobh Tuath). Genealogical research service, local history, geology, flora and fauna. By the roadside three miles west of Leverburgh.

MacGillivray Centre. Unmanned centre with small natural history display one mile into Northton.

HARRIS AND LEWIS: TARBERT TO STORNOWAY (37 MILES)
Continue to follow the A859 north out of Tarbert for Stornoway.

Terrain: Not far out of Tarbert the road embarks on yet another epic climb over the pass to the east of Clisham, the highest mountain in the Outer Hebrides. It is dauntingly steep to begin with. There is a long downhill on the far side. There are numerous small but tiring climbs before reaching Stornoway.
Detours/Day trips from Stornoway: The Butt of Lewis, 27 miles one-way – the most northerly point on Lewis. A trip out to Na Gearrannan Blackhouse Village and the Carloway Broch, on the coast 12 miles west of Stornoway could also include the standing stones at Callanish.

ACCOMMODATION
Balallan (01851–)
 Hotels and B&Bs: Clearview (–830472); Burnside (–830326).
Stornoway (01851–)
Hotels and B&Bs: The Old House, 4 Lewis Street (–704495); Park Guest
 House, 30 James Street (–702485); Mrs J. Morrison, 11 Columbia Place
 (–704194); Alexandra's, 14 Goathill Road (–703247); Fairhaven, 28
 Francis Street (–705882).
Hostels and Camping: Stornoway Backpackers, 47 Keith Street (–703628);
 Laxdale Caravan Park and Bunkhouse (–703234).

WATCH OUT FOR!
Whaling station, Bunavoneadar. Ruined whaling station about three
quarters of a mile along the B887.
 Museum nan Eilean, Francis Street, Stornoway. History of island life.

6

MACHO
LANARKSHIRE, GALLOWAY
AND CARRICK

The south-west of Scotland is to visitor itineraries what contraception is to casual sex: left off in the heat of the moment. Well, in the heat of the rush north to the Highlands, in the case of the south-west. As a result cycling in the south-west should be peaceful and safer, at least, than casual sex.

Not that any kind of sex was likely, especially when I was travelling with two guys with broken noses. When you don't look that braw you have to find other outlets for your masculinity and for my good friends, Stewart and Hugh, cycling big distances with lots of hills at a fast and uninterrupted pace is their chosen relief.

You'd think that with broken noses deep breathing would be something they'd want to avoid but the huge downhill out of the old county town of Lanark to cross the River Clyde, and the steep climb that followed to reverse the height loss meant that the first two miles were cycling ecstasy for my two companions.

There were other reasons to be ecstatic. It was a fine summer's evening, so still as to accentuate the peace and heavy with scent. Once we were in the Douglas Valley life was as easy as it could be. The lane wound between fields of green and gold. Sometimes Tinto Hill was in full view, sometimes beeches in full leaf towered over and sometimes birches whispered in the gentle breeze. I find it hard to think of another occasion when the cycling was this good.

Unfortunately I got a bit carried away and forgot myself and the nature of my company. I happened to suggest that it was the kind of evening on which idylls came into being. I went further, saying I thought it the kind of evening on which to film a sentimental pop video or a promotion for funeral services featuring a maiden dressed in flouncy white linen dreamily brushing the tall grass with her hand in an excess of golden sunlight as she made her way over to sit by an old oak. The mention of a maiden in white linen made them a little edgy and they suggested that the scene might be better minus the linen.

It was clearly time for a big hill but apart from the clad or unclad maiden the description was accurate. Were it not for curvaceous Tinto Hill with her huge summit cairn we could have been cycling in the Cotswolds or Burgundy or some other rural idyll. Tinto Hill is an icon in this part of the world and pinned our location down to rural Lanarkshire. Pastoral or bucolic are not adjectives you'd normally associate with Lanarkshire but they are apt. There is much more to Lanarkshire than smoke stacks and staggeringly ugly townscapes.

Once we were under the M74 motorway and onto the cycle path that runs with the M74 to Carlisle but at a big enough distance to be pleasant, Tinto Hill was behind us. Now it was the soft, green and rounded Lowther Hills bubbling up before us.

From this side of the Southern Boundary fault they look unremarkable. Most people's experience of the Lowthers will be from the M74 and will amount to no more than a need to retune their car radios, and virtually no one will recognise the name.

Up close the Lowthers consume the visitor and close off the outside world behind them. There was no doubt that the boundary fault had been crossed and that we'd left the Central Lowlands for the Southern Uplands, the wider range of which the Lowthers are part. Some travellers have complained of a feeling of claustrophobia in the Lowthers and it was not hard to see why. The hills abut tightly to the road and a view ahead never really opens up. There is always another corner to turn. Only the giant golf ball radar structures could be seen on the highest summits ahead.

Gradually the gaps between us grew as Hugh and Stewart pushed on to really enjoy the exertion of the hill that would take us through Scotland's highest villages and over the watershed between the Clyde and the Nith.

The silence and the loneliness of the Lowthers were sudden. There is no compelling reason to come by the Lowthers nowadays and that was apparent. Any cars that did pass by could be heard approaching for quite some time. Initially the road climbed only moderately and the discomfort of ascending was tempered by a slow steady rhythm to the point where it was almost therapeutic. At the village of Leadhills, however, the rhythm had to be abandoned for undignified grunting and groaning.

Fortunately there was no one about to witness such an undignified sight. The streets of Leadhills were deserted. Leadhills may be a little lifeless but it was a pleasant and un-contrived time warp. Leadhills has remained pretty much the same for 250 years and there was no doubting its purpose. The very name Leadhills, the squat white cottages that line up on the hillsides and the piles of grey spoil say it all. For seven centuries gold, silver and zinc, but mainly lead, were mined from these hills, earning the Lowthers the nickname of 'God's own Treasure House in Scotland'.

There are no knick-knack shops or second-hand bookshops or other ventures that thrive on quaint environments. Leadhills, high up in the hills, is much too raw for that but it could do with the lift and the visitors to justify such outlets.

Beyond Leadhills the climb started to feel long and legs began to tire, but it never felt tedious. The summits in the Lowthers are never far off and they approached eye-level until eventually I could see over them to the west. Under a sky of duck-egg blue, crests unfolded into the distance, the sun obscured by cloud sent only shards of light to the ground, suggesting that God was communicating with his people at the treasure house. Crucially there was to be no red sky.

The sign heralding Wanlockhead as Scotland's Highest Village at 1,531 ft also said exertion over. Ironically the village lies below the level of the road in a hollow. Again little white cottages spill up the sides and again grey spoil heaps haven't been cleared away and wagons still sit on rails at the entrance of a boarded-up pit. Normally such industrial detritus would have been removed from such a beautiful spot but somehow the pit-bings seem in keeping and perhaps they remain to help the village retain an identity. It's rather a former mining village than just a village.

A red kite flew from telegraph pole to telegraph pole as if to show me the way out of Wanlockhead's hollow and into the Mennock Pass. The entrance was narrow and small rocks had trickled off the hillside and onto the road. The red kite flapped to the next pole reassuring me that this was the way on.

The pass has very steep sides and was by now sunless. The stream that started by my side dropped away to a deeper course. A car parked on its roof on the valley floor was proof of the need to be careful. For eighteenth-century traveller Maria Riddell it was only her travelling companion Robert Burns' 'fascinating conversation' that made her forget the 'profound precipice'. The kite was now missing out a pole to keep ahead of me as I sped my way deeper into the hills.

In the Mennock Pass, claustrophobia could reach panic proportions as the hills became so overbearing that it seemed inevitable they would close over and form a roof. It is just at the point where your speed will be greatest that the hills squeeze in and throw the road into a difficult series of bends. Heavily laden, it was not easy to control the bike quickly and find a comfortable line and I was forced onto the other side of the road. Fortunately the road settled onto a level grassy floor and my considerable momentum petered out. The kite had gone.

It was here that we would camp on a little oasis of green grass and level ground by the Mennock Water. The hills are very steep and feel huge for such a diminutive range. The Mennock Pass rivals any Highland glen for imposing grandeur.

By the time I arrived, Hugh had the stove on for tea and was busily pitching his tent. Meanwhile Stewart sat on his mat waiting for his tent and pitcher to arrive. All three of us were buzzing with the pleasure of such an evening in such a place. Not for long though.

A gentle breeze blowing from the south suddenly dropped. It was like waiting for the explosion of a falling bomb. Seconds later they were out and we fumbled frantically with midge nets as if they were life-saving gas masks.

Just because you stop feeding them doesn't mean the midges go away. Pulling the net up and down in between gulps of supper was not easy and I lost count of the times I tried to gulp with the net still down so that I had to lick my finely minced supper from the inside of the net.

The next morning Hugh attempted a reveille at 5 a.m. but had to settle for seven. We were enticed up by a shoestring breakfast of muesli or porridge; Hugh gave us the distinct impression that he considered the porridge a special treat and the offer only remained open for a limited time. However it was a breeze pulling at the tent that persuaded us it was safe to come out.

Rain wasn't far away so we packed rather than ate and were underway before eight. Five minutes later we stopped to don waterproofs and a few more layers. None of the summer had survived from the evening before. Early morning starts and wet weather are necessary solace for the macho brain so Stewart and Hugh, at least, were happy.

Fortunately, or unfortunately, it was more pleasant once we were out of the Lowthers and over the River Nith. The road was level and the trees hung low, giving a measure of shelter – except for the huge drips that found their way down the back of my neck with uncanny accuracy.

Between the frothing river and the rain beating down on the trees, a kind of white noise filled our ears so conversation was sparse, even though we were cycling three abreast. We raised our pace to match the tempo of the Nith and to counteract the cold. It was July but it was barely 10 °C.

The relative comfort of the banks of the Nith was short-lived, for an unexpectedly steep climb took us away from the Nith and out of the trees. The slower pace and the lack of shelter meant that I was now shipping water. The view from the high rib of land should have been good but a grey drizzly haze obliterated the whole world except for the field on our right.

Drumlanrig Castle could have offered some respite and heat, but, of course, it was closed, since it was barely after nine. Drumlanrig is more chateau than it is castle – a frilly pink seventeenth-century renaissance creation completely lacking in defensive features, although the admission charge was likely to keep the likes of Hugh at bay: '£6 tae get in? Ye're not on!' The sentiment however was likely to have been reciprocated: 'Three dripping-wet cyclists? You're not on!' I tried to shake as much water as possible from my jacket and panniers but somehow I seemed to disturb stagnant water trapped between the layers and push it through to new depths.

There would have been more trees to shelter beneath had it not been for the 4th Duke of Queensbury. He caused outrage when he had the woods cut down to pay his gambling debts. Local resident Robert Burns hated the duke for such an act of vandalism and attacked him as the 'Discarded remnant of a race'. Moreover, Wordsworth thought the man a 'degenerate'. The locals apparently bought up some of what was left to prevent him from felling them as well.

Galloway nonetheless is still very green. The verges were burgeoning with growth and the grass flopped over under the weight of rain to slap at my shins. The fields were so deep in green grass that the cows looked short. I imagine that when it rains in Galloway watching the grass grow is a viable pastime. Where trees hung low and moss furs the stone dykes, the visible spectrum shifted to green and even a passing Royal Mail van had a greenness about it.

The rain abated but the temperature and the sky remained stubbornly low. Spirits on the other hand were high, boosted by brunch from a mobile bakery van and hot tea courtesy of Hugh; although it was Hugh's preference to brew up by the side of the road, there was no indoor alternative.

We would have drifted apart again were it not for the delicate navigation that was required to locate first of all Glenmidge and then the correct route to Dunscore. The roads tend not to be signed and sometimes the turnings are anti-intuitive. Glenmidge was particularly easy to miss. Surprisingly, people do live in a place with such a terrifying name.

On our way up and over to Glenkiln a south-westerly wind met us head on. Out of the trees and the shelter of the valley of the Cairn or the Nith we realised just how easy a time of it we'd been having. This road, as far as I can make out, constituted part of the only direct route from Edinburgh to Kirkcudbright in the eighteenth century. However, it was clear that there weren't many people coming this way any more. Grass was growing thickly up the middle of the road, bracken was colonising the ungrazed hillside and the dykes were tumbledown.

There was more to the downhill than the much anticipated exhilaration. There was art. Art in the form of stainless-steel sculptures by the likes of Renoir, Rodin and Sir Henry Moore. This is no local authority art project. Henry Moore's *King and Queen* have sat on their bench in the bracken by the Glenkiln reservoir since 1952. The two sharp-featured figures greet you as you round the bend at the foot of the hill.

Not only did we feel obligated to stop but we felt we had to come up with a reason why art by such august individuals should be here. Irony, freedom from the constraints of the gallery or somehow drawing an analogy between the art critic and the sheep were just three of our attempts to hit the nail on the head with a knowing and erudite thump.

Rodin's naked *John the Baptist*, who steps towards you with a curled come-hither finger, was altogether more perplexing and riled Stewart into an outburst: 'Artists urr obsessed wi' willies.' The stone sculpture that Moore alleges are two figures reclining was entirely ignored despite the huge phallus filling our view ahead on a painfully slow uphill.

As I passed, a German stepped out. 'Halt! You must stop! This is very important! Do you know what it is?'

'Uh huh?'

'It is a Henry Moore!' he said, clearly not believing me. Why else would I be going past?

'Vee have come all the way from Germany to see it. It is truly remarkable.'

He needn't have come the whole way – you can see it from quite a distance.

By the time I caught up with Stewart and Hugh they were gingerly making their way past a horny bull who was blocking the road. Fortunately he was more interested in a cow on the other side of the dyke and was attempting to knock the wall down. Stewart and Hugh were in a state of high agitation, which they put down to the length of time I was taking, when really it was all that homoerotic art. With them and the aroused bull there was enough testosterone leaking out to stiffen the limpest of wrists.

'Galloway [. . .] a district which has remained unknown to the world longer than any other part of Scotland,' wrote the Rev. C.H. Dick in 1916. When visiting writers described Galloway for their readers they had to describe it in terms of everywhere else – a common ploy – but Galloway would appear to have had more than its fair share. To the Scots it was described as the 'Southern Trossachs'. To the English, Keats described it as being in the 'Westmorland fashion' with 'a little of Devon'. The Welsh would be reminded of 'the wild beauties of Caernarvonshire', according to Richard Ayton, anyway. The Irish would find it a home from home. As we emerged from the hills onto what can only be described as cultivated moor, I hoped for the 'little of Devon' to show itself.

Keats, it would seem, was not a reliable witness. He'd put it down to poetic licence, I'm sure, as I can't imagine that Devon has ever been this cold in July. The whitewashed village of Kirkpatrick Durham was all too brief a respite from the cold wind and the damp that seemed to creep from the fields. The village says all that needs to be said about the prevailing weather in these parts. Kirkpatrick Durham huddles together and hunkers down and it's only the church that is daft enough to stick its head in the air. The warm glow emanating from the Drovers' Inn was almost too much to bear. Oh, and did I mention that I was hungry?

In Castle Douglas, Hugh thought a picnic by the loch a good idea on a day when shoppers were dressed as if the next thing they were going to do that day was go to sea. We had our picnic, which essentially amounted to hot tea. Hot tea is to Hugh what chicken soup is to a Jewish mother: it cures everything.

Castle Douglas is not a castle, it's a town, and Kirkcudbright (Cur-coo-bree – say it quickly) is not a convincing candidate for the Venice of Scotland. There is more to Venice than a proximity to water, which was what prompted Lock Cockburn to claim Kirkcudbright as its Scottish equivalent. The crucial difference, I'd say, is the sun.

A glimpse of the sea had been much anticipated all day. As we sat at our picnic bench on our hillside campsite eating our rapidly cooling dinner and overlooking the roofscape of Kirkcudbright, we still couldn't see it for the gloom. I did have something to be grateful for – we had meat for our dinner. Hugh had thought it decadent but Stewart and I had overruled him. So, like Robert Burns who composed his 'Selkirk Grace' in Kirkcudbright, 'We hae meat–' but only just '–so let the Lord be thankit'!

Kirkcudbright bestowed patience on us all and the sunny Sunday morning helped. Its colourful and elegant Georgian streets preferred an unhurried dignity. Even though MacLellan Castle casts a dark and craggy shadow over the town centre, it is the Georgian quarter that sets the tone. Kirkcudbright came across as a bright town with poise, and one that's not at all provincial. It is a surprise to find such a place in an area where bumpkins must have outnumbered burghers.

If the spirit of a place rather than the physicality were to produce a sobriquet then Kirkcudbright would be the 'Montmartre of Scotland'. Artists made the town their own at the turn of the twentieth century, living not in garrets but in the fine Georgian townhouses. E.A. Hornel was the pioneer and the rest followed so that a colony of artists formed around him.

Kirkcudbright is still an artists' town; the quality of the light in Galloway is apparently the real attraction for the many artists who turn up to paint. I think it would be fair to say that it would definitely be the quality and not the quantity of light.

One artist, Jessie M. King, said it was, 'a happy wind that blew her into Kirkcudbright'. It was a happy wind, that is the one at our backs, that blew us out of Kirkcudbright by the iron swing bridge, that doesn't swing any more, over the Dee and by the road to Borgue, which, said the Rev. C.H. Dick in his encyclopaedic *Highways and Byways in Galloway and Carrick*, 'will appeal to the connoisseur of roads'. He described a road between a dark wood and the shining water and 80 years on it is still as he said it would be. The wreck of a cutter in the bay would probably have been a bit more substantial but other than that he wouldn't be aware of any difference.

Out in the open, the countryside was just as it had been the day before. The road ran between two sturdy and grey stone dykes, the grass beyond was coarse and rocky, but today the cows stood rather than sat and the incessant greenness was at least towards the livelier shades. Behind us we could see the dark shadows of the Lakeland Fells, in the distance was the Isle of Man and ahead of us was the next day's route down the length of the next peninsula to Whithorn.

The energetic grunting of the day before was replaced by contented sighing. The road twisted round the coast and the way ahead was often obscured by high hedges or a dip in just the way that motorists hate. Cyclists appreciate a road such as this and have therefore a stronger claim to be road connoisseurs. When the Rev. C.H. Dick was on his bike in Galloway he felt there was a certain 'propriety' to his journey. These roads weren't created for the modern car but, to quote the reverend, for 'the landau, the horse-drawn cart and caravan' – and, of course, the bicycle.

We dismounted to explore the churchyard at Borgue and again to wander round the strange structure at Corseyard, which turned out to be a 'Coo Palace'. The building, adorned in ornate ironwork and crenellations, sits somewhere between a French railway station and a schoolboy's toy fort. The tower is impressive but is merely a water tower. As well as water towers they disguised silos. These sumptuous farmyards, as this was by no means the only one, were for the comfort of cows. A brief brush with affluence in the early twentieth century produced these follies; money was something the Galloway farmers were clearly not used to.

Cows have to do something to deserve such opulent surroundings. The 'Cream of Galloway' is a much more practical celebration of the cow and its produce, and a pleasant surprise on the anonymous back road. It is an imaginative complex of an adventure park for children, a small brewery and a restaurant. This kind of enterprise, which makes the direct link between the countryside and its produce, is commonplace on the continent but still quite rare in Scotland. Every product is distinctive and we bought organic, brewed-on-the-premises beer for later and three huge ice creams to celebrate the weather.

The brilliant white buildings of Gatehouse of Fleet make too much of the sun and dark glasses were an essential accessory for those enjoying a drink at pavement tables. My brief brush with Gatehouse of Fleet could have led me to christen it the Paris of the North or Barcelona on Fleet. Yet on another day I might have seen the truth of its preferred alter ego, the 'Glasgow of the South', but I doubt it.

You'll have begun to realise that Galloway has an esteem problem, preferring to be described as an imitation of elsewhere rather than as it is. Gatehouse of Fleet is a conventional little village all in white but a pleasant place to be and if it hadn't been for the huge ice creams we'd have stopped to enjoy an al fresco pint.

Galloway is nevertheless very proud of its roads. The Rev. C.H. Dick managed 500 pages on the subject. Thomas Carlyle tried to convince Queen Victoria that the road from Creetown to Gatehouse of Fleet was the loveliest in all her kingdom, with the second loveliest being the return.

There are three roads from Gatehouse of Fleet to Creetown. The A75 Euroroute, which is the one Carlyle was on about, a steep military road and the road which goes via the old railway station. We chose the last for, despite Carlyle's reference, the A75 is not a safe option. The road that follows the Water of Fleet inland, like so many of the roads in Galloway, no longer has a purpose. The road linked Gatehouse of Fleet with its railway station six miles away and high on the moor. Of course, the station and the line are long gone.

Horse and carriage would have provided the link between the station and the village, therefore it was a well-graded road that climbed from the pastures of the valley floor through the old broad-leafed woodland onto the moors. Objectivity was another side effect of such a sunny day. We looked on the hills and moors ahead as somewhere we wanted to be.

The drama in the landscape is the Big Water of Fleet Viaduct, an immense 20-span structure, redundant but immense. Its red brick, added in the Second World War, is incongruous in this land of granite but it is all the more the spectacle for it and it does not jar quite as much as the 'natural' commercial forestry that covers the lower summits. This was the bridge that Buchan had in mind when Hannay jumped from the train in *The Thirty-Nine Steps*. Certainly the wild, lonely setting is ripe for sporting pursuits and adventure. Buchan chose Galloway as the setting but Hollywood chose the Forth Bridge and Glen Coe. It seems that Galloway can't even be itself.

Poor old Galloway. Buchan was specific enough to have Hannay walk up to the remote Gatehouse of Fleet Station by the road which we descended to Creetown. It was a fast and exhilarating descent that left

Hugh gasping, 'How would you be able to tell someone how good that was?'

It would be equally difficult to describe how bad the route is from Creetown to Newton Stewart. SUSTRANS has gone to considerable effort to avoid the need to cycle on the A75 but the cycle path is symptomatic of how short of cash they are. The steep ascent to join the cycle path is difficult, even on foot, as our heavy panniers caused our bikes to rear up like agitated stallions. Beyond the cycle path the route returns to back roads for a couple of miles but then joins a forestry road so steep and loose that we did start to wonder if we'd come the right way. No matter how tempting it may be to use the A75 it is not something you are likely to do twice.

This whole tour of the south-west would fall down if it wasn't for these unpleasant few miles on the forestry track and things should improve in time but care must be taken, especially on the downhills. There were a couple of times when I felt I wouldn't be able to stop.

The next morning the roads were still wet from an overnight downpour, a vindication of Stewart's decision to stay in the youth hostel at Newton Stewart. The wind was blowing stiffly from the south-west, which was exactly the direction we were going in. The light was watery and weak making it feel earlier than it was.

Hugh was determined that the day be about cycling rather than stopping. A decadent pace was fine on a Sunday but this was Monday morning and we should be more businesslike. The pace along the low road by the Cree was furious. Like migrating ducks we each took our turn at the front and fought the wind for progress.

This was the Machars and 'machars' means flat land. So, unhindered by the relief, the rain clouds were zipping over our heads and gathering on the Galloway hills behind us. Ahead of us sat Wigtown on its knoll.

We paused in Wigtown, a former county town and now Scotland's National Book Town. The merchants' houses and shops that form a continuous townscape on either side of the wide marketplace are mostly devoted to the second-hand book trade and publishing. It is a town very much in the mould of ancient county towns but at the head of the marketplace there is a town hall that is unmistakable as a French *mairie* and gives the town a bit of an identity crisis, but it is still a wonderful building. We thumbed some books because we thought we should but when presented with so many I couldn't think of one that had eluded me.

Legislation has been unkind to Wigtown. In the 1970s it was robbed of its county town status. Throughout the seventeenth century several acts of Parliament passed by successive Stuart kings turned its Presbyterian citizens into Covenanters – men and women who pledged their support for the reformed religion through the National Covenant and were prepared to fight and die for the right to practise according to their beliefs.

Presbyterianism rejected the authority of bishops and the right of the gentry to select their minister. They abandoned their parishes and took to the hills to continue their chosen form of worship with their ministers. These feral Christians were hunted down and usually executed. In Wigtown's churchyard there are a few of the well-maintained graves of the martyrs. Memorials to summary executions are to be found in many remote spots throughout the whole of the south-west but just as you come into Wigtown there is a memorial to two women tied to stakes by the Cree and left to be drowned by the rising tide.

The sixteenth-century Reformation did the most damage economically. Wigtown was en route to Whithorn and the shrine to St Ninian. Many thousands of pilgrims from all over northern Europe would pass through Wigtown on their way to Whithorn. An act of Parliament outlawed pilgrims as idolatrous and that was the end of that.

I suppose that since we were headed for Whithorn we could consider ourselves pilgrims. Pilgrimage shouldn't be easy but we were pilgrims making no progress. In the strong wind everything in the landscape was moving apart from us. I'm sure I'd have gone backwards if I had stopped pedalling even for a second.

Our schedule slipped. Rather than having lunch at Isle of Whithorn, we had to stop short in Garlieston. Garlieston is so forgotten that it displays a picture signpost at the main road to make passers-by aware of the gem that lies so close. In fact Garlieston attracts so little attention that the Mulberry Harbours to be used on D-Day were tested here.

An eighteenth-century planned town and port, the harbour and town look little changed and are very evocative of a time when barques would have unloaded their cargoes of lace, tea and brandy and exported wool and sailcloth.

After lunch we cycled on into the wind through the juicy green fields that really do make this the land of the happy cow. Cyclists going the other way flew past us with big smiles, oblivious to our purgatory. I reckon it took us about an hour to cover the five miles from Garlieston to Isle of Whithorn.

Isle of Whithorn is not an island, it is a very picturesque fishing port. The houses form a continuous wall around the harbour leaving no room for the church, which has to stick its bum out over the high-water mark. I barely managed to persuade Hugh and Stewart to walk to the thirteenth-century ruined church built on the same spot as St Ninian's Candida Casa and on to look down on the coastline where St Ninian may have first landed in Scotland. Looking down on the rocks and the swelling Irish Sea I reckoned he crashed because you wouldn't pick this spot.

Even though we'd turned north at Isle of Whithorn, the wind was still giving us trouble. Perhaps we wouldn't be free of it until our pilgrimage was complete. Whithorn, two miles to the north, was the ultimate goal of the pilgrim.

The thought of finally getting onto the end of that wind and hurtling north made Stewart and Hugh impatient, so it was a whirlwind tour of the Priory, the Whithorn Dig, the visitor centre and the small museum. It was a lot to squeeze into half an hour. I didn't even get time to try on a horse-hair shirt on sale in the Whithorn Penance shop, although Hugh was almost tempted by the self-flagellation kit.

At last a tail wind was our reward. The miles just clicked by as we cycled north on the A747. Once on the coast the road was flat and we were only feet away from a seething grey sea. Ahead and to our right the sky was black.

It is probably fair to say that the folk down this way weren't particularly keen on the authorities, remote in far-off Edinburgh and London. If they couldn't make a living legally then they were well placed to take advantage of smuggling, especially since the tax haven of the Isle of Man was close by.

This coast was perfect for the smugglers' purposes. There are caves to the south and smugglers could land easily on this relatively gentle coast where boats, if need be, could be landed on the beach. Until the government got its act together and built barracks along this coast, the smugglers could out-gun and out-man the excisemen and so they could land their cargoes in the harbours with impunity. Once landed the contraband would be unloaded from the luggers onto the backs of ponies. Trains of up to 200 ponies could set off at night from Port William or Monreith or the beach at Auchenmalg with 100 or so escorts across the moors for Glasgow and Edinburgh.

Between the black rocky beach and the soft grassy cliffs we cycled effortlessly north. Very little changed. There was no livestock about, there were few buildings and even fewer cars. With the spray from the sea regularly reaching us and the black skies above, the dramatic weather was as enjoyable as any sunny day. There was a nervous anticipation that the clouds would suddenly burst. The speed and the pumping adrenaline induced by the race against the weather made for an exhilarating cycle.

Hugh pushed on and beat the weather but Stewart and I failed. We arrived in Glenluce drenched. As soon as we arrived, a smugly dry Hugh informed us that dinner was ready and that it had only cost £3. Dinner, in fact, cost me and Stewart £20 in the Kelvin Hotel as Hugh's meal of cold boiled eggs, cold boiled potatoes and cheddar didn't appeal to either of us, especially the cold part.

The rain persisted into the next morning. Apparently at 5 a.m. it had stopped but I hadn't responded to a decision to get up and go so it was my fault that we were cycling in the rain. At 5 a.m. we wouldn't have been able to visit Glenluce Abbey, founded by the Cistercians in the twelfth century, but that was not a concern of Stewart's. The Cistercians, a particularly austere order, would have thoroughly approved of our suffering.

If we had been smugglers despatched with our ponies, weighed down with brandy and tobacco, to take this route from New Luce into Ayrshire, we'd have had the fags smoked and the drink drunk before we'd gotten very far. This was the most disconsolate country and our spirit craved succour. The featureless moor is rough, wild and wet. An old signal box by the Glasgow to Stranraer railway line was a rare landmark.

I was going to recommend an alternative route until we met an older couple resting by a bridge over the Stinchar. They had cycled over the moors as we had, having caught a ferry from Belfast. 'Oh! It was beautiful country, don't you think?' They'd seen it in the worst weather, yet they had found the scenery beautiful and although they were in their 60s they hadn't found the climb too challenging. So don't be complaining.

It would have been easy to give up at Barrhill and catch the train to Glasgow but we persevered and the day got better. Ayrshire's green miles were comfortable and warm.

Later in Maybole, a group of boys stopped to ask where we'd come from, how far we'd cycled and how long it had taken us. They looked at us in silent disbelief until one of them asked, 'Why did ye no jist take the train or a motor, it'd only taken ye a couple o oors? Eeejits so ye's ur!'

Ach well, it was three happy eejits that cycled into Ayr.

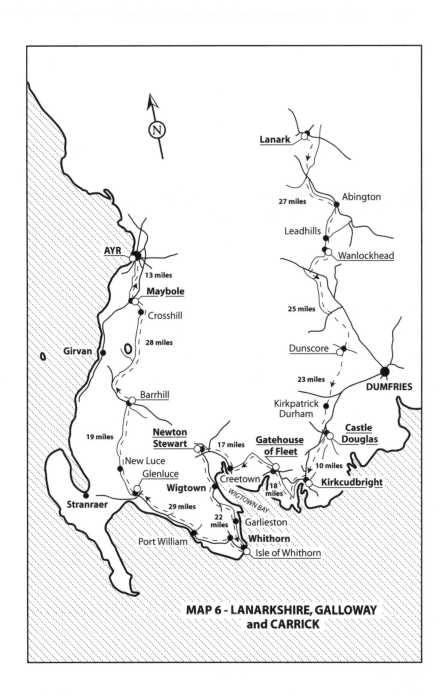

N

Lanark

Abington

27 miles

Leadhills

Wanlockhead

AYR

13 miles

Maybole

Crosshill

25 miles

Girvan

28 miles

Dunscore

Barrhill

23 miles

DUMFRIES

Kirkpatrick
Durham

**Newton
Stewart**

17 miles

**Gatehouse
of Fleet**

**Castle
Douglas**

19 miles

10 miles

New Luce

Creetown

Kirkcudbright

Glenluce

Wigtown

18
miles

WIGTOWN BAY

Stranraer

29 miles

22
miles

Garlieston

Port William

Whithorn

Isle of Whithorn

**MAP 6 - LANARKSHIRE, GALLOWAY
and CARRICK**

Distance: 233 miles

Maps: OS *Landranger* series (1:50,000); sheets 70, 71, 76, 78, 82, 83, 84. OS *Road Map 3: Southern Scotland and Northumberland.*

Banks/Cashpoints: Lanark, Sanquhar, Castle Douglas, Kirkcudbright, Newton Stewart, Wigton, Maybole, Ayr.

Cycle Repair: Castle Douglas Cycle Centre, Church Street, Castle Douglas (01556 50 45 42); W. Law, 19 St Cuthbert Street, Kirkcudbright (01557 330 579); Carrick Cycles, 87 Main Street, Ayr (01292 269 882).

General Stores: Every town and village has at least a small shop, except between Wanlockhead and Castle Douglas where Dunscore is the only possibility and opening hours are limited.

Traffic: There are a few points at which care should be taken. These are on the A70 near Douglas, the A76 at Mennock, the A711 from Tongland to Kirkcudbright, on the A714 from Barrhill to Pinmore. These stretches are very short or traffic is moderate. Elsewhere you will experience virtually no traffic at all. It may be tempting to take a short cut on the A75 on occasions but I would not recommend this.

GETTING THERE AND BACK

Train: Glasgow Central Low Level (lift to High Level) to Lanark – hourly train service seven days a week. Journey time is one hour.

Ayr to Glasgow Central – half-hourly train service. Journey time is 50 minutes.

There is no designated cycle space on either of these services but bikes can be carried in the passenger areas; it is best to avoid busy periods – before 9 a.m. and between 4 p.m. and 6 p.m.

ROUTE INFORMATION

LANARK TO WANLOCKHEAD (27 MILES)

Starting at Lanark Railway Station turn right out of station car park. Go straight on at traffic lights. Descend High Street and follow road through narrow gap at church. Continue downhill for a half mile and turn left for Hamilton A72.

Descend steeply to Clyde and take first left once over the bridge. After 300 yards take left fork and follow lane uphill. At top of hill swing sharply to right and follow lane to T-junction and turn left. Ignore turnings for Lesmahagow and Sandilands, rather follow signs for Douglas Water. However do not take the first left for Douglas Water, take the next left. Follow road to T-junction with B7078. Turn left and follow B7078 to roundabout.

Turn right at roundabout for Ayr and Douglas. At next roundabout go straight through and then turn left. Join cycle path. Cycle path ends just short of Abington; join road and follow through Abington. On the other side of Abington turn right for Leadhills and Wanlockhead, B797. Follow all the way to Wanlockhead.

Terrain: There are three notable climbs: the first is early in the route and is steep but short; the other two are long and moderate. The climb to Wanlockhead does become steeper at Leadhills. Otherwise the route is undulating.

ACCOMMODATION
Lanark and New Lanark (01555–)

Hotels and B&Bs: West Port House, West Port, Lanark (–660263); Cartland Bridge Hotel, Glasgow Road, Lanark (–664426); Bankhead Farm, Braxfield Road (–666560); Duneaton, 159 Hyndford Road (–665487); Jerviswood Mains Farm, Cleghorn Road (–663987); New Lanark Hotel (–667200).

Hostels: New Lanark SYHA (–666710).

Camping: Kirkfieldbank on the right just before you cross the Clyde.

Abington, Leadhills and Wanlockhead

Hotels and B&Bs: Abington Hotel, Abington (01864 502 467).

Hostels: Wanlockhead SYHA (01659 74252).

WATCH OUT FOR!

New Lanark. World Heritage Site, eighteenth-century mills and village. Follow signs in Lanark.

Falls of Clyde and Nature Reserve. Follow signs in Lanark for New Lanark. Reserve is well known for its bats and badgers.

Curfew Bell, Leadhills. Near the centre of the village, has sounded emergencies and the change of shifts since 1770.

Allan Ramsay Library, Leadhills. Scotland's oldest subscription library (est. 1741).

Leadhills and Wanlockhead Railway. Signed from Main Street, Leadhills. Wanlockhead and Mining Museum (seasonal) (01659 74387). Fascinating village gives a real flavour of the life of a lead miner, museum offers the background and a trip underground.

WANLOCKHEAD TO DUNSCORE (25 MILES)

Follow the B797 south out of Wanlockhead and descend into the Mennock Pass. It is a long downhill to junction with A76. Turn right onto A76 and follow through Mennock. Take first left beyond Mennock and cross Nith on stone bridge. Keep left to continue with the route (turn right for Sanquhar). Follow Nith for three miles to T-junction, turn right and climb away from Nith. At cottage take left fork and climb steeply. After a level section with good views, road descends through a difficult S-bend. At bottom turn right at T-junction and follow avenue to Drumlanrig Castle.

At castle go off to the left and turn right at T-junction. When road forks take left and follow to junction with A702. Turn right and then left at disused church and follow lane into Keir Mill. In Keir Mill turn left.

Stick with this road for four miles or so. When road starts to climb look out for right for Glenmidge. Descend into Glenmidge and take right at campsite. Follow road to junction with B729 and turn left for Dunscore.

Terrain: An easy start, followed by a stiff climb away from the Nith. A difficult descent returns you to level ground. Nothing too demanding beyond Drumlanrig.

ACCOMMODATION

Sanquahar (01659–)

Hotels and B&Bs: Frances Barbour, Newark (–50263); Blackaddie House, Blackaddie Road (–50270).

Camping: The Casteview CP (–50291).

Dunscore

Hotels and B&Bs: George Hotel, Main Street (01387 820 250).

WATCH OUT FOR!

Sanquhar Castle. Eleventh-century ruin.

Post Office, Sanquhar. Oldest in the world, from where Robert Burns posted 'Ae Fond Kiss' to Clarinda.

Tollbooth Museum, Sanquhar. History of Upper Nithsdale, summer only.

Drumlanrig Castle (01848 330 248). Castle with works by da Vinci and Holbein, crafts, cycle museum and woodland walks.

DUNSCORE TO CASTLE DOUGLAS (23 MILES)

In Dunscore, turn right at church and continue downhill ignoring left turn. Follow road round to the left at telephone box. One mile further on, turn right for Glenkiln and Shawhead. It is a long moderate climb followed by short descent to Glenkiln reservoir. Turn right a quarter of a mile beyond dam and climb. It is a long descent to crossroads with A712. Go straight over for Kirkpatrick Durham. At Drovers Inn in Kirkpatrick Durham go straight over and keep right at church. At next crossroads at Old Bridge of Urr go straight over for Castle Douglas. Follow road through Clarebrand. Go straight over at crossroads with B795 for Castle Douglas. Go under A75 and proceed into Castle Douglas. At next T-junction turn right and follow signs for Town Centre at roundabout.

Terrain: A long climb over to the Glenkiln reservoir is followed by a couple of short stiff climbs. There is however plenty of downhill to compensate.

ACCOMMODATION

Castle Douglas (01556–)

Hotels and B&Bs: The Crown Hotel, 25 King Street (–502031); Imperial Hotel, King Street (–503009); Kings Arms (–502626); Albion House, 49 Ennespie Road (–502360); The Market Inn, 6–7 Queen Street (–502105).

Camping: Lochside CP (–502949).

WATCH OUT FOR!

Sulwath Brewery, Castle Douglas (01556 504 525). Conducted tours and tasting.

CASTLE DOUGLAS TO KIRKCUDBRIGHT (10 MILES)

Follow High Street to Carlingwark Loch and join cycle path. At the end of cycle path turn left for Kelton Church and Threave Gardens. Take right fork at entrance to Threave for Rhonehouse and follow road all the way to junction with A711 at Tongland. Turn left and take next left over the

Tongland Bridge and cycle short distance into Kirkcudbright.

Terrain: The route climbs steadily to begin with. There is nothing too demanding.

ACCOMMODATION

Kirkcudbright (01557–)

Hotels and B&Bs: Gordon House Hotel, 116 High Street (–330670); Selkirk Arms Hotel, High Street (–330402); No. 3 B&B, 3 High Street (–330881); Mrs Durok, 109a High Street (–331279); Mrs Black, 1 Gordon Place (–330472).

Camping: Silvercraigs Campsite (–331079).

WATCH OUT FOR!

Threave Gardens (NTS), Castle Douglas (01556 502 575). 1,200 acre estate of horticultural excellence. There is also a wildfowl centre.

Threave Castle. Fourteenth-century tower on island in the Dee. Follow the B736 out of Castle Douglas to roundabout and over to the right.

Galloway Hydros Visitor Centre, Tongland (01557 330 114). Guided tours mid May to mid September.

Broughton House (NTS), Kirkcudbright (01557 330 437). Eighteenth-century town house and home to artist A.E. Hornel.

Tollbooth Arts Centre, Kirkcudbright (01557 331 556). Seventeenth-century prison and court. Audio visual show and art exhibition.

The Stewartry Museum, Kirkcudbright (01557 331 643). The history of Stewartry.

Wildlife Park, Kirkcudbright (01557 331 645). Zoo one mile out of town on the B727.

McLennan's Castle (HS), Kirkcudbright. Ruin of castellated town house that dates from 1577.

KIRKCUDBRIGHT TO GATEHOUSE OF FLEET (18 MILES)

Leave Kirkcudbright on the A755, Bridge Street, for Gatehouse of Fleet. Once over the Dee take first left for Borgue, B727, NCN 7. In Borgue follow road round to the left in the direction of the church. Follow road for five miles and turn left for Sandgreen and the Cream of Galloway, NCN 7. At next T-junction turn right, away from Sandgreen. One mile further on between Girthon and the A75 follow NCN sign left onto cycle path and follow signs through woodland to tarmac drive. Turn right and proceed past the Cally Palace Hotel. Turn left, signed NCN 7, beyond the Hotel and follow signs into Gatehouse of Fleet.

Terrain: On the whole quite a gentle section. Hills are mostly short and fairly laid back.

ACCOMMODATION
Gatehouse of Fleet (01557–)

Hotels and B&Bs: Bank of Fleet Hotel, 47 High Street (–814302); Murray Arms Hotel, Ann Street (–814370); Bobbin GH, 36 High Street (–814229); The Bay House, Ann Street (–814073).

Camping: Sandgreen CP (–814331). Two miles off route. Left at next junction after Cream of Galloway.

WATCH OUT FOR!
Nun Bay. Very pleasant spot on the road to Borgue.

Cream of Galloway (01557 81 40 40). Place to sample Galloway's wonderful fare en route, especially own brewed beer and ice cream.

The Mill on the Fleet, Gatehouse of Fleet. Crafts and tearoom in eighteenth-century mill.

GATEHOUSE OF FLEET TO NEWTON STEWART (17 MILES)
From the clock tower head downhill and over the River Fleet. Turn right onto the B796 and follow for six miles to T-junction at former railway station. Turn left for Creetown. It is a long descent to a T-junction opposite the Ellangowan Hotel. Turn right and climb out of Creetown. On the downhill turn right onto cycle path. At the end of cycle path turn right over bridge. After one mile turn left over bridge and proceed to crossroads. Go straight over for Stronard Outdoor Centre and Kiroughtree Forest Visitor Centre. Beyond outdoor centre road becomes rough and extremely steep. The descent to the A75 is just as steep. At this point there should be a new cycle path to the junction for Newton Stewart and the B7079. Follow B7079 into Newton Stewart.

Terrain: It is a long but moderate climb to former railway station. It is a terrific downhill to Creetown. The cycle path between Creetown and Newton Stewart is almost impossible in places.

ACCOMMODATION
Creetown (01671–)

Hotels and B&Bs: Ellangowan, St John Street (–820201); The Haven, 23 Harbour Street (–820546); Cherrytrees, 59 St John Street (–820229).

Camping: Creetown CP, Silver Street (–820377).

Newton Stewart (01671–)

Hotels and B&Bs: The Galloway Arms Hotel, 54–58 Victoria Street (–401653); Corsbie, Corsbie Road (–402124); Creebridge Lodge, Minigaff (–402319); Kilmartin, 4 Corsivel Road (–403047).

Hostels: Minigaff SYHA (–402211).
Camping: Creebridge CP (–402324).

WATCH OUT FOR!
Creetown Gem Rock Museum (01671 820 357). Collection of gems, crystals, fossils and minerals.

Newton Stewart Museum (01671 402 039). Natural and social history of Galloway.

NEWTON STEWART TO ISLE OF WHITHORN (22 MILES)
It is left once over the River Cree in Newton Stewart. Follow the A714 out of Newton Stewart for Wigton. At roundabout go straight over for Wigton, A714. After two miles turn left for Cartyport and Moss of Cree. Follow the level road but with a short steep climb at the very end into Wigton. At the far end of Market Square follow the A714 to the left for Whithorn. At the distillery by the River Bladnoch turn left over the river and follow the A746 for Whithorn round to the right. A half mile beyond Kirkinner take the left for Garlieston, B7004. At next T-junction turn left for Garlieston and right to continue to Isle of Whithorn. Ignore B7052 and follow B7004 round to the left. At fork in the road take the left for Isle of Whithorn B7063. Follow to Isle of Whithorn.

Terrain: A gentle section over rolling countryside.

ACCOMMODATION
Wigtown (01988–)
Hotels and B&Bs: Craigenlee, 8 Bank Street (–402498); Galisnock House, 20 South Main Street (–402249); Brora Lodge, Station Road (–402595); Old Coach House, 34 Bladnoch, Bladnoch (–402316).
Isle of Whithorn (01988–)
Hotels and B&Bs: Steam Packet Inn (–500334); Dunbar House, Tonderghie Road (–500336); Queens Arms Hotel (–500369).

WATCH OUT FOR!
Martyrs' Memorial. Memorial to two women tied to stakes to be drowned by the rising tide, to the left just before you climb into Wigton.

Wigton Bay RSPB Nature Reserve. Saltmarsh, mudflats and sandflats.

Garlieston. Eighteenth-century planned village. Look out for evidence of D-Day exercises.

ISLE OF WHITHORN TO GLENLUCE (29 MILES)

Follow the A750 out of the Isle of Whithorn for Port William and Whithorn. Take the right two miles out of Isle of Whithorn for Whithorn – still the A750. At T-junction it is right for Whithorn town centre and it is left to continue with the route signed Monreith A746. At next T-junction turn right for Monreith and Port William, A747. Follow the A747 for a relatively easy 22 miles to a junction with the A75. At junction turn right then immediately left for Glenluce.

Terrain: A few up and downs until you reach the coast where the road is more or less level until it climbs inland again to Glenluce.

ACCOMMODATION
Whithorn (01988–)
Hotels and B&Bs: Balteir Farm (–600241); Belmont, St John Street (–500890).
Glenluce (01581–)
Hotels and B&Bs: Kelvin House Hotel, 53 Main Street (–300303); Rowantree GH, 38 Main Street (–300244).
Camping: Glenluce CP (01581 300412).

WATCH OUT FOR!
Whithorn Priory, Museum, Northumbrian Monastery and Archaeological Dig (01988 500 508). A series of exhibitions and ruins that try to get across the importance of this site.

Monreith Animal World (01988 700 217). Goats, owls, reptiles and lots of other stuff.

Chapel Finian (HS). A ruined tenth-century resting place for pilgrims en route to Whithorn, signposted from the A747.

GLENLUCE TO BARRHILL (19 MILES)

Descend through Glenluce on Main Street and once out of Glenluce turn right for New Luce, Barrhill and Glenluce Abbey. Follow this road all the way to Barrhill. You can catch the train to Glasgow from Barrhill. The station is on the left on the downhill to Barrhill.

Terrain: The hill between Glenluce and Barrhill is slow to get going and the top is a long time coming.

ACCOMMODATION
New Luce
Hotels and B&Bs: Kenmuir House Hotel (01581 600 218).
Camping: There is camping available.

Barrhill (01465–)

Hotels and B&Bs: The Trout Inn (–821244); Blair Farm (–821247), one mile east on the A714.

Camping: Queensland Holiday Park (–821364), one-and-a-half miles west on the A714.

WATCH OUT FOR!

Glenluce Abbey (HS). Twelfth-century Cistercian Abbey.

Martyrs' Graves, Barrhill. Graves of two Covenanters summarily executed for carrying bibles.

BARRHILL TO MAYBOLE (30 MILES), MAYBOLE TO AYR (13 MILES)

At Barrhill and junction with A714 turn left for Girvan and Ayr. Follow the A714 for seven miles and turn right on the uphill from Pinmore for Tormitchell. Follow to T-junction with B734.

Turn left onto the B734 for Dailly and then after 200 yards leave the B734 on the right for Dailly and Maybole. Turn right at next T-junction again for Dailly and Maybole. Continue past Dailly and join the B741 and follow to Crosshill.

Turn left in Crosshill for Maybole, B7023. Five hundred yards out of Crosshill turn left, signed NCN 7. Follow road into Maybole. At first T-junction in Maybole turn right. Climb to junction with A77. Go straight over A77 signed, NCN 7, Ayr 13 miles.

Turn left at railway station, another point at which to catch the train to Glasgow, and then take first right. After 300 yards turn left into Gardenrose Path. Climb steeply out of Maybole. Descend through crossroads and then climb again. At top follow road round to the right. There then follows an exasperating sequence of ups and downs. At T-junction turn left for Carrick Hill Road. The road descends at first then climbs to viewpoint. Long descent on twisting road to T-junction. Turn right for Ayr, A719. Beyond Haven Holiday Park look out for cycle path off to the left. Take cycle path and emerge in residential area on Castle Street. Follow Castle Street to seafront car park. Just beyond car park cycle path resumes. Follow cycle path over bridge and along seafront into Ayr. Turn up right at Ayr Pavilion to Wellington Square. Turn right at T-junction onto Alloway Place then turn left onto Miller Road (A70) and follow to convoluted road system. Station is on the far side. It's maybe best to get off and walk round.

Terrain: A lot of ups and downs on this section, some of which are draining. The NCN from Maybole onwards is demanding and requires a lot of patience. There is, however, the reward of fine views.

ACCOMMODATION

Pinwherry (01465–)

Hotels and B&Bs: Daljarrock Hotel (–841224); The Auld Creamery, 9–11 Main Street (–841669).

Crosshill and Maybole (01655–)

Hotels and B&Bs: Royal Hotel, 57 King Street, Crosshill (–740209); Holmlea, 62 Culzean Road, Maybole (–882736); Enoch Lodge, Culzean Road, Maybole (–883328).

Ayr (01292–)

Hotels and B&Bs: Leslie Ann GH, 13 Castlehill Road (–265646); Arrandale Hotel, 2–4 Cassillis Street (–289959); Deanbank, 44 Ashgrove Street (–263473); Garth Madryn, 71 Maybole Road (–443346); Horizon Hotel, Esplanade (–264384).

WATCH OUT FOR!

Burns' Cottage, Kirk Alloway, The Tam O'Shanter Experience. All the best Burns sites within a short distance of each other. Follow the A719 into Ayr and turn right at roundabout and follow road to junction with B7024 and turn left.

7

DRINK
SPEYSIDE

Aviemore is Scotland's adventure capital. Climbing, skiing, canoeing, hill walking and mountain biking are all enthusiastically pursued in and around the unique wilderness of the Cairngorm Mountains. For some, a retail adventure on Aviemore's Grampian Road is enough. Basically, Aviemore can provide you with everything you could need for that perfectly colour coordinated outdoor experience, as well as burger and fries to go.

The stench of frying foods is all-pervasive in Aviemore. I suppose that if you were lost in the mountains you need only follow your nose as opposed to your compass. However, on this day it was the mountains that were lost, lost in a thick blanket of mist. What did I care! I was going the other way. Anyway, the venerable Scots pines of the Rothiemurchus Forest were a sight in themselves. Spaced out over a thick mat of heather and juniper, these are trees of character and individual beauty. Standing separately and with their branches stretching out and curling, the trees resemble the citizens of Beijing doing their morning t'ai chi.

In the forest it is calm and the pine-fresh smell just about purged the odour of hot oil and vinegar from my nostrils. The scent of the forest was at the same time invigorating and relaxing. There should be a sign for motorists: 'You are now entering a scented zone, throw away those magic trees and roll your windows down!' But the motorists would argue that the air conditioning doesn't work with the windows down.

The calming influence was lost on the mountain bikers whose fast-moving heads I could see through the trees. Occasionally a group of them would appear in a cloud of dust, their faces splattered with mud like Russian tank commanders. Smooth tyres and a puny frame are not quite de rigueur in the Cairngorms and they looked at me as if I were a different species, unsure whether to say hello or not. I received a sort of a nod from one of them but he may have been choking on his drinking tube.

When I turned north at Coylumbridge everything changed. All the busy wizziness had gone and all was quiet. A steam train was chuffing out steam and blowing on its whistle but I didn't count that as noise. The Spey was still and brown, sedated by a week of dry weather. Once the train had gone the only sound was the whirr of fishermen casting out their lines.

I decided to follow the clouds of steam and found myself in Boat of Garten. Boat of Garten is a village that wears the local look of granite cottages very well. Aviemore, on the other hand, has always tried to be the quintessential mountain resort. At first it had something to learn from the French and everything was built in concrete in the style of those alpine resorts that only exist in winter. Then they turned to log cabins and Scandinavian pine lodges and these still persist. However, they overlooked what was already there. The buildings constructed in granite have a rugged quality and are in themselves mini-mountains. Boat of Garten has done well to avoid a makeover.

I missed the train at Boat of Garten but it was a very happy 20 minutes I spent waiting on its return. Flowers in beds and boxes and holiday posters in primary colours were intoxicating reminders of a more civilised era of rail travel. When the train chuffed in I almost got on just for a bit more.

Beyond Boat of Garten I had no more than the occasional decision to occupy me. Should I take the direct route to Nethy Bridge or saunter through the Abernethy Forest and pay a visit to the Loch Garten ospreys? The ospreys were, I suppose, always going to win.

The Abernethy Forest is much denser than the Rothiemurchus Forest. Lichen-coated trees suggest that light is generally in short supply. The forest has the feel of an intimately lit room and I relaxed further still. The road was undemanding and the trees would have excluded anything likely to hinder me. I was content with the pine-fresh smell and trying to catch the ephemeral sounds of the forest.

I stopped by Loch Garten to take in the mountains and their reflection. The gloomy light in the forest was due in part to the cloudy skies and spots of rain were causing ripples on the loch, although some were created by jumping fish. They must be big fat fish, for insects were definitely not in short supply.

The Loch Garten ospreys were predictably out to lunch. I just have no luck with big birds. Before I set off I returned to the loch in case they were trying to catch one of those fat trout while my back was turned. Nah!

I was so relaxed that I didn't care. In fact I was probably well over the inner-calm cycling limit. I wonder how they would test for that – maybe they would see how many wedding videos you could sit through without getting up in a state of agitation. Sit through more than three and you're looking at a year's ban.

When I emerged from the forest I realised that I had only been vaguely aware of the weather. Out in the open there was very much more rain hitting the ground – and me. Not only that, I was experiencing withdrawal symptoms now that I had left behind the heady scents and comfort of the forest. It wasn't so much cold turkey as frozen-stiff turkey.

I couldn't see very much of what was around me but 'wild heathery moor' would be a good guess. The road climbed and the trees thinned to one isolated pine. My vague plans for the day were becoming firmer as the rain beat down and every foot of ascent brought a drop in temperature. I would spend the night in Tomintoul rather than Dufftown.

I did know what lay ahead of me: a big dip. Looking down from the top of the hill to the Bridge of Brown is not for the squeamish. The ascent on the far side of the bridge was laid bare and I winced in advance at the agony it would involve.

The road down to the bridge was tortured and I gave up my attempts at building up speed, indeed I was desperately trying to control it. I wasn't far up the other side when I called it a day and got off and pushed. The Italian drivers of a convoy of motor homes would have got out and let someone drive in much the same way as a pilot steers a ship into port. The grimaces from drivers and passengers alike said it all.

In the end the hill was steep but quickly overcome. I was no sooner up than I was going down again. At the bottom of the hill a measure of comfort was regained. The purple heather remained high above, coating the hilltops like a psychedelic snow. Now I was on a road lined by birches and among green fields of chewing cows.

The Hills of Cromdale and the Ladder Hills create this discrete pocket of comfort between them in which Catholicism survived the Reformation and it would seem that not a lot else has happened since Percy Toplis, a First World War mutineer, shot and injured a local PC and a farmer.

I was very glad to reach Tomintoul. The poor light had wound forward my body clock to early evening and I was cold and I was wet. Queen Victoria wasn't impressed by Tomintoul at all – she thought it 'poor' and 'tumbledown'. The royal put-down must have got to them because I found it to be a spruce little place built of grey granite and, as there was no room at any of the three inns that lined the village square, a popular little place as well. She must have been referring to the youth hostel. The roof felt was flapping loose and I had to plough through deep wet grass to confirm what I already suspected – it was out of order. Fortunately I had my tent and the locals pointed me in the direction of their highland games field.

The next morning, cold and stiff as I struggled from my tent, I noticed a hint of blue sky and a big cat. At first I took it for a dog or a fox but it was definitely a cat. Had I been lucky enough to see a Moray wildcat or was it just an overfed moggie? I'd like to think it was the former. I am assured that, big though they are, they do not pose a threat to humans.

Tomintoul at one point saw itself in the Aviemore mould but the signs above the empty ski-hire shops suggest that skiing at the nearby Lecht has not brought the hoped-for benefits, mainly down to the recent run of mild winters. Even though it was early August, I wasn't ruling out snow as I left Tomintoul.

Tomintoul may curse its luck for being too cool in the summer and just not cool enough in the winter but this means that it has a good all-year-round climate for the consumption of whisky. Just as aspirin is found in the bark of the damp-loving willow, the same logic is upheld by the fact that these high glens should produce most of the best whisky and, like aspirin, whisky is most often consumed for medicinal reasons.

A bit of a bump separates Tomintoul from Glen Livet, the *Côtes Nuit* of the whisky world. Whisky distilling has thrived both legally and illegally in the glen. George Smith was the first of the moonshiners to jump the dyke and apply for a licence in order to supply King George IV. The whisky produced by Smith is today referred to as *The Glenlivet*.

Glen Livet is a glen subjected to many adjectives by the advertising and PR people. The glen is described as wild and untamed, as silent and unforgiving. I daresay that this narrow glen fills easily with snow in the winter but in just a few short miles it completed the transformation from exposed heathery hills to pleasantly pastoral. I would say it was on the comfortable side of wild and untamed. Certainly it was silent, as most highland glens are, but as I freewheeled and enjoyed the shelter of the glen I didn't feel it was unforgiving at all.

In the eighteenth century Glen Livet had two major exports: whisky, of course, and Catholic priests. The Scalan Seminary educated 100 priests despite constant harassment from government troops which reached a peak in the aftermath of the Jacobite defeat at Culloden. These days Glen Livet has difficulty retaining one priest shared between three parishes.

Not even the long-horned Highland Cows with that cute dopey look can distract you from the fact that the Glenlivet Distillery is an eyesore. The great grey barns are, I suppose, an indication of just how good business is, but it just doesn't fit with the PR or the image projected on the label. As I descended from my vantage point on Gallowhill I was met by the wonderful smell of fermenting yeast; one whiff and I was mellow as a

Rastafarian and quite forgot about the look of the place. I did the distillery tour, finding that the length of time between the start and the tasting room was longer than was decent.

However there was no chance of overdoing it – this is Scotland after all and the whisky isn't exactly thrown at you. Unless you've got someone to share with, you only get to taste the one, which is a pity for I would have liked to make the comparison with their new Chardonnay cask-aged whisky. The 17 year old was most impressive.

The calm I was experiencing as I cycled out of Glen Livet and into Glen Rinnes was much deeper than that induced by the pine forests. Now my nostrils were burned with the scent of fermenting wort. Or was it the angels' share – the whisky that evaporates from the casks at the rate of 3 per cent a year must constitute at least as much of the atmosphere in these parts.

In Glen Rinnes the hills formed a continuous ridge that bumped along with me. To look at, the hills were unremarkable really but not unpleasant. Noisy clouds of tiny birds would rise from the hedgerows. Hares and rabbits, which seemed to know that there were no cars coming this way, would run ahead of me.

Dufftown, the whisky capital, offered more distillery tours but one in a day is more than enough. Dufftown has the light-hearted feel of a seaside town. Colourful signs above the shops create a pleasant variation on the grey granite uniform worn by all of the towns in this area. There was probably the smell of fish and chips but I was still only aware of the odour of the inside of the distillery's wash-back tub.

Beyond Dufftown all I had to do was pedal and it was quite refreshing not to be weighed down by having somewhere to visit or somewhere to be. I was stepping off the tourist trail and into serious farming country. A banner attached to a fence advertised the cows as prime beef, even though they were still walking around.

Every square inch of this land has a crop or a use. Cows graze and barley grows on the valley floor while conifers are harvested on the hilltops. It was only since the distillery tour that I was aware that the fields of barley were not fields of waving wheat. It was only then, when I saw the acres of land given over to barley, that I realised how important the whisky industry is.

Keith claimed to be the 'Friendly Toun' but I found it to be the 'Traffic Toun' and I was glad to be out the other side and on my way to Cullen, but I regretted the missed opportunity to visit the town's Museum of Tartan.

It did rain on the way to Cullen but there was plenty of space between the raindrops. Although I was keen for the change that being on the coast would bring I wasn't inclined to rush. I detoured to the pretty medieval village of Fordyce and the wonderfully hugger-mugger fishing port of

Portsoy. When I finally reached Cullen and had pitched my tent in the clifftop campsite, the sun was already preparing to set.

In Cullen be careful that you don't do anything you might regret. Don't be carried away by the town's steep Seafield Street unless you intend to visit the town's harbour or Cullen's seaside quarter, Seatown. You'll only have to come back up again. Cullen Skink may sound like something that you'll regret but 'Skink' is not a misspelling of skunk and neither is it some other horror that only people living this far north could find delectable. Skink is Gaelic for 'essence' and the 'Cullen Essence' manifests itself as a salty and creamy soup bulked out with smoked haddock and potatoes. Basically the soup uses all the ingredients that would have been at the town's disposal. Ensure that your water bottles are filled, for Cullen Skink will induce a raging thirst

The most striking thing about Cullen is its viaducts, one arch of which straddles Seafield Street and frames the town's sea view. The local gentry didn't want the trainline running too close to their property so the hard-up Great North of Scotland Railway Company were forced out onto the coast where they had to build several expensive viaducts. The trains have now gone and the track bed has been turned over to cyclists and pedestrians.

It could be said that the route is better suited to the cyclists, for they miss little of the delights of this journey. The route westwards was a treat of good views, clifftops matted with flowers and bizarre coastal features. Soft sediment acts as the meat which the sea is eating away to leave the bones of greywacke and quartzite. The path called at pastel Portknockie with its tiny picturesque harbour and Findochty with its scimitar beach and landmark white church on a low headland.

At Buckie the cycle path gets confused with back lanes and footpaths so I abandoned the cycle path that seemed to want to take me behind the town, braved the town centre traffic and took the much more interesting route by the town's working harbour. Buckie is unmistakably Victorian but cycling by the shore through Yardie you can see the cramped cottages once typical of north-east herring fishing communities. Here the houses are built as close to the sea as they dared and at right-angles to the sea so that only the windowless gable-end would be exposed.

The Caithness and Sutherland coast on the far side of the Moray Firth grew sharper as I made my way westwards, with Ben Wyvis remaining a dark and large shadow. To my left the North Sea was still there and even although the weather was clearer there was nothing more to see – a dead space really. Along both these coasts, which pinch at Inverness to create the Moray Firth, it was herring that was the salvation of those who were replaced on the land by sheep.

If the locals were to be believed these waters would have resembled

Hong Kong harbour – a floating morass of wood and mast. Even today there are those who struggle to find an analogy to convey the awesomeness of the herring fleet. The most common one is that you could walk right across some expansive bay or harbour without putting a toe in the water.

Between Buckie and the River Spey the countryside grew gentler still. Any flatter and a dyke would have to be built. Interest was maintained by a village of free-range pigs and the overgrown runways of Dallachy Airfield. The south-east of England may have been the frontline for the war across the channel but there was a war fought in the North Sea and in Scandinavia. It was only in 1992 that someone remembered to remember those who died fighting with the Dallachy Strike Wing.

Again the cyclist and the pedestrian benefit from the departure of the railways. The Spey Viaduct has to take a big step over this most capricious river. As it thundered under the bridge it had more of a Highland character than the Spey at Aviemore, where it is as a river with time on its hands. The river is disconcertingly visible flicking in and out of sight through the slats of the railway bridge.

Two legs and two wheels had been a rare sight until now. Surely the river was not the attraction for the cycling families hovering on the banks. A thrown stone would make no impression on this beast. It was on the other side that all was revealed.

'Did you see the osprey fishing on the river?'

Shit! I was mesmerised by the configuration of iron girders and hadn't thought to look closely at the river. I turned to go back but the woman added, 'It has gone now, I'm afraid.'

For a while on the coast there was a touch of The Fens but as I made my way inland the land dried out quickly to resemble the *Ile de France* or Champagne, dry and golden. Only the farms had none of the shambling charm of French farms, instead they were trim and grey and businesslike.

Elgin Cathedral, however, bears an uncanny resemblance to the cathedral at Reims at the heart of Champagne, with the Notre Dame look of two imposing towers (it once had three but we won't dwell on that). Even as a ruin it was a striking sight as I approached from the west on unusually high ground.

Samuel Johnson and James Boswell came by way of Elgin on their way to tour the Hebrides. Johnson said that the cathedral, 'afforded us another proof of the waste of Reformation'. Nearly all of Scotland's abbeys and cathedrals are in ruins but the remains at Elgin are so tantalisingly beautiful that you do regret its state a little bit more than the others. I have always wondered why those who plundered these cathedrals for their stone stopped when they did.

Despite building his cathedral out of stone, the Bishop of Moray still succumbed to the Big Bad Wolf of Badenoch. After much huffing and puffing over being ex-communicated for mistreating his wife, the Wolf, aka Alexander Stewart, bastard son of Robert II, burned the place down.

Elgin would have been a good place to stop. It is an elegant town with an eclectic mix of medieval and neo-classical buildings and it hasn't lost all of the kudos that a cathedral brought.

Not far out of town a serious accident had blocked the main road and I understood immediately why the SUSTRANS route goes to such lengths to keep you off the B9012. Unfortunately, all of the traffic was being directed my way, but once it had found its way round the blockage I was left in total silence. I wondered at first if this was the man-made silence of modern agricultural methods. There was a semblance of a hedge lining the large golden fields but there were no birds and nothing else for that matter. The way the cows were walking towards the fence to stare at me and moo menacingly I thought that maybe there was a more sinister reason. Perhaps in cow language they were not just mooing but chanting, 'Four legs good. Two legs bad!' So the birds had copped it and I was next.

I was sufficiently spooked by the whole experience to pedal as fast as I could. I just kept pedalling, hoping I wouldn't have to stop and get the map out. I kept looking round to check that they weren't following but what if they had alerted another herd up ahead? Should I change my route? They'd probably have all options covered. I decided to keep going and work a double bluff.

It was dusk when I reached Kinloss, breathless and distressed. My plan had worked. I shouted to a perimeter guard on the RAF Kinloss airbase that if he were to see any cows following me to shoot 'em. God knows what would happen if they got their hands on military hardware.

To arrive at the Findhorn Campsite by bike is to wear a halo, for this is not just a campsite and the bike is valued for its sustainability. This is the HQ of the Findhorn Community. It isn't anything quite as formal as a religion or as sinister as a cult but there are elements of both, I suppose. I believe they refer to themselves as a spiritual community with sustainability and respect for the environment as core aspirations.

The community was formed on the campsite 40 years ago by Eileen Caddy and her husband Peter. At first it may seem a bit naff but this is a serious outfit developed under God's guidance. God spoke to Eileen and Peter followed the advice. The Findhorn Community has many tentacles reaching out across the world so I suppose this is their Vatican. Instead of, 'Peter, on this rock you will build my church.' It was, 'Eileen on this grass and sand you will form a community.'

The community own the campsite now but it is a secular affair and despite the proximity it feels quite separate. The RAF base, on the other hand, doesn't feel at all separate. The constant noise of jets taking off and landing was a bit like playing Wagner as background music at a dinner party. Wagner would be quite inappropriate; a Mozart Piano Concerto would be more in keeping the mood of the community.

In actual fact it is the perfect environment in which to read the Sunday newspapers and that is exactly what I did with a mug of tea and a slice of something from the community's café. They, however, thought Bob Dylan did the trick musicwise.

At 2 p.m. I was still around so I decided to do the tour. With a loaf of organic San Francisco sourdough bread under my arm I joined Rory, the guide. As did four Italians. Starting at the best deli outside of Chelsea we went back to the beginning with Rory to the caravan where it all started, the vegetable plot that produced huge vegetables, the retreat centre, the impressive theatre, café, pottery, the eco-village and the meditation areas.

I could swear there was time I couldn't account for – Rory's quiet New York accent just lulled me to the point where I was gone. I had always assumed that it would be very difficult to attain a meditative state but in the right circumstances it was remarkably easy and I wanted to go deeper. There was another thing I couldn't quite explain: a sudden craving for lentils.

There was a time when the Findhorn Community was viewed with suspicion and even derision, but the big brown tourist signs that point it out suggest that the locals know when they're on to a good thing. The economic impact it has on this area is considerable and it is all down to taking life from a different angle. Others can't help but be curious.

Out in the world again, everything seemed so conventional. The actual village of Findhorn is pretty and very traditional, but I was unlikely to encounter buildings of flowing lines of wood and stone so redolent of California or the striking New England eco-houses in sunshine yellow or bright blue.

Even the nearby River Findhorn relaxes as it enters the sea. It spreads out into a wide circular bay with only the momentum of its journey getting it through the marshy land that rings the bay. For me there was absolutely nothing to get worked up about – the road ahead was empty and once again perfectly level; oh, but it was raining, and heavily.

The Culbin Forest was denying me a sea view. This forest was planted to keep the sandy coast in place. The locals refer to this area as the Culbin Desert, as this is one of the driest places in the British Isles. In the lee of the mountains not much rain makes it over here; however, it made it today.

I winced at having to cross the busy A96 and the railway line to visit Forres and Sueno's Stone and then having to do it again to return to the route west. Like every other day, I was cycling far later in the day than I would have liked. Brodie Castle was already closed to visitors though the gardens were still open, but that didn't quite appeal in the rain. Within an hour I was in Nairn and I decided to stop.

The campsite, or rather caravan park, at Fishertown in Nairn claims to welcome tents but I couldn't see any. Apart from that I prefer my campsites not to welcome me with flashing neon lights so I grabbed a fish supper and cycled another mile and half out of town to an altogether more peaceful spot. Peace was what I would insist on from now on.

The peace was such that I slept late. I emerged to a bright sunny day and my tent was already dry. Three Texans had pitched their tent alongside mine, having arrived late in the night. They had a huge hire car which they had filled with large polystyrene boxes. The boxes had contained all their food for two weeks in Scotland. They had brought it all the way from Texas – their defence: 'The food's so darned expensive here and your cows are mad.' They weren't however put off and intended to return the following summer to do some climbing. Indeed they considered their experience in Scotland 'awesome' and were going to spend their last day reflecting on it.

I would have to reflect while I cycled. I knew that today would be different. Almost immediately I was climbing and it wasn't long before I had a good view of the Moray Firth, the huge sheds of the oil rig fabrication yard at Ardersier, the town of Nairn and the hills to the south. For the last few days I had cycled among fields that were dry and odourless and now I was in country that reeked of turnips and manure. The hedges were thicker and heavy with raspberries. Not only did the road climb but it constantly changed direction to find the easiest gradient. I gave up the mountains for the coastal plains and was now returning to the mountains.

For the time being I was in the pretty interim of quaint cottages with a view and mossy dykes. Cawdor, the village complete with gas lighting and fairytale castle, was especially pretty and well worth the detour from the National Cycle Network even although I had to reverse a big height loss to regain it.

On 4 April 1746 the army of the Duke of Cumberland marched from the town of Nairn following the River Nairn westwards to meet the Jacobites on Culloden Moor. From my position on the opposite bank I would have had a good view across the shallow valley of the Nairn of the 15 battalions of 10,000 men and the heavy artillery. I would probably have even been able to pick out the fatboy duke himself.

I squandered my height to visit the battlefield on Culloden Moor and wander the mass graves of the clans. This has to be the most misunderstood event in Scottish history, even at the time most Highlanders didn't really know why they were there. Bonnie Prince Charlie wanted the crown of England for his father, while the Highlanders thought they would have a Catholic Stuart king in Edinburgh.

The Jacobites never managed to charge the Hanoverian lines

convincingly and the screaming charge was the Highlanders' most effective weapon. They stood for too long and endured the volleys of grape shot that were devastating their lines. One thousand Highlanders died in battle and one thousand more in the butchery that followed. The Highlands of Scotland were kept on a very short leash after the '45 Rebellion and the defeat effectively ended the Highland way of life.

Like Bonnie Prince Charlie, I was bound for the hills, only I could afford to take my time about it. Apparently the stench of his flight was so strong that even today bloodhounds would be able to pick up the trail.

There was now more gorse than grass and more sheep than cows. There was also more climbing than descent. Each descent was bittersweet because I knew that I had to overcome Slochd Summit at 1,320 ft, so whenever I gained height I wanted to keep it. Ahead of me were bald hills, too high to have their summits coated with conifers. Occasionally there was a view ahead to the Cairngorms. I crossed the River Findhorn again, this time closer to its source in the empty Monadhliath than its mouth.

It was a beautiful evening, the final ascent to Slochd was not as bad as I'd feared and the cycle path that runs with the A9 was surprisingly pleasant. The cycle path is essentially the old A9 and just beyond Slochd it drops below the current road. It was hard to believe that the A9 was ever so narrow, slow and winding. Scots pines, stretched out over the old roads – a situation that modern haulage wouldn't be able to live with.

I had done my work and I was now reaping the benefits; if I didn't want to pedal I didn't have to. Only once did the road go back up again. It had been a long day of almost 50 miles and again it was twilight when I arrived in Boat of Garten. So I decided to stop and take the steam train the last few miles to Aviemore in the morning.

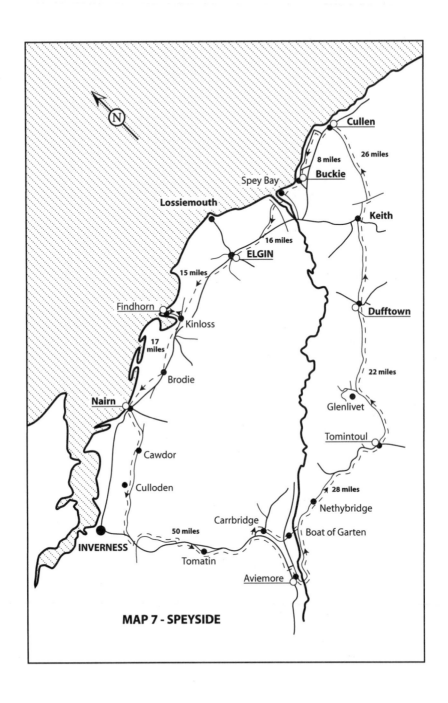

MAP 7 - SPEYSIDE

Distance: 180 miles approx.

Maps: OS *Landranger* series (1: 50,000), sheets 27, 28, 29, 35, 36, 37. OS *Road Map 1: Northern Scotland*. SUSTRANS *Aberdeen to John O'Groats: NCN 1* and *Lochs and Glens Cycle Route: NCN 7*.

Banks/Cashpoints: Aviemore, Dufftown, Keith, Cullen, Buckie, Elgin, Forres, Nairn.

Cycle Repair: Bothy Bikes, Aviemore Shopping Centre (01479 810 111); R. Cockburn, 62 West Cathcart Street, Buckie (01542 831 493); Bikes and Bowls, 7 High Street, Elgin (01343 549 656); Bike and Buggy, Leopold Street, Nairn (01667 455 416); Ian Bishop Cycles, Slochd (01479 841666).

General Stores: You'll have no problems finding a general store anywhere along the route.

Traffic: Expect some traffic on the roads around Aviemore and on the A939 into Tomintoul. Also expect traffic in and around Buckie, Keith and Elgin. There is a short stretch on the very fast A95 just beyond Keith where extreme care should be taken.

GETTING THERE

Train: Frequent trains from Glasgow Queen Street Station or Edinburgh Waverley for Inverness stop at Aviemore. Typically two bikes per train. Advanced booking of spaces is essential. Journey time for Glasgow/Edinburgh to Aviemore is three hours.

ROUTE INFORMATION

AVIEMORE TO TOMINTOUL (28 MILES)

From Aviemore Railway Station turn left and proceed south out of Aviemore. Turn left after 500 yards for Coylumbridge and Cairngorms, B970 and NCN 7. Just beyond the Hilton turn left for Boat of Garten, Nethy Bridge, B970 and NCN 7. Follow B970 into Nethy Bridge or turn right 700 yards beyond Boat of Garten junction for Loch Garten, Tulloch and Tulloch Moor. Follow road through the Abernethy Forest ignoring turnings for Tulloch and Tulloch Moor. Eventually you turn right for Grantown on Spey rejoining the B970. Go through Nethy Bridge. Cross the Nethy and take next right and follow road to crossroads. Go straight over for Tomintoul. Follow road all the way to junction with A939. Turn right and follow all the way to Tomintoul (eight miles).

Terrain: Very easy going at first, nothing more than gentle ascents. There is a stiff climb to join the A939 followed by a moderate ascent. Road descends steeply to the Bridge of Brown and climbs away even more steeply but it's shorter than it looks.

ACCOMMODATION

Aviemore (01479–)

Hotel and B&Bs: MacKenzie's, 125 Grampian Road (–801672); Ravenscraig, Grampian Road (–810278); Vermont, Grampian Road (–810470); Cairngorm Hotel, Grampian Road (–810233); Ardlogie, Dalfaber Road (–810747).

Hostels: Aviemore SYHA, 25 Grampian Road (–810345); Mountain Supplies Bunkhouse, 111 Grampian Road (–810903).

Camping: Rothiemurchus Caravan Park, Coylumbridge (–812800).

Tomintoul (01807–)

Hotel and B&Bs: Bracam House, 32 Main Street (–580278); Findron Farm (–580382); Auchriachan Farmhouse (–580416); Gordon Hotel (–580218); Richmond Hotel (–580206); Glenavon Hotel (–580777).

Hostels: Tomintoul SYHA – contact SYHA HQ for details (01786 891400). There is a bunkhouse attached to Gordon Hotel (see above).

Camping: There is no official campsite so ask locally for a suitable spot. Glenlivet Estates is sympathetic to discrete and responsible wild camping.

WATCH OUT FOR!

Strathspey Steam Railway, Aviemore (01479 810 725). Trains run between Aviemore and Boat of Garten and will carry bikes.

Auchgourish Gardens, Boat of Garten (01479 831 464). Millennium and Japanese Gardens.

Loch Garten RSPB Osprey Centre, Tulloch, Nethy Bridge (01479 831 694). Watch the nesting Opsreys, March to August.

Tomintoul Museum (01807 580 285). Local history and heritage in tourist info centre.

TOMINTOUL TO DUFFTOWN VIA GLENLIVET (22 MILES)

From the square in Tomintoul continue east between the Clockhouse and Richmond Hotel. Take left for Dufftown, Braemar and 'The Glenlivet', B9008. Cross the A939 continuing to follow the B9008 for Dufftown.

Just beyond Tomnavoulin, turn left uphill over Gallowhill. At Glenlivet House turn right and descend through distillery complex. At next junction turn right away from the Drumin Museum. Once over the River Livet go round to the right to follow the B9008 back towards Tomintoul for about one mile. Take the left on the bend Dufftown (11 miles), B9009. Follow B9009 all the way into Dufftown.

Terrain: There is some climbing but it is nothing more than moderate.

ACCOMMODATION
Dufftown (01340–)
Hotel and B&Bs: Fife Arms Hotel, 2 The Square (–820220); Morvern, The Square (–820507); Davaar Church Street (–820446); Nashville, 8A Balvenie Street (–820553); Mrs Robertson, 11 Conval Street (–820818).
Hostels: Loch Park Adventure Centre (out of Dufftown on the road to Keith), Drummuir Castle Estate (01542 810 334).

WATCH OUT FOR!
Glenlivet Distillery, Ballindalloch (01342 783 220).

Balvenie Castle, Dufftown. Ruin of thirteenth-century Stewart stronghold.

Glenfiddich Distillery, Dufftown (01340 820 373).

DUFFTOWN TO CULLEN (26 MILES)

Continue downhill past old tower following signs for Rhynie, A941. At bottom of hill follow signs for Keith, B9014. Follow the B9014 all the way to Keith.

At T-junction in Keith turn right for Aberdeen, A96 and towards town centre. On short uphill turn left for Newmill and St Rufus Park B9116.

Proceed downhill past park, after 500 yards turn right in residential area for Newmill.

Turn right once over railway line and river just before Newmill. At next junction turn right and follow to junction with A95. Turn left onto the A95 and follow for a half mile. Take care: this road is very fast and can be busy. Turn left for Cullen. B9018. Follow NCN signs off to the left before encountering A98(T) and follow Findlater Drive, Cathay Terrace and then South Desmond Street. Turn right onto Grant Street for Cullen Town Centre.

Terrain: There is a bit of a climb out of Dufftown. Beyond that the going is easy, unless you detour to Fordyce and Portsoy, which involves big hills.

ACCOMMODATION
Cullen (01542–)
Hotels and B&Bs: Cullen Bay Hotel (–840432); Seafield Hotel, Seafield Street (–840791); 11 Seafield Place (–840819); Mrs Phimister, 13 Olgivie Park (–840017); Lily Cottage, 1 Cathay Terrace (–840132).
Camping: Cullen Bay CP (–840776).

WATCH OUT FOR!
Strathisla Distillery, Chivas Brothers, Seafield Avenue, Keith (01542 783 044).

Scottish Tartans Museum, Keith (01542 888 419).

Fordyce. Follow signs from B9018, involves a climb. Fordyce is a pretty village with an interesting churchyard and tower.

St Mary's Collegiate Church, Cullen. Medieval church. Robert the Bruce's second wife is said to be buried here.

CULLEN TO BUCKIE (8 MILES)
From main square Cullen follow Grant Street (west) and then turn right onto North Desmond Street. Descend steeply to cycle path. Turn left onto cycle path and follow to Portknockie. Go straight over onto Admiralty Street at the end of cycle path. Continue straight over Falconer Terrace and then take next left onto Commercial Road. Follow Commercial Road to junction with Harbour Road and turn left. Wander round bay on Harbour Road. Leave Harbour Road for Cliff Terrace. At the end of Cliff Terrace join cliff-top path.

Leave cycle path in Findochty and follow Cliff Street then Mackenzie Street. At the end of Mackenzie Street turn left steeply uphill. Turn right onto cycle path by the A942. After a short distance follow NCN signs off to the left. At next junction turn right then left. Within sight of Buckie turn right past storage tanks. Follow signs through the industrial estate. At T-junction go straight over onto shared footpath/cycle path and continue past garages. Turn right onto Commerce Street and then turn left for town centre. Follow East Church Street to Cluny Square.

Terrain: Easy going along cliff-top path. Just one or two short climbs.

ACCOMMODATION
Buckie (01542–)
Hotels and B&Bs: Rosemount, 62 East Church Street (–833434); Mrs E. MacMillan, 81 High Street (–832367); Cluny Hotel, 2 High Street (–832922); The Old Coach House, High Street (–836266).
Camping: Strathlene CP (–834851).

WATCH OUT FOR!
Buckie Drifter Museum, Freuchney Road, Buckie (01542 834 646). Maritime heritage museum.

BUCKIE TO ELGIN (16 MILES)

At the roundabout in Cluny Square, turn right and then turn left on the bend. Follow road through Yardie. A half mile beyond town limits join the cycle path on the left and follow cycle path to Portgordon. At the end of the cycle path turn right for Dallachy and Spey Bay. Follow road west along sea front. Road drifts away from sea front and after two miles turn right for Spey Bay on Beaufighter Road. Continue around disused airfield and into Nether Dallachy. After 300 yards turn left onto Spey Road. At next T-junction turn right. A half mile beyond the post office turn left onto dirt track between fields. In trees turn left and then after a short distance turn right and join cycle path over the Spey Bridge.

Continue to follow track to emerge in Gartmouth. Turn left onto road. Proceed to T-junction and turn right. Take left for Lochhill and Milton.

After about two miles follow road round to left for Elgin, ignoring turning for Lochhill. Go straight through next set of crossroads. At next set of crossroads turn right for Milltown and Lossiemouth. Follow road to T-junction with B9103 and turn left and then after a half mile turn right over humpback bridge. Enter Elgin on the downhill. At T-junction turn left. After a short distance turn left onto Newmill Road. Beyond Johnstone Cashmere Centre turn right onto North College Street for Library and Cathedral. Turn right into King Street for Cathedral.

Terrain: Very easy going. There is a bit of up and down between Gartmouth and Elgin.

ACCOMMODATION

Elgin (01343–)

Hotels and B&Bs: Southbank, 36 Academy Street (–547132); West End, 282 High Street (–549629); Julie;s, 12 Culbard Street (–541870); Richmond, 48 Moss Street (–542561); Braelossie Hotel (–547181).

Hostels: The Saltire Bunkhouse, Pluscarden Road (–551467).

Camping: Riverside CP, West Road (–542813).

WATCH OUT FOR!

Moray Firth Wildlife Centre and Ice House, Spey Bay (01343 820 339).

Dallachy Airfield. There is a memorial to those members of the Dallachy Strike Wing who attacked German shipping in Scandinavian waters.

The Elgin Museum, High Street, Elgin (01343 543 675). More than usual local heritage, such as shrunken heads and a Peruvian grinning mummy.

Elgin Cathedral (HS). Ruin of thirteenth-century cathedral easily spotted as you come into Elgin.

ELGIN TO FINDHORN (15 MILES)

From Cathedral go straight into Cooper Park and follow path round by duck pond. Signs are quite confusing. Do not go over red iron bridge but follow river upstream through underpass. Follow path between playing fields and river – fairly rough. At swimming pool turn right over Bailey Bridge. At Rugby Club go to the right and then right again into trees. Follow track through woodland to emerge in residential area. Turn left and then right onto quieter road. At next T-junction turn right and proceed up steep hill out of Elgin.

Just short of B9012 road swings to the right. At this point take the cycle path that goes downhill to the left. At the end of cycle path turn left onto road in the direction of Kintrae. After 800 yards turn right and follow road steeply downhill. At the bottom of the hill turn left. Go straight over at crossroads with B9013 for Longhillock. At next set of crossroads go straight over for Coltfield. At Coltfield go straight over for Miltonhill.

At next T-junction beyond Miltonhill turn left. Once over railway line turn right for Newton Struthers. After one mile come to T-junction and turn right for Kinloss. In Kinloss at T-junction with B9089 turn left and join cycle lane. For Findhorn turn right onto the B9011. Follow all the way to village or Foundation.

Terrain: A steep climb out of Elgin is followed by miles of level cycling.

ACCOMMODATION
Findhorn (01309–)
Hotels and B&Bs: Findhorn Foundation Visitor Centre will give you details of B&Bs (–690310); Heath House (–691082).
Camping: Findhorn Foundation CP (–690203); Findhorn Sands (–690324).

WATCH OUT FOR!
Kinloss Abbey. Ruin of abbey and the graves of 200 airmen and women.
   Findhorn Foundation (01309 690 310). Remarkable community based on the teaching of Eileen Caddy. There is a tearoom, incredibly well stocked deli, arts venue, an eco-village and somewhere to meditate.
   The Findhorn Heritage Centre (01309 690 349). Pre-history to present and natural history.

KINLOSS (FINDHORN) TO NAIRN (15 MILES; DETOUR 17 MILES)

From Findhorn make your way back to the B9089 at Kinloss. Turn right onto the B9089 for Forres and join cycle lane. Cycle lane ends at garage but a shared footpath/cycle path continues for 200 yards. At the end of cycle path cross the road for right turn. Stay on this road all the way to the Ben Romach Distillery. To visit Forres go over the level crossing and take care crossing the A96. To continue with the route turn right at distillery and then left after a short distance onto broad rough track. Follow track and cross River Findhorn on Bailey bridge. Re-emerge in Broom of Moy. Follow long, straight, tree-lined road to T-junction and turn right for Kintessack. Take next left for Kintessack, Dyke and Culbin Cloddymoss.
   Continue to follow signs for Dyke and Brodie. At T-junction at level crossing turn right away from the level crossing. After about one mile turn left for Nairn at T-junction. After about a half mile the road forks; follow road to the right for Nairn. Follow road through Kingsteps into Nairn on Lochloy Road. Watch for cycle path leaving Lochloy Road on the right. Follow cycle path down to riverbank. Turn right for Fishertown, cross river for Town Centre or turn left to continue with the route.

Terrain: A level cycle.

ACCOMMODATION
Nairn (01667–)
Hotels and B&Bs: Clifton House, Viewfield Street (–453119); Invernairn Hotel, Thurlow Road (–452039); Ascot House, 7 Cawdor Street

(–455855); Bracadale House, Albert Street (–452547); Ceol Mara, The Links (–452495); Greenlaws, 13 Seafield Street (–452738).

Camping: Spindrift CP (two miles out of town on B9090), Little Kildrummie (–453992).

WATCH OUT FOR!

Sueno's Stone. Twenty-foot Pictish carved stone on the eastern side of Forres.

Bendromach Distillery, Forres (01309 675 968).

Falconer Museum, Forres (01309 673 701).

Nelson Tower, Cluny Hill, Forres. Furthest north memorial to Lord Nelson.

Brodie Castle and Gardens (NTS). Z-shaped sixteenth-century castle and home of the Earl of Brodie.

NAIRN TO AVIEMORE (50 MILES)

On the right bank of the River Nairn follow the cycle path upstream and under St Ninian Bridge. Join cycle path by the Nairn and follow under railway viaduct. When the cycle path ends turn right onto A939 or cross road to cycle path/footpath and leave Nairn. Take next right for Housemill Meadows and Gate. At T-junction with B9101 turn right and then left for Geddes Trout Fishery. After one mile turn left. After a further two miles turn right.

At next set of crossroads NCN goes to the left, continue straight on for Cawdor. After a short distance turn right for Cawdor. Fast downhill to T-junction with B9090. Turn left for Culloden and Inverness. Turn left after a short distance. At junction in village turn left and follow road round bend past post office and out of village past the church.

Just beyond church turn left. Three-quarters of a mile further on, turn right. Fast downhill through trees brings you to a T-junction in the open. Turn left and follow the road to crossroads. Go straight over to rejoin NCN1 in the direction of Galcantray.

After about three miles turn right for Clava Bridge (continue straight on to avoid big downhill and uphill). Go under huge viaduct and descend very steeply. Take next left for NCN7 for Carrbridge, Tomatin and Clava Cairns. Follow road past Clava Cairns, then steeply uphill to the left and under railway line. Turn right at T-junction at Culdoich Farm for Carrbridge and Tomatin.

Follow road for three miles to T-junction with B9154 and turn left for Carrbridge and Tomatin. Longish uphill takes you past Loch Moy to junction with A9. Follow cycle path that runs parallel to A9. After a short distance you have to cross the A9 and continue following A9 on the other side. At Tomatin Services turn right for Tomatin and Carrbridge. Go under railway viaduct and follow road round to the right over River Findhorn. Follow road uphill to Slochd summit then follow intermittently cycle path and former A9. Join A938 and follow into Carrbridge. Go round to the right at Carrbridge Hotel and cross River Dulnain. Follow this road out of Carrbridge to T-junction with A96. Cross A96 and join excellent cycle path and follow to Boat of Garten. At Boat of Garten railway station, go round to the left and then turn right. Proceed to junction with B970 and turn right. Retrace outward route to Aviemore.

Terrain: Not far out of Nairn the climbing begins. Most climbs are moderate but some are steep. The climb to Slochd summit is long but well graded. It is almost downhill the whole way into Carrbridge. Carrbridge to Aviemore is gentle.

ACCOMMODATION
Cawdor (01667–)
Hotels and B&Bs: Fairview, Culcharry (one mile east of Cawdor) (–454382); Dallaschyle Farm (two miles west of Cawdor; en route) (–493422).
Tomatin
Hotels and B&Bs: Millcroftt, Old Mill Road, Tomatin (01808 511405).
Camping: Auchnahillin Camping (by the B9154; en route) (01463 772286).
Carrbridge (01479–)
Hotels and B&Bs: Carrmoor, Carr Road (–841244); Craigellachie, Main Street (–841641); Caberfeidh, Station Road (–841638); Moorfield House, Deshar Road, Boat of Garten (–831646).

WATCH OUT FOR!
Cawdor Castle (01667 404615). Home of the Cawdors for 600 years. Links with Macbeth and there's a maze in the grounds.

Culloden Moor Visitor Centre (NTS). Detour north for about a half mile from the point at which NCN 1 and NCN 7 meet. Site of the defeat of Bonnie Prince Charlie and the end of the Jacobite rebellion of 1745.

Landmark Heritage Park, Carrbridge. Heritage, natural history, forest walks and mazes; good for kids.

8

FOOD
THE FIRTH OF CLYDE

Arran is the big guy when it comes to islands in the Firth of Clyde, a giant 'sleeping warrior' no less, with a compact, muscular and well-defined physique. On the map it is shaped like a huge baked bean; from the Ayrshire coast I suppose it does have a passing resemblance to a 'sleeping warrior', with the jaggy hills at the northern end his rugged features and the low-lying land to the south as his legs and body. He does however seem to have at least two noses – or is it that his eyes are out on stalks?

The Highland Boundary Fault cuts Arran in two, which accounts for the low-lying south and the mountainous Highland north. As a result Arran is often described, especially in tourist board brochures, as 'Scotland in Miniature'.

Wheeling my bike off the ferry and up the slipway I reckoned that if this is Scotland in miniature then Brodick must represent, allowing for a suitable scale factor, Edinburgh. A big town on the east coast, overlooked by a castle – yes, that fits. Brodick is even the island's capital – another similarity. My God, it's true, Arran really is 'Scotland in Miniature'.

Really Brodick couldn't be more unlike Edinburgh, as the Scotland in Miniature thing only works from a distance. Anyway you're likely to meet Glaswegians in Brodick and the same couldn't be said for Edinburgh.

It was a Glaswegian who accosted me on my way up the slipway.

'Is that a bike you're oan?' he shouted over. To state the obvious is a

Glasgow conversation starter but still it was enough to panic me into looking down to make sure.

'Yes, aye!'

'So where ye aff tae?'

'Oh round the island, well almost. I'll be catching the ferry to Kintyre from Lochranza.'

'How faur's that then?'

'About 40 miles or so.'

'Ye're a bloody liar, naeb'dy kin pedal a bike that faur! N'you wi' aw that stuff tae!'

With that he went off to rejoin his wife standing in the queue for the open-top bus tour. If I hadn't seen the open-top bus with my own eyes then I might have called him a bloody liar had we got round to talking about his plans for the day, but, yes, such a thing exists. It must be the first time I've ever hoped for it to rain and rain heavily.

Rain seemed a possibility. Dark clouds were gathering just the other side of Goat Fell so that the rocky peak and its neighbours were difficult to make out. The air was thick and warm and if anyone harboured plans to sell genuine Arran fresh air, this was the day to do it, for I was sure it could have been cut into cubes, packaged and sold in two flavours: fresh sea air and fresh mountain air.

I was no match for the first hill out of Brodick. Within minutes I was breathless and greasy with sweat. I could've blamed the climatic conditions but my condition maybe had something to do with the bumper fried breakfast I'd eaten on the Calmac Ferry. To make matters worse a group of cyclists clad in pink Lycra passed me on the hill, chatting effortlessly amongst themselves, whereas I was wrestling with gravity to keep my full belly out of the way of my pedal action.

The rain clouds seemed unable to make it over the mountains to the east of the island. The west side of the island looked as if it was having a terrible time but on the east side it was developing into a sunny day. Of course there are times when the rain clouds do make it over but there is enough of a rain shadow for Brodick, Lamlash and Whiting Bay to be viewed as credible holiday resorts.

Before I descended the steep hill into Lamlash I looked out over the bay sheltered by the Holy Isle. Hundreds of pleasure craft were swinging on their moorings in the bay where King Haaken gathered his fleet for the attack on the Scottish mainland in 1263 and where the Royal Navy's North Sea Fleet regularly lay at anchor.

A small boat was ferrying people out to the Holy Isle. Perhaps they were new recruits to the community of Tibetan Buddhist Monks that has set up on the island or perhaps they were going out to climb the 300 metres to the island's high point; it didn't much matter I suppose. The town was busy with visitors aimlessly pawing second-hand books or flicking through prints of local scenes. Most of the hotels and guest houses were displaying 'No Vacancies' – a good sign so late in the season.

Between Lamlash and Whiting Bay it seemed as though every barn and farmhouse had become self-catering or B&B accommodation. Highland Cows in a field usually mean that there isn't any serious farming going on. Arran needs tourists and has done for over 150 years when well-to-do Glaswegians started taking houses for the summer on the island. Mother and children stayed for the whole summer and father came down at weekends; after all, the journey was not much more than two hours by steamer from Glasgow. Arran also needs tourists who want to spend money but I had no need for a local artist's artwork or a jar of Arran mustard or handmade candles.

As far as Whiting Bay, Arran belongs to the motorist, but from Whiting Bay onwards the island belongs to the cyclist. No one followed me out of Whiting Bay. I didn't encounter anyone on the difficult bends, the road narrowed to single track, the white line disappeared and the verges were no longer clipped to please tourists who value tidiness. The verges were full of the late-summer colour of blackberries, cats' ears and thousands of bluebells or harebells (if we use English nomenclature).

The view inland was unremarkable: rough grazing fringed by conifer forest in the process of being felled, which also meant that the strong smell of pine sap obliterated any scent that might be emanating from the verges. The road was high as it turned onto the south coast, while the fields to my left rolled over a cliff so that I couldn't see the coastline.

In terms of 'Scotland in Miniature' the view made no sense; where I suppose 'England in Miniature' should have been were the tiny islands of Ailsa Craig and Pladda. Ailsa Craig is the distinctive semicircle of rock that can be seen from the Ayrshire coast; from Arran it is a sharp and slight island and looks a bit like a sinking Sugar Loaf Mountain. Pladda is low, green and flat and dominated by its lighthouse. The Ayrshire coast was completely hidden in the haze but Kintyre's shades of green were vivid in the west.

At Torrylinn I pulled over for the Arran Creamery – the home of Arran cheese. I should have been reassured by the dental-surgery cleanliness of the creamery but it left me rather cold and unengaged. No bacteria, no stench of mould and no samples. What kind of cheese factory is this?

The road sank into Kilmory where people were enjoying an unhurried lunch in the garden of the Lagg Inn under towering Scots pines and within earshot of an energetic stream. Leafy green bushes and trees abound in this little hollow and the cool green worked with the mugginess of the day to create a perfect little microclimate.

On Arran, the view ahead is constantly changing, open sea with

Northern Ireland just a shadow in the distance is replaced by the growing arm of Kintyre and then the mountains to the north appear once again. Beinn Bharrain was scuffing the underside of the dark cloud that was still sitting over the island and hiding Goat Fell entirely. There was no evidence that it had ever rained on the west coast and it was a pleasant surprise to find that it was just as sunny a day as on the east.

Beyond Blackwaterfoot the road dropped right down to the level of the water and only a grey pebbly shore lay between me and the barely lapping waters of the Kilbrannan Sound.

There were tourists and holidaymakers on this side of the island too but I judged from the fact that the fields were now full of sheep and cows that these were tourists who didn't shop. Rather they were enjoying Arran as it should be enjoyed – as a getaway. There were at least half a dozen artists spaced out along the shore painting the clearer scenes on offer over the Kilbrannan Sound to Kintyre. In the gardens of little holiday cottages men and women snoozed or had their heads in books.

For many miles the road was so perfectly level that I must have slipped into the cycling equivalent of cruise control and I was so switched off that I forgot to pedal harder when a small rise did present itself.

The Catacol Bay Hotel's position right on the shore and yet backing onto the mountains sums up what it is that makes Arran special: the compelling coming together of sea and mountain environments. The hotel was full to overflowing with diners and drinkers when I arrived. However, I was their only resident and I was shown to a room with a sea view without any prompting.

The hotel and especially the bar had the atmosphere and décor of a students' union. The food was along those lines as well: cheap and in once-a-week portions. The menu was the usual international fare. The only concession to the locality was that it served Arran Ale. The crisp fresh flavour of the Arran Blonde mimics the qualities of continental beers and was perfect for a sultry evening.

It was a very quiet night in the Catacol Bay Hotel, although the hotel is renowned for its Friday-night folk nights, and there was no incentive to stay out of bed. Breakfast was predictably huge, designed for at least two plates. Every time I tried to remove something from the plate I sent a wave of beans over the side. The weather, on the other hand, was looking as unpredictable as ever.

Lochranza, just around the corner from Catacol, is the village with the unenviable title of the shadiest place in Britain. The sun has to be very high in the sky to shine over the mountains that wall Lochranza in on three sides. The lack of sunlight has two possible effects. One, it makes the setting of Lochranza all the more dramatic, and two, it keeps the tourists away because, despite having a photogenic castle out on a gravel spit in the loch, the island's only distillery, a decent golf course and a few arty-crafty outlets, the tourists don't come round in quite the numbers you'd expect.

If it's any consolation it does mean that Lochranza is the most genuine-feeling place on the island. Perhaps, though, they could develop a niche market among vampires, luring them with such novelties as daytime TV and all-day breakfasts.

On the ferry from Lochranza to Kintyre I preferred to look back at Arran rather than forward to Kintyre. Loch Ranza, from which the village takes its name, although short, was a convincing fjord, the mountains on either side rising so steeply into the low cloud that you could imagine that they were of great height. The weather hadn't quite decided what it was going to do yet so it was doing nothing. No wind, no rain, no sky, just low flat cloud.

I shared the ferry with a Swiss backpacker who was leaning over the edge looking into the black waters of the Kilbrannan Sound for submarines. He was also very perplexed that the ferry would arrive at nowhere in particular. 'There must be something there,' he complained. 'Look,' he said holding out his map, 'the town is called Claonaig.' Unfortunately Claonaig is no more than a concrete slipway, a couple of port-a-loos and a bus shelter but I thought I'd let him find out for himself.

There was at least a bus to go with the bus shelter and he hopped on without even checking where it was going. A bus, unlike a ferry, I suppose, always goes somewhere. Behind the bus shelter there was a big colourful sign advertising the 'Seafood Cabin' which said to me: affordable seafood. When it comes to good seafood money is rarely a problem but on this occasion, an appetite was. I would have to acquire one cycling the one mile out of the way to get to it.

One mile of easy cycling to Skipness and still no appetite, a big long wander round the not inconsiderable ruins of Skipness Castle and still no appetite, a walk down to the beach and the ancient St Brendan's church and there was a decision – I was going anyway.

The Seafood Cabin is just that. There were indoor eating facilities available but the view from my picnic table was truly sensational. The mountains of Arran were now clear, as the weather seemed to be deciding on a fine day. The view down the Kilbrannan Sound probably stretches all the way to Ireland on a haze-free day. The view would be the reasoning behind building such a large castle on this spot. An invading force would be able to get very close to the Scottish mainland by using Arran as cover. Skipness Castle would have been built as a deterrent as well as lookout.

There were a few who did use Arran as some sort of bridgehead. The Vikings assembled in Lamlash, Robert the Bruce returned to Scotland via Arran by first landing at Lochranza and Edward I was prone to attacking Brodick Castle.

Before the defeat of King Haakon at Largs in 1263 – some say it was a draw – most of the western seaboard of Scotland was disputed with the Vikings, therefore it was in the spirit of both nations that I ordered Scottish salmon gravadlax and washed it down with two glasses of Sauvignon Blanc (because I couldn't leave out the French).

The lingering taste of pickled salmon and the enduring mellowness brought about by the Sauvignon were a comfort as I made my way over Kintyre. Kintyre looked almost flat when compared with Arran but it didn't feel flat.

Nevertheless it wasn't the climb over the peninsula that I was dreading, it was five, maybe six miles, on the A83. I had agonised over these miles and even thought about ruling out the whole route but it was only five miles out of potentially 150 miles. In the end there was nothing for it but to try it. I counted 20 cars, there was more level or downhill than up and there was plenty of space. I didn't feel threatened at any point but I was still relieved to be in Tarbert. Maybe someone somewhere will agree that this route is a compelling one and put in a cycle lane.

I could smell Tarbert long before I could see it. The woods that lined the A83 and kept West Loch Tarbert mostly out of sight also trapped the smoke from Tarbert's smokehouses. The smell of smoking fish was a wonderful welcome to town and an appetite was suddenly activated. This was a time when I wished I had my tent and stove and could rustle up a couple of smoked haddock for dinner.

Loch Fyne, on which Tarbert sits, is renowned for its smoked fish, largely because it sticks with the traditional method of actually using smoke rather than the commercial preference of using a yellow dye to achieve a similar but inferior effect. I am told that it is common in Loch Fyne smokehouses to mix the beech chippings with the chippings from old whisky barrels to imbue the fish with a flavour that dyes will never be able to recreate.

Needless to say, Tarbert is a fishing port and has been for over 1,000 years. The Dutch are reported turning up as early as the ninth century to buy salted herring. Nature has created the perfect harbour at Tarbert. In fact it is so sheltered it is difficult to detect the way in. The harbour is ringed by a continuous façade of tall narrow buildings which adds an extra touch of cosiness.

From Tarbert I was catching my second ferry of the day, this time to connect me with another part of the mainland, namely the Cowal peninsula – or peninsulas really. The sea lochs, peninsulas and islands of the Firth of Clyde are the domain of the amphibian. It was common practice for ships to be taken out of the water at Tarbert and pushed for the mile across the peninsula to save sailing round the Mull of Kintyre. King Magnus did it because a treaty with the Scots said that he could claim all the land he could sail around, so his boat was pushed across under full sail with King Magnus at the tiller. Robert the Bruce did it in order to sneak up on his enemy Lame John of Lorn.

In a reversal of the logic of reducing the need to sail, the ferry over to Portavadie on Cowal saves about 100 miles of driving. The ferry left Tarbert under a darkening sky. Several times bow waves made it over the side to drench me but then I was too keen to stay out on the car deck and take in the view.

Once again the ferry connects somewhere with nowhere. On Cowal the landscape was of the type that Scotland has in surplus – rough heathery, coarse and always wet. Perfect for conifers and, bizarrely, an oil rig fabrication yard. There were never any rigs built here despite the government spending lots of money digging a huge hole for the dry dock and a village for the workers who'd have to come from elsewhere. The village out of the same packet as the inner-city estates built in the '60s has fared just as badly as the inner-city versions even though no one has ever lived here. Cycling past this slightly eerie ghost town was a drain on my good spirits. They should flatten it as soon as possible.

Thus far I'd cycled for one hour, spent one hour sitting on my arse on ferries and one hour lunching, which makes two hours sitting on my arse. In order to tip the balance in favour of cycling I had to take in the detour to Ardlamont Point rather than go straight on for Kames and Tighnabruaich, which were just over a mile away from Millhouse.

It didn't seem possible but the road to Ardlamont Point was narrower than the one I'd left. There were a couple of farmhouses but no sign of life. The fields looked untended and ungrazed. The trees and vegetation by the road was dense and oppressively close. In the almost sub-tropical atmosphere insects were thriving. Had I been a wide-mouthed frog I'd have been well fed on each downhill.

The Firth of Clyde's favourite amphibian was Neil Munro's Para Handy, Master Mariner and captain of the Clyde puffer the *Vital Spark*. When Munro wrote about Para Handy's exploits sailing between the ports and piers of the Firth of Clyde for the Glasgow *Evening News*, places that are now obscure backwaters were very much part of the familiar. Places such as Skipness and Ardlamont Point were as familiar to Glaswegians as the Spanish costas are today.

There being absolutely no need to come via Ardlamont Point was in itself a good reason for coming and so was the good view down between Arran and Bute to the mainland. The topography of land and water is so complex that it was some time before I was sure of what I was looking at.

From the high point the road dropped to be right by the Kyles of Bute, the narrow and sheltered stretch of water between Cowal and the Isle of Bute. Yachts were motoring north and south rather than under sail, for in contrast to the wild conditions earlier on Loch Fyne there wasn't a breath. The road into Kames was perfectly level, and rather worryingly, I was at my destination and I wasn't feeling even slightly hungry.

Kames and nearby Tighnabruaich are villages devoted to sailing. Hotels and houses alike hang buoys instead of baskets of flowers, flagpoles look suspiciously like masts, lifebelts are attached to walls and telescopes sit in windows even though you can only see a couple of hundred yards over to the blank green hillsides of Bute.

I was staying at the Kames Hotel, where the nautical theme is continued on the inside. At the Kames Hotel it is the bar that is the star. Decked out in dark wood, superfluous brass instruments and fixed furniture, it is a captain's cabin without the annoying rocking sensation. The captain is Tom Andrew, complete with eye patch, piratical dark hair and a five-o'clock shadow. The bar's atmosphere is so convincing that it was filled with nautical types and it has made landlubbers of the lot of them. Few were of the boat shoes and flannels variety, most were swarthy individuals with their jeans tucked into their wellies, darned woolly jumpers pickled in brine – well, maybe not brine. The spirit or at least the dress sense of Para Handy was alive and well in Kames and Tighnabruaich.

I left the next morning with a belly full of bacon and a head full of yarns to tour Cowal unencumbered by panniers. I had to stay two nights at the Kames Hotel. A tragedy, I know. The Cowal Highland Gathering was taking place in Dunoon so everything over that way was fully booked.

Roads have never found an easy way into Kames or Tighnabruaich and consequently there is no easy way out. Great globules of sweat poured off my forehead in impossibly close weather. A steep uphill followed every downhill and sunshine followed bursts of rain. Forestry and bracken covered the rough country and green fields and cows squeezed in where they could. Occasionally there was the glimpse of higher hills through the gloom but on the whole it was unremarkable countryside but very, very peaceful.

At the top of my final descent to Loch Fyne, which was long and straight, I waited for a tractor to labour up towards me. I bumped up onto the verge to let it pass. Aargh! The verge was an illusion. It was like falling through the bamboo into the tiger pit. I lay in the ditch looking up through the bracken and the brambles at the sky while water seeped through my clothes. To his credit, the farmer asked if I was OK before laughing hysterically. I saw the funny side until I had to go back up the hill to retrieve my map from the ditch.

I thoroughly enjoyed the hill the second time around as I hurtled past the expensive Kilfinnan Hotel, an eighteenth-century hostelry that has a formidable reputation for seafood, to another restaurant at Otter Ferry which specialises in oysters harvested from its own oyster beds in Loch

Fyne. If you'd rather have a picnic there is a great wee gravel beach by the pier at Otter Ferry.

The 15 miles from Otter Ferry to Strachur are among the easiest miles you'll find anywhere. The road is level and the prevailing south-westerly, which brings in the rain and persuades people to live elsewhere, pushed me north with such force that pedalling was optional.

As well as being exposed to the wind and rain there is little space for life on this side of Loch Fyne. Rocky outcrops and steep water-oozing hillsides mean that the road is confined to a narrow ledge just above the water. For most of the 15 miles I couldn't have been any more specific about my location than that I was on the east side of Loch Fyne.

A rare landmark was the ruin of Castle Lachlan. It became a ruin in the aftermath of the '45 rebellion. It was very easy for navy frigates to sail up to these coastal castles and blow them to smithereens and a similar fate befell most of the castles in this area.

I had lunch in the tearoom attached to the post office in Strachur, not because I was hungry but because it was raining heavily. When the rain stopped I had to make a decision. I could return to Kames via Glendaruel, which I reckoned would generate an appetite that could manage at least a main course and a starter. Or I could go south by Lock Eck and then return west by a very hilly route which would mean that the chocolate pudding in a light toffee sauce could be added comfortably to my evening meal. I plumped for the pudding route.

There was a little hump to get over before I could see Loch Eck and from then on it was flat for the whole length of the loch. Beinn Mhor on the far side of Loch Eck was, as always, made up of heather, rock and coarse grass but this time high enough and shapely enough to be photogenic. Loch Eck at its foot is long and slender.

In all it is a classic highland glen which I am sure Sir Harry Lauder appreciated when he bought the Glenbranter Estate at the northern end of the loch. As the most prominent Scot of his time, no ordinary glen would do. Sir Harry sold his estate in 1926, for he had bought it for his son who was killed in the Great War. The memorial he erected by the side of the road to his son and to his wife adds that air of melancholy and sadness that no highland glen should be without.

The road down the glen was busier than normal, due largely to the Cowal Highland Gathering which was being held in two days' time. Up to 150 pipe bands and 40,000 spectators have been known to attend. Towards the southern end of the loch the skirl of bagpipes playing a hundred different tunes could be heard. I sought peace in the Younger Botanic Gardens. I wouldn't normally add botanic gardens to my list but the awesome peace of the avenue of giant redwoods rivalled that of a great cathedral.

Dunoon was not the place to be on a bike so I fled west into Glen Lean. Glen Lean is another example of a fine but overlooked highland glen. The hill to the south had a fine corrie and as I climbed, the view to the north took in more shapely peaks.

For a road to run from east to west on Cowal is to go against the natural lie of the land. The climb to Loch Tarsan at the top of Glen Lean wasn't too bad but the descent to Loch Striven was still welcome. The next hill however, was a stoater.

The road that climbs away from Loch Striven has no art to it. The Swiss would have constructed lovely sweeping bends to keep the gradient reasonable. Basically this road had tarmac thrown at it to see if it would stick. I doubted whether I would stick to it.

It is one of the steepest highways in the whole of Britain. Car manufacturers used to hold hill climbs on it and the time it took their cars to climb the hill was used in advertisements. The building at the bottom was a coaching inn where the horses had to be changed before the coach could carry on up the hill. I didn't even bother to try to cycle up although walking up wasn't especially easy either.

At the foot of the downhill that followed I joined up with the road that comes south via Glendaruel so these hills are avoidable. The next hill was the one I would have avoided had I not being staying another night at Kames. The road was only opened in 1970, which was around the time that puffers and steamers were sent to the breakers' yards by sensible people who decided that roads were the future. This road is not sensible.

Since this hill is not part of the route I won't bore you with the details except to say that the top was a long time coming and I'd have to do it again the next morning. The view from the top is considered to be one of the best in the country. It belongs to the National Trust who want to make sure that it never becomes obscured. The view is over the Kyles of Bute and it is one of perfect balance between open hillsides, wooded shores, tiny islets and water. After this I had an appetite, all right.

The first night at the Kames Hotel was no one-off and I left the next morning with the folk song 'Always Argyll' ringing in my ears. I tried hard to remember the words to go with the tune that was going round and round in my head but couldn't recall more than two: 'always' and 'Argyll'. The night before I seemed to know the words as I belted it out along with the locals as if it were a national anthem. I wondered if this was the tip of a hidden desire for independence for Argyll. No, the Tighnabruaich folk were more concerned with saving their pier – one of the original steamer piers and possibly the last one standing. They have a song about the pier as well.

I was glad I'd had the view over the Kyles of Bute the evening before because it was obscured by mist, a phenomenon that not even the

National Trust can do anything about. It was only when I was within yards of the ferry at Colintraive that I could actually see it. There were two other passengers but three crew to guide the ferry the 200 yards over to Bute. By the time I had walked the length of the ferry I was one third of the way over.

Seasickness may have been unlikely but some rain-induced malady seemed certain. The rain was falling heavily and there was no obvious place to shelter. There was absolutely no wind to move it on and the sails of boats on the Kyles hung about their masts like wet washing. I thought it possible they could sink under the weight of water from above.

I sat in a tearoom overlooking Ettrick Bay watching the rain rolling down the huge glass windows, consoling myself with toasties and multi-coloured cheesecake for as long as I could get away with. In the end I had to go back out into it and find a hotel.

A seemingly endless line of hotels and guesthouses stretches along the front in Rothesay and I cycled much further than I would have liked to find exactly the right place to stay. I chose the Ardyne/St Ebba because it had a restaurant built in.

Exquisite Bute lamb helped to make the meal in the Ardyne the best one of the trip. Second to the meal was a sensational view through the restaurant's big picture window of an angry Firth and the moody mountains of Argyll. The calm atmosphere of the Ardyne was a pleasant antidote to the relatively raucous two nights at the Kames.

It was a good decision to wait until the next morning to explore Bute properly. The wind was blowing strongly from the south-west so there was no telling how long the sunny weather would last. I had barely picked the last bone from my breakfast kipper than I was off.

Despite the sun and the palm trees, the dog walkers on Rothesay's colourful esplanade were dressed in heavy jackets and woolly hats. Thirty or forty years ago, regardless of the weather and relatively early hour, several steamers would probably have been vying to tie up on one of the piers to the strains of German bands getting the Glasgow holidaymakers into the holiday mood.

Rothesay is a town built in Glasgow's image. Sandstone tenements make up much of the townscape and there is an Argyle Street and a Gallowgate, two of Glasgow's better-known thoroughfares. Glaswegians, it would appear, didn't like to feel too far from home until, that is, you could get a full Scottish Breakfast and read your *Daily Record* in the Spanish sun. Rothesay might have got the visitors in, in the past, but now the town has to look to the rest of the island for inspiration.

Most visitors to Rothesay in the past wouldn't have dreamed of venturing very far round the island for there is nothing on offer but peace, good views of Arran, wildlife and, as it happens, excellent cycling. The road oscillates between acceptable limits, never steep, never dull, mostly sheltered and always quiet. There were enough cows and enough green grass to suggest that cream teas should be available locally but there were no visitor facilities on this side.

Just about everyone I'd met on Bute insisted that I should visit Mount Stuart. They enthused about the incredible home of the Marquis of Bute but pulled a face when warning me not to be put off by the Visitor Reception Centre. 'The Grey Box' was how it was most often described.

My expectations had been lowered to such an extent that when I turned off the road and into the car park I was pleasantly surprised by the contemporary design of the visitor centre. It has an understated style and I can't think what would have been more appropriate. The outside is slick and businesslike and the inside feels like the foyer of a large corporation's tower block.

Beyond it was a sublime experience. Three hundred acres of ordered gardens isolate the gothic masterpiece from anything mundane. First impressions are of a stoic and sensible sandstone building but on the inside it is the pinnacle of taste, comfort and frivolity.

It was just as well that visiting Mount Stuart was the last act of my trip for nothing was likely to come close. Well, maybe a pee in the preposterously opulent gents' toilets on the pier in Rothesay could run it close.

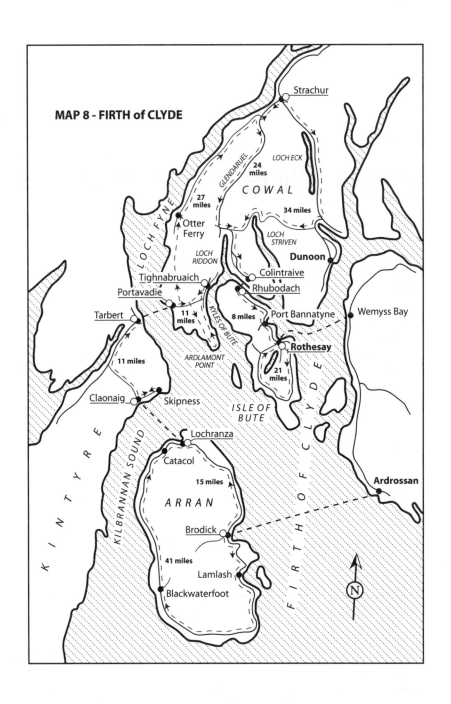

MAP 8 - FIRTH of CLYDE

Strachur

LOCH ECK

GLENDARUEL

24 miles

COWAL

27 miles

34 miles

Otter Ferry

LOCH RIDDON

LOCH STRIVEN

Dunoon

Tighnabruaich

Colintraive

Portavadie

Rhubodach

Tarbert

11 miles

KYLES OF BUTE

8 miles

Port Bannatyne

Wemyss Bay

11 miles

ARDLAMONT POINT

Rothesay

21 miles

ISLE OF BUTE

Claonaig

Skipness

KINTYRE

KILBRANNAN SOUND

Lochranza

Catacol

15 miles

ARRAN

Ardrossan

Brodick

41 miles

FIRTH OF CLYDE

Lamlash

Blackwaterfoot

N

FIRTH OF CLYDE: ESSENTIALS

Distance: 155 miles maximum.

Maps: OS *Landranger* series (1:50,000), sheets 52, 55, 56, 63, 69. OS *Road Map 2: Western Scotland*.

Banks/Cashpoints: Brodick, Tarbert, Rothesay.

Cycle Repair: Brodick Cycles, Roselynn, Brodick (01770 302 460); Bute Cycle Centre, 24 East Princes Street (01700 502 333).

General Stores: Not a problem on Arran. Kintyre – Skipness and Tarbert. Cowal – Kames, Tignabruiach and Strachur. Bute – Rothesay and Port Bannatyne.

Traffic: There is light to moderate traffic on Arran as far as Whiting Bay, beyond which the roads are very quiet. On Kintyre there is a six-mile stretch of the A83(T). The traffic is fast but not especially heavy, however the road is wide and mainly downhill or level. Much of the roads on Cowal are empty. The A815 is the busiest between Strachur and Dunoon. On Bute the roads are only busy around the towns.

GETTING THERE AND BACK

Train: Glasgow Central Station to Ardrossan Harbour for ferry to Brodick. There is a service to meet all but the earliest sailing to Brodick. Journey time is 55 minutes. Return journey, Wemyss Bay to Glasgow Central. There is a train for every sailing to Wemyss Bay. In each case the ferry terminal is adjacent to the railway station. There is no cycle space but bikes may be carried in the passenger's area; it is best to avoid peak periods.

Ferry: Island Hospscotch tickets 4 and 5 cover all ferries. There are six ferries daily from Ardrossan to Brodick. Journey time is 55 minutes. On the return journey there are about 20 ferries daily from Rothesay to Wemyss Bay. Journey time is 35 minutes.

ROUTE INFORMATION

ARRAN: BRODICK TO LOCHRANZA. CLOCKWISE (41 MILES); ANTI-CLOCKWISE (15 MILES)

From the slipway either follow the A841 left for Lamlash and Whiting Bay or right for the short route to Lochranza via Sannox.

Terrain: Arran is hilly. There are many ups and downs between Brodick and Blackwaterfoot but from then on it is essentially level. The short route starts off level enough but there is a big climb followed by a very fast descent to Lochranza.

ACCOMMODATION (01770–)
Brodick
Hotels and B&Bs: Glenartney Hotel (–302452); Roseburn Lodge (–302383); Douglas Hotel (–302155); Tigh-na-Mar (–302538).
Camping: Glen Rosa Campsite (–302380).
Whiting Bay
Hotels and B&Bs: Royal Hotel (–700286); Swan's Guest House, Rowallan (–700729); Invermay (–700431).
Hostels: Whiting Bay SYHA (–700339).
Kildonan
Camping: Sea Shore (–820320).
Kilmory
Hotels and B&Bs: Lag Inn (–870255).
Blackwaterfoot
Hotels and B&Bs: Morvern House (–860254); Glen House (–302092); Kinloch Hotel (–860444).
Hostels: Lighthouse Bunkhouse, Pirnmill (–600249).
Catacol
Hotels and B&Bs: Catacol Bay Hotel (–830231).
Lochranza
Hotels and B&Bs: Castlekirk (–830202); Apple Lodge (–830229); Fairhaven (–830237); Croftbank; (–830201); Belvaren (–830647).
Hostels: Lochranza SYHA (–830631).
Camping: Lochranza CP (–830273).

WATCH OUT FOR!

Brodick Castle (NTS), Brodick. A home of the Duke of Hamilton, known for its furniture, gardens and tearoom.

Arran Heritage Museum, Brodick.

The Arran Brewery, Cladach, Brodick (01770 302353). Tours and tasting, daily.

Torrylinn Creamery. Home of Arran cheese. It's best to go in the morning.

Torrylinn Cairn, Kilmory. Neolithic chambered cairn.

King's Cave. The cave where Robert the Bruce was inspired by the spider, allegedly; two miles north of Blackwaterfoot.

Machrie Moor Stone Circles. Bronze Age stone circles, three miles north of Blackwaterfoot.

Lochranza Castle (HS). Fourteenth-century ruin, connections with Robert the Bruce.

Isle of Arran Distillery, Lochranza (01770 830264). Visitor centre, tours and tasting.

KINTYRE: LOCHRANZA TO CLAONAIG TO TARBERT (11 MILES); CLAONAIG TO SKIPNESS (1 MILE)

Ferry: There are typically nine ferries daily from Lochranza to Claonaig. Journey time is 30 minutes.

From the slipway turn left for Tarbert and follow the B8001 (A83) round to the right (turn right for short detour to Skipness). Follow B8001 over the peninsula to T-junction with A83 turn left for Tarbert (six miles) and follow to Tarbert. In Tarbert turn right onto Harbour Street, A8015 and follow round harbour to slipway.

Terrain: Level out to Skipness. The climb over the peninsula is of moderate length and tough in one or two places. The A83 is level or downhill mostly but there is a climb into Tarbert.

ACCOMMODATION
Tarbert (01880–)
Hotel and B&Bs: Columba Hotel, East River Road (–820808); Tarbert Hotel, Harbour Street (–820264); Victoria Hotel, Barmore Road (–820236); Kintarbert Lodge, Kilbery Road (–820237); Glenorchy, Pier Road (–820263); Springside, Pier Road (–820413).

WATCH OUT FOR!
Skipness Castle (HS). Substantial ruins of thirteenth-century castle and chapel, one mile north of Claonaig.

Seafood Cabin. Fresh seafood served in the shadow of Skipness Castle.

COWAL: TARBERT TO PORTAVADIE TO TIGHNABRUAICH VIA ARDLAMONT (11 MILES)

Ferry: There are typically 12 ferries daily from Tarbert to Portavadie. Journey time is 25 minutes.

Follow road uphill away from slipway, go to the left at T-junction. Follow road steeply uphill and then steeply downhill to peculiar junction at Millhouse. Turn right for Ardlamont and follow road round the peninsula. On entering Kames go straight on past tenement building when road veers to the left. Go uphill past the Kames Hotel. At T-junction turn right and then at next T-junction opposite post office turn right.

Terrain: Long climb away from Portavadie. Fast descent to Millhouse. It is mainly up but never too steeply on the east side of Ardlamont; on the west side it is more or less level.

ACCOMMODATION
Tighnabruaich and Kames (01700–)
Hotels and B&Bs: Kames Hotel, Kames (–811489); Piermount, Kames (–811218); The Royal Hotel (–811239); Tighnabruaich Hotel (–811615); Ardeneden (–811354).

WATCH OUT FOR!
Tighnabruaich Pier. One of the original piers built for the Clyde steamers.

TIGHNABRUAICH TO STRACHUR (27 MILES)
Leave Tighnabruaich to the south and follow B8000 for Millhouse and Strachur. Follow the B8000 round to the right at Millhouse. Follow the B8000 through Kilfinan and Otter Ferry for about 25 miles. At T-junction with A886 turn left and proceed into Strachur.

Terrain: There are a few stiff climbs between Millhouse and Otter Ferry. From then on the road is generally level with just the occasional uphill.

ACCOMMODATION
Strachur (01369–)
Hotels and B&Bs: Barnacarry, Strathlachlan (–860212); The Creaggans Inn (–860279).

Strachur to Colintraive: via Loch Eck (34 miles); via Glendaruel (24 miles)

Turn right at junction of A886 and A815 for Dunoon. Follow A815 beyond Loch Eck. Turn right at head of the Holy Loch just short of Sandbank for the B836 for Colintraive, Glendaruel and Tighnabruaich. Follow road up Glen Lean and over to Loch Striven and then continue to T-junction with A886. Turn left for Colintraive. After about two miles turn right for loop of B886 that has been by-passed by A886. This avoids a climb. After three miles turn right to rejoin the A886 and follow to Colintraive.

To go via Glendaruel follow the A886 south from Strachur all the way to Colintraive.

Terrain: There is a small climb away from Strachur but from then on it is an easy cycle for the length of Lock Eck. Once on the B836 life becomes difficult. There is long climb up Glen Lean to the reservoir followed by a fast descent to Loch Striven. The climb away from Loch Striven is very steep. The A886 and B886 to Colintraive involve short moderate ascents.

Via Glendaruel – when the road swings away from Loch Fyne the road climbs fairly steeply, about 800 ft in just over 2 miles. Fast descent after which road undulates to the head of Loch Riddon.

ACCOMMODATION

Hotels and B&Bs: Whistlefield Inn, Lock Eck (01369 860 440); Coylet Inn, Lock Eck (01369 840426); The Anchorage Hotel, Shore Road, Sandbank (01369 705108); Colintraive Hotel (01700 841 207).
Hostels: Whistlefield Inn Bunkhouse (as above).
Camping: Glendaruel CP (01369 820 267); Lock Eck CP (01369 840 472).

WATCH OUT FOR!

Millhouse Gunpowder Mill Memorial. Roadside memorial between Kames and Millhouse to the many who died working at the mill.

Castle Lachlan. Ruin of ancient home of the Maclachlans destroyed in the aftermath of the 1745 rebellion view from B8000.

Strachur Smiddy. Restored eighteenth-century smiddy, now a museum and craft shop; open 1 p.m.–4 p.m.

Lauder Monument. Memorial to the son and wife of Sir Harry Lauder, accessed by steps from the A815 just south of Glenbranter.

Benmore Botanic Garden, Lock Eck (01369 706 261). A satellite of the Royal Botanical Garden in Edinburgh.

BUTE: COLINTRAIVE TO RHUBODACH TO ROTHESAY (8 MILES)

Ferry: There is a regular service between 5 a.m. and 8 p.m. Journey time is five minutes.

From slipway follow A886 into Port Bannatyne and then to Rothesay.

Terrain: Completely level road.

ACCOMMODATION
Rothesay (01700–)
Hotels and B&Bs: Ardyne/St Ebba, 37–38 Mount Stuart Road (–502052); Craigmore Hotel, Chricton Road (–503533); Glendale Guest House, 20 Battery Place (–502390); Waverly, 37 Argyle Street (–502390); The Moorings, 7 Mount Stuart Road (–502277).
Camping: Roseland CP, Canada Hill (reached by a big climb) (–504529).

ISLAND LOOP (21 MILES)
From Winter Garden head north from Rothesay through Port Bannatyne to junction at Kames Bay. Turn left onto the A884. When the road forks for Ettrick Bay take left. At each junction keep right and follow the coast. At turning for Kilchattan at Kingarth either follow the road to the left or extend journey with small loop in the direction of Bruachag. Follow the A884 north to Rothesay.

Terrain: There is nothing more than short moderate climbs on the way round.

WATCH OUT FOR!
Rothesay Castle, Rothesay (HS). A moated thirteenth-century castle at the centre of Rothesay.

Victorian Toilets, Rothesay. Have a pee on the pier in marbled opulence.

Bute Museum, Rothesay. Wildlife, Clyde steamers, geology and archaeology.

Isle of Bute Discovery Centre. The building that is most evocative of Rothesay's heyday, the centre puts Bute and Rothesay into context for the visitor.

St Blane's Chapel. Detour for two miles from A844 at southern end of island to the thirteenth-century chapel/monastery in a serene spot.

Mount Stuart (01700 503 877). One of Scotland's must-see attractions, a spectacular Victorian Gothic house.

Ascog Hall Fernery. Sunken Victorian fern house, two miles south of Rothesay.

9

MEAN ABERDEENSHIRE

The north-east of Scotland is not one of Scotland's regular calendar girls. If, however, one of the usual girls let them down, say Glen Coe didn't dry out in time and a replacement for August was needed, then the north-east would be the place to call on. The scene that lay before us was summer, in the popular sense of the word. Golden fields of wheat and barley aren't the product of a good spell of weather, they are only to be found where the sun reliably shines and the air is warm and drying.

The sky for its part was deep blue, save for the odd patch of brilliantly white cloud. There was a heat haze shimmering off the road and little swirls of dust were swept up by a breeze so gentle that it wasn't clear where it was coming from. I suppose people don't come to Scotland to do flat and at first it did seem a little strange and unsettling but once we realised there wasn't going to be a sting in the tail or a downside that would suddenly present itself, we relaxed into it.

My companion, Hugh, and I had started our journey at Dyce Station on the fringe of the City of Aberdeen. Normally when I arrive at a place the direction in which I want to go is obvious. I just look to the landmarks, the hills, a castle or the coast, orientate my inner compass and set off. In Dyce I was flummoxed. I couldn't see anything higher than a house and nothing more distinctive than a bus shelter; well actually, it was a train shelter but who knows what that is.

One of those little blue signs with a bike on pointed past a chip shop, so we dutifully followed. It was about a half mile later that it occurred to me that we were in fact on our way to Aberdeen. We should have left from the other end of the station car park and cycled out past the playing fields and an industrial estate. How awfully mundane!

When we eventually located the Formartine and Buchan Way, our escape was simple enough. A perfectly level strip of grey ash led us out of town into a parched landscape of golden fields and haystacks. However, it was only when we were out of earshot of the helicopters that fly continuously out of Dyce Airport ferrying men out to North Sea oil rigs that we felt we'd really escaped.

Now the map was superfluous, there was no doubt as to the way ahead and we were hooting our way along the track-bed of the former Formartine and Buchan Railway like the midday express, not pausing for any of the grass-grown platforms that still line the way. I think we may even have resorted to making engine noises.

After about ten miles the choo-chooing wore off and the railway path was spending more time in cuttings than out in the open. At the first opportunity we fled for the back roads. Railway paths have their place and we could have followed this one all the way to Peterhead or Fraserburgh, but you do start to feel a bit disconnected.

Out on the roads, Hugh was overcome by a wave of euphoria. Even the high quality of the road surface was giving him cause for delight and so he felt justified in repeating his mantra – 'the best things in life are free' – over and over. I know Hugh well and I know that what he really means is that the free things in life are best and the very cheap things are next best. Hugh is the King of Mean. He was probably born with his fists tightly clenched. He had only agreed to come along on condition that I agreed to meet his tight spending targets – £30 to be exact, and that was between us.

Hugh had in mind an experiment. He hoped that we could somehow prove that, were we to adopt the lifestyle of cycling gypsies wandering forever carrying all we needed with us, it would be infinitely sustainable. In the circumstances it would have been easy to sign up for life. The easy terrain and the promise of warm dry weather for days to come were very seductive.

We were barely aware of our loads but a tent and a warm sleeping bag seemed overkill. We could see ourselves sleeping in the shelter of a wood and cooking on an open fire, recapturing something of the spirit of the pioneers of cycle-touring who lacked gear and money but had plenty of enthusiasm for the outdoors and sought adventure in their own backyard. We were weaving quite a Utopia for ourselves as we pedalled along, completely unimpeded, even by better judgment.

Ellon was on us quicker than we'd imagined; golly, Aberdeenshire wasn't going to be big enough for more than a couple of days of cycling. At this rate of progress we'd have to find somewhere else or go home early.

The long descent into Ellon was also a surprise, for it suggested that we'd been climbing. The novelty of going downhill was welcome as was the novelty of the River Ythan flowing through Ellon. It highlighted that the landscape we'd just cycled through really was dry, drier even than Hugh's mouth when he handed over the £40 for his train ticket to Dyce. The trim granite town held us up long enough for us to buy our evening meal from a supermarket – and believe me it wasn't long.

Boswell and Johnson breakfasted in Ellon on their way from Aberdeen to Slains Castle to stay with the Earl of Errol, which was basically what we had in mind. Johnson complained that the road was stony. A minor inconvenience when you consider what lay ahead of him in the West Highlands. We had no such complaints but we did have difficulty locating the bridge over the Ythan further downstream from Ellon.

The bridge was clearly marked on the map but a sign indicated that the road was a dead end. We cycled down it anyway, past an old church and manse amongst big leafy trees at Logie Buchan. The road was getting progressively greener with grass growing up through the tarmac. Even though the map shows the road continuing over the Ythan, the bridge was in fact a footbridge and much too narrow for vehicles.

Below the bridge, which doubles as a war memorial, flowed the beautifully tranquil Ythan. Tall reeds encroached well into the river which ducks were darting in and out of. Further downstream we could see a huge flock of birds resting on a larger body of still water.

Some would say that standing on a bridge looking down at the river for so long was foolhardy because there could be a kelpie waiting to pounce from its watery hideout. Kelpies are waterhorses that are to be found mainly in rivers in the north-east. Sometimes they appear as a horse, other times as a dark-haired man, but before you wait around hoping to meet the dark-haired man version bear in mind that they have been known to dismember and eat up passing travellers.

Hugh knew that a kelpie wasn't going to eat him. He knew that if there was a kelpie about it was more likely to opt for someone slower and meatier like, shall we say, me. Little did Hugh know that the road ahead could be smeared with witches' butter and he'd be the first to encounter it, and wheels coated in witches' butter could result in a calamity.

As far as I know witches didn't smear their butter on roads but on door handles – especially those belonging to fishermen – and for them to get it on their hands was very bad luck. Apparently fishermen who had to return to the house after setting off for their boat would climb in the window rather than open the door. Rabbits, hares, trout, salmon, the minister and people dressed in black could all result in bad luck for the fisherman.

We'd seen enough rabbits, and for that matter, people dressed in black including one stern-looking minister and yet we didn't feel unlucky – quite the opposite, in fact. Perhaps these things only affected fishermen. When we arrived at the tiny fishing village of Collieston at least one source of bad luck was obvious. The way out of the harbour into the open North Sea looked extremely treacherous as waves broke on particularly jaggy rocks and kept them hidden for several moments at a time. Calamities must have been commonplace. In much earlier times, if you were unlucky enough to fall overboard there was no question of you being rescued for the 'sea maun had his nummer', which meant that you had to let a certain number drown in order to satisfy some sea spirit.

The village is squeezed into the cove that surrounds the harbour and all the houses look inward. We wandered between the houses pushing our bikes on the narrow foot-worn paths. Most of the villagers seemed to be elderly, which is surprising when you consider that you can't get a car anywhere near most of their homes. A fair number were sitting out in their gardens, looking out to sea.

They happily exchanged greetings but despite Hugh's best efforts no one was keen to chat – they just kept their eyes fixed on the sea. They might have been watching for the annual migration of the bodies of those drowned to heaven or hell. The sea did seem to have its own darkness and an agitation that wasn't in keeping with the day's general tenor. It seems entirely appropriate that the jagged rocks that lie just offshore should be called the Skares of Cruden.

We travelled to Cruden Bay on a narrow lane that followed the coast from Collieston. Fringed in green and far from straight it was a pleasant contrast to the roads of the interior. The lane also climbed sufficiently to give a good view of Cruden Bay, a scimitar of sand at the tip of which was the village of Cruden Bay and a little way beyond the village the imposing ruins of Slains Castle, or should I say Castle Dracula.

Was it the dead bodies rising from the sea and the common perception that there were a large number of witches living in the area that attracted Bram Stoker to Cruden Bay for several summers? Certainly there are those who suggest that Cruden Bay and its environs brought out the horror writer in him, which is not hard to understand when you consider how warped the collective imagination was in these parts.

The argument goes like this: Bram Stoker had his holidays in Cruden Bay, he was invited to Slains Castle, he wrote the book *Dracula* and therefore Slains Castle is Castle Dracula. It must be! Not as far as Whitby, the setting for Stoker's book, is concerned and a few other folk who claim to be Dracula experts. The fact that Dracula didn't ever exist seems to have been overlooked in the battle for tourists. As Hugh pointed out, there did seem to be a shortage of young maidens in Cruden Bay for the Count to feed on.

We waited until morning before checking out Slains Castle, as you can't be too careful about these things. You can freely wander its roofless rooms and corridors. Unfortunately there were no shivers, no spine tingles, nothing. If you want your nerves to jangle look down into the deep sea chasms that cut into the cliff in front of and behind the castle. Johnson, who along with Boswell, stayed the night at Slains, described the walls of the castle as 'a continuation of the perpendicular rock'. It's not garlic or a stake that will keep you safe but the good sense not to wander too close to the edges.

Boswell and Johnson were next shown to the Buller of Buchan by their hosts. Slains Castle was a bit of a disappointment so I had to persuade Hugh that the one-mile detour was worth it. The Buller is a 200 ft deep sea chasm into which the sea enters through a small archway; it was probably once a large cave but the roof has at some point collapsed. On a wild day the sea seems to boil as it is forced through the archway.

It's a precarious wander round the narrow edge of the chasm and I felt very uncertain indeed in my slippery cycle shoes – there is no guard rail. Boswell and Johnson walked all the way round and were taken inside by boat, and Johnson seems to have been genuinely in awe at what he saw. Forget Dracula, the coastal scenery of long slender ridges of rock and sea chasms are indisputably spectacular and terrifying. Please take extreme care!

Once we were on our way Hugh conducted an audit of monies spent so far. We had spent £4 on food and £6 on the campsite at Cruden Bay. The owner had tried to charge us £9 but Hugh beat her down and he was glad he did when he found out that you had to pay an extra 20p for the shower. Needless to say we didn't shower that night, especially since I didn't fancy sharing one with Hugh.

The fields were busy with combine harvesters, tractors and crop sprayers. Instead of a landscape of swaying wheat it was a landscape of cylindrical bails of hay. In every direction the scene was the same. If you stared at it long enough the bails of hay in the distance became slots so that the scene resembled endless sheets of old computer card or the music for a fairground melodeon.

I was guessing that cows aren't crazy about hay as winter fodder – it must be akin to eating a Pot Noodle without first adding the boiling water. Maybe if they didn't store it in black plastic it would be a bit more appetising. Perhaps someone could come up with a snazzy design and a slogan. Instead of the calves saying, 'Oh no not hay again!' They'll say, 'Oh goody, Bison Bites. Yum, yum!'

I wasn't bored with the cycling but I may have been a touch delirious, and thanks to Hugh, my calorie intake was lowered in the drive to make me a more efficient cyclist and at the same time save money. Any kind of change was welcome. A bridge to cross was notable, a patch of rough heathery moor among the fields exceptional and trees were very rare. Several times we went a different way from the one we had intended, which was down to a reluctance to continually stop and check the map to make sense of the maze of roads. Although whether we went via Toddlehills or Nether Kinmundy didn't much matter.

In between repeating his mantra that the best things in life were free, for the conditions were no different from the day before, Hugh would throw in a line or a verse from a Bothy Ballad, such as the 'Battle of Harlaw'. The bothies were attached to the farms and were where the unmarried labourers, known as 'bothy loons' lived while they worked on the farm. The ballads were the epic songs that were composed and recited for entertainment. Out of the bothies emerged a culture and a sense of identity as strong as that of the Gaeldom.

It grew so hot that little bubbles were forming on the tarmac. The sound of our tyres bursting them was actually quite pleasing. I even started to look for them ahead of me so that I could steer my bike over them. The only challenge we faced was the one to stay cool, hydrated and motivated. Any kink there was in the terrain was working its way out as we made our way back towards the coast and the cycling just got easier.

There was a definite change once we were on the coast. Any notions we had of snoozing on the beach at St Combs while we let the heat of the day pass were quickly abandoned. The wind coming off the North Sea was cold enough to cause us to chitter.

Fraserburgh ahead of us looked like a huge grey fortress, the enemy being the weather from the cold north-east. From a distance and close up it looked grim and grey. Close up it is not the look of the town that underwhelms you but the smell of fish that overwhelms you. There seemed to be miles of fish-processing firms lining the approaches to the harbour area and the gentle hum of refrigeration units was a constant presence.

The all-pervasive smell of fish was to our benefit because two days of sweaty cycling and the lack of a shower meant that even we were becoming aware of the odour. I'm sure that when we passed through, without stopping, the oppressively neat villages of Longside and St Combs, a collective sigh of relief was breathed.

The fishing boats in Fraserburgh harbour are on a scale I have never seen before. They look like the kind of boat that Robert Maxwell fell off. A fisherman on the quayside informed us that they cost £14 million each but they were able to catch so much fish the bank loan could be paid off in two and a half years.

Thousands of tonnes of herring, mackerel and haddock can be chilled and stored on board throughout a voyage lasting many months, so gone are the days of buying freshly caught fish on the quayside. 'Aye it's state o' the art,' said the fisherman on the quay, 'the fish have got no chance!' Fraserburgh or the 'The Broch' as the locals like to call it would not be on many people's list of places to see but if you want to understand why modern fishing is so controversial it's a must.

The smell of fish followed us for some way out of Fraserburgh. Beyond Rosehearty our free and easy sojourn suddenly became hard graft. The road turned uphill but my leg muscles were too relaxed and floppy to cope. Psychologically I just wasn't prepared for the change in the nature of the trip. I'd known the change was coming but it didn't stop me wanting to avoid it and resenting it. Hugh, however, was delighted with the challenge.

Hills rolled up to the road from the south which meant that we lost the sun prematurely. The road fluctuated between sea level and near enough the top of these hills. Every time there was a river to be crossed the road swooped down into the valley to almost sea level to cross it. Not content with the steep climbs to be had on the road that was taking us west I insisted on visiting the village of Pennan.

The incline of the road down to Pennan is insane and Hugh found it especially frustrating to be hanging onto the brakes rather than being able to let the hill carry him down. To let go would mean that you'd become the new mural on the gable end of the village hotel or the first sub-sea cyclist.

The village is a must-see. Firstly, because of its incredible location at the foot of the cliff with the houses built only feet from the sea and backing into the cliff face. Before the tiny harbour was built the boats would have been launched from the shore and it would have been the women's job to carry the men out to their boats on their backs. It was imperative that if the men were to spend hours at sea that they remain dry. The women would also have carried the catch in baskets up the hill and inland to barter with farmers for eggs and butter. Clearly these would have been women not to be trifled with.

The second reason for visiting Pennan is that it was the location for the film *Local Hero*. The village phone box featured prominently in the film so we each decided to phone home. We were quite happy with this and taking cheesy tourist photographs until one of the locals informed us: 'You know that they used a prop for the film, don't you!'

Pennan was not the only village positioned at the bottom of the cliff. There are two others, Gardenstown and Crovie. The road down to each of them is just as preposterous as the one down to Pennan but it is only Gardenstown that is a viable village.

It's a long way down to Gardenstown and with every bend there came a fresh view of the roofs of the next tier of houses. Again there was no question of free wheeling and the smell of the melting rubber was wafting up from below. Hugh couldn't contain his annoyance: 'This is not a road, it's a cliff!' Indeed the Coastguard Reserves had commandeered a stretch of road to practice cliff rescue.

As a village it is very appealing. The narrow sunless streets, the hugger-mugger houses and the quaint harbourside backed by the pink sandstone cliffs made this easily the most photogenic place we'd visited. By chance Hugh ran into a man with a van full of fish from whom he purchased some smoked haddock and he also bought a freshly baked loaf from the village bakery. This kind of shopping appealed to Hugh and he was pleased with his purchases.

There was no question of me going back up the hill or cycling on to Banff until I had had a long rest, overnight even. Hugh was not going to pay for a B&B when he had a perfectly good tent with him so we found a spot down by the shore where we could bed down for the night. Facing north, we were unable to see the sun set but the change in colour of the light reflected off the sea was just as spectacular. In darkness we enjoyed a meal of smoked haddock and onion, soaking up the juice from the haddock with the bread. Once inside my sleeping bag I was as warm as I wanted to be and tiredness meant that there were no lingering anxieties about sleeping outside. Hugh was in his element, for this was the kind of experience that money couldn't buy, and I had to agree.

Hugh decided that the money saved by sleeping rough the night before could be spent on cakes. We chose a local variety called 'Rankins' which are gingerbread wrapped in puff pastry. We had two for breakfast and kept two for lunch.

Apart from the hill out of Gardenstown there was only one more hill to overcome on the way to Macduff and Banff. We were back in our stride and very pleased with the way our night under the stars had gone; in doing so we were truly touching base with the early cycle tourists, although with modern sleeping bags and self-inflating mats we were probably a damn sight more comfortable than they ever were.

Macduff was a fishing port on a more familiar scale and its fishing boats were recognisable as fishing boats. Banff is its non-identical twin on the other bank of the River Deveron. Banff is an attractive town with many fine merchants' buildings and lots of Georgian touches. I was glad that we hadn't reached it the night before, as staying in Banff would have been just another night in a campsite. But a night in a campsite would have cured the odour problem, as another night had passed without the opportunity to wash.

Banff was to provide us with a great spot for a picnic. I did the tour of Duff House, a satellite of the National Gallery in Edinburgh, while Hugh snoozed under a tree in the grounds. It was one of the guides in the Duff House who suggested that we cycle out to the Bridge of Alvah following a rough road through the estate.

Sitting with my back against the warm stone parapet I ate my Rankin and supped my tea. It was a beautiful spot, low in a wooded gorge through which the River Deveron moved only sluggishly. The day was warm but there was much less light as a thin layer of cloud hid the sun. It was clear the weather was about to change but nevertheless I was in no hurry to get up and get on my way.

I might have hurried had I known what a delight the Deveron Valley would be. The countryside had a bit more texture to it and the farming was mixed rather than exclusively arable. We knew that we had to be cycling uphill because we were following the river upstream but there were enough twists and turns and ups and downs to hide the road's true intention. Above all, the road was completely empty of traffic for the 14 miles to Turriff where we had to leave the Deveron in search of the Don.

In Turriff we caused a commotion. I just happened to get the map out when a woman approached me and asked me where I wanted to go.

'Alford,' I replied.

'Oh you want to go to Alford. I'll have to ask someone else.'

So she did but she had to ask someone else. They then both shouted to a man crossing the road who then went and fetched a friend. In the end there were at least eight people standing round us discussing the way to Alford. Their considered opinion was that we first had to go to Aberdeen. We thanked them for their advice and followed the road that went to Alford without first going to Aberdeen.

The throb of grain driers was always with us as we made our way into the hills that we knew were lurking over the horizon to the west when we were enjoying the easy cycling of the coastal plain. Progress seemed painfully slow as we made our way through the tiny hamlets of Fisherford and Culsalmond and the villages of Insch and Auchleven.

The long climb over the shoulder to the west of Bennachie's distinctive Mither Tap was indeed slow and Hugh had a long wait for me at the top. Crucially, we arrived at the campsite in Alford too late to get a key for the shower block.

I for one couldn't stand it any longer. There were no other campers so I stripped off and tried to shower as best I could under the cold standpipe. The sight of my big white body looming in the gloom was too much for Hugh and he laughed long and hard. It was worth it, though.

We woke the next morning to the sound of heavy rain battering on our tents. We set off without breakfast and without paying – there was still no one to pay. Anyway we hadn't even managed to get showered. Hugh was very keen to depart before he was asked to pay for facilities he hadn't used.

The rain was heavy but trees provided partial shelter. We left Alford and followed the sign for 'My Lord's Throat'. I was curious to find what it was but we never ever got there. In amongst dense birch woods and the towering oaks and beeches just showing the slightest hint of autumn was a good place to be on such a wet day. The trees, along with the venerable River Don, gave this landscape a stately feel.

In Monymusk, a village that was designed to be pleasing with its little village green and little cottages all with leaded windows, we had a cooked breakfast of sausage and beans. Breakfast was cooked on the stove, of course, in the shelter of a doorway. Everyone who passed by stopped to pass the time of day with us; we'd half expected frowns, but no one did.

Everything about this trip had delighted Hugh, including the fact that Castle Fraser was closed when we called in, saving him at least £4. I was mad that I'd climbed the steep drive to find it shut. He even stopped at a road gang to congratulate them on the condition of the Aberdeenshire roads. However, the witches' butter finally got him. Only a few miles from Dyce his bike inexplicably slid from under him and he crashed into the road and me, sending me into a hedgerow. I was OK but Hugh had a few sore bits to rub. You just can't be too careful, especially when there are witches about. Incidentally, our total spend came to £34.

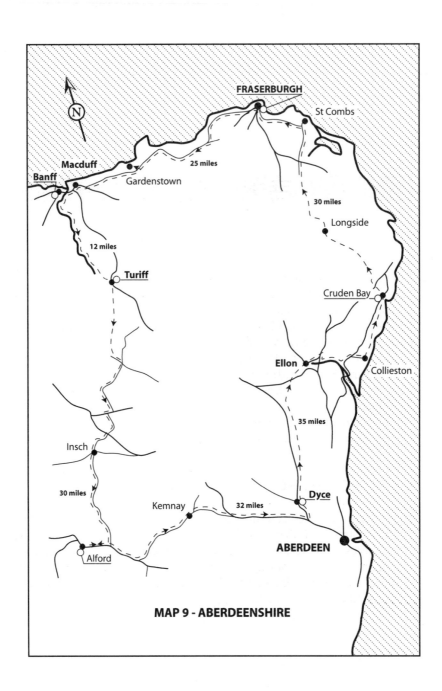

N

FRASERBURGH

St Combs

Macduff

Banff

Gardenstown

25 miles

30 miles

Longside

12 miles

Turiff

Cruden Bay

Ellon

Collieston

35 miles

Insch

30 miles

Kemnay

32 miles

Dyce

Alford

ABERDEEN

MAP 9 - ABERDEENSHIRE

Distance: 164 miles approx.

Maps: OS *Landranger* series (1:50,000), sheets 29, 30, 37, 38. OS *Road Map 3: Northern Scotland*.

Banks/Cashpoints: Dyce, Ellon, Fraserburgh, Banff, Turriff, Alford, Kemnay.

Cycle Repair: Cycling World, 57 Cross Street, Fraserburgh (01346 513355); Wheels, 6 Main St, Turriff (01888 562122); Budget Bicycles, Craigearn, Kemnay (01467 643957).

General Stores: Most villages have a shop. Notably there is no shop in Pennan.

Traffic: The roads around Fraserburgh, Dyce and Banff are busy. Otherwise there is very little traffic to speak of.

GETTING THERE

Train: There are regular trains between Edinburgh Waverley, Glasgow Queen Street and Aberdeen. Some services continue to Dyce, otherwise it is necessary to change at Aberdeen. Aberdeen Airport is immediately adjacent to Dyce Railway Station. There is typically space for two bicycles on each train; advance booking is essential. Journey time is 2 hours 40 minutes to 3 hours.

ROUTE INFORMATION

DYCE TO CRUDEN BAY (35 MILES)

From platform turn left through car park. Follow cycle path signed at the corner of the car park for Peterhead, Fraserburgh, Ellon and NCN 1. Ash path runs parallel to railway line by football pitches and industrial units. Follow the Formartine and Buchan Way for about 12 miles.

Leave the 'way' when it dips steeply to cross road. Turn left onto road and then follow round to the right past Mains of Orchardton Farm. Just beyond farm there is a T-junction with the B9000. Turn right. Take third on the left for Esslemont (ignore the other lefts for Mill of Torry and Esslemont. Ellon, 4 miles). Follow road all the way to Ellon.

In Ellon you come to a T-junction with Riverside Road, turn right. After 300 yards turn right for Fraserburgh, Peterhead, Aberdeen, A948 (A90T) (left for Ellon town centre).

About 600 yards out of Ellon turn left for Kirkton of Logie Buchan. Take extreme care at crossroads with A90. Cross straight over A90.

At Kirkton of Logie Buchan turn left at converted stables, signed as a dead end. Descend past Manse and Church. Road becomes rough and grassy. Cross concrete bridge and follow road on far side to Denhead. At crossroads turn right for Collieston. At crossroads with A975, go straight over for Collieston, B9003. Turn left at Slains Church for Whinnyfold to continue with route (for Collieston continue round bend and uphill).

Follow narrow road and coast north past Cruden Bay Oil Terminal to crossroads with A975. Turn right into Cruden Bay.

Terrain: A very gentle ride with just the occasional hill. The Formartine and Buchan Way can be muddy and narrow in places.

ACCOMMODATION

Ellon (01358–)

Hotels and B&Bs: Station Hotel, Station Brae (–720209); Brackenbrae, Ythanbank (–761222).

Cruden Bay (01779–)

Hotels and B&Bs: Kilmarnock Arms Hotel, Bridge Street (–812213); Red House Hotel, Aulton Road (–812215); St Olaf Hotel, Aulton Road (–813130).

Camping: Craighead CP, one mile out of town en route (–812251).

WATCH OUT FOR!

Forvie National Nature Reserve, Collieston. Internationally important colonies of breeding Eider and Tern; follow signs for Forvie Reserve and

Stevenston Visitor Centre on the approach to Collieston.

Slains Castle. Extensive ruin of nineteenth-century house on the very edge of a precipitous cliff reached by footpath from Cruden Bay.

Bullers of Buchan. Spectacular coastal scenery, sea rushes into sea chasms hundreds of feet deep through natural archways, three miles north of Cruden Bay. Take extreme care.

CRUDEN BAY TO FRASERBURGH (30 MILES)

Continue north on the A975 through Cruden Bay. Just beyond the limit of the town turn left for Auchiries and Craighead Caravan Park. Go straight over A90(T) for Gask and Longside and then after a short distance turn right. After one-and-a-half miles turn left at West Gask for Longside. Follow this road for about four miles to Toddlehills – a collection of brown bungalows. Turn left for Kinmundy and after 100 yards turn right. Road rises and then descends to T-junction. Turn right. At the crossroads at the Bruce Arms Hotel go straight over for Auchlee and Rora. At triangular junction, turn left in the direction of Mintlaw. After one mile turn right for Balearn and Backfolds. At next T-junction turn right for Rora and Hyvie. After 500 yards turn left.

At crossroads, at house dated 1881, go straight over. At the next junction at Ridinghill turn right and then left for St Combs. Follow road to crossroads with A90(T); go straight over for St Combs, B9033 (Coastal Trail).

Just short of St Combs the B9033 goes to the left for Fraserburgh. Follow the B9033 into Fraserburgh. Cycle path crosses the B9033 follow off to the left for harbour and town centre. Otherwise follow B9033 to T-junction at cemetery.

Terrain: Cycling continues to be easy. Hills are gentle or exceptionally short.

ACCOMMODATION
Fraserburgh (01346–)
Hotels and B&Bs: Saltoun Arms Hotel, Saltoun Square (–518282); Madge Cumming, 14 Hanover Street (–517393); Clifton House, 131 Charlotte Street (–518365).
Camping: Esplanade CP, The Esplanade (–510041); Rosehearty CP, The Harbour Rosehearty, four miles west of Fraserburgh (–571658).

WATCH OUT FOR!
Maggie's Hoosie, Inverallochy. A fisher cottage that remains just as it was in the nineteenth century.

Fraserburgh Heritage Centre, Quarry Road, Fraserburgh (01346 512888).

Waters of Philorth Nature Reserve, Fraserburgh. Variety of breeds and habitat; access adjacent to golf course.

FRASERBURGH TO BANFF (25 MILES)

At T-junction at cemetery turn left for Aberdeen and Peterhead. At roundabout at Tescos take the exit for Inverness (A96), (A98). At next roundabout go straight over for Inverness. At next roundabout go straight over. At T-junction with A98 turn right towards Fraserburgh for Rosehearty and Sandhaven. At the Shell garage turn left on to B9031 for Sandhaven and Rosehearty.

Follow the B9031 through Sandhaven and Pitullie. In Rosehearty follow signs for New Aberdour, Macduff and Banff, B9031.

Follow the B9031 west. At T-junction with B9032 turn right for New Aberdour, Banff and Macduff. Continue through New Aberdour. Follow road along the coast to T-junction turn right onto the A98(T) and enter Macduff. Follow road downhill to the harbour and to bridge over the River Deveron. Cross the bridge for Banff and Duff House.

Terrain: The easy cycling ends at Rosehearty. From then on the road goes through some considerable contortions, though once beyond Gardenstown it gets easier.

Detours: The remarkable villages of Pennan, Gardenstown and Crovie are all worth the detour from the B9031; however, it is very steeply downhill into them and very steeply uphill out of them.

ACCOMMODATION
Gardenstown (01261–)
Hotels and B&Bs: Palace Farm (–851261); Lucy Smith, Bankhead Croft (–851584).
Camping: Wester Bonnyton Farm Site, by the B9031, four miles west of Gardenstown (–832470).
MacDuff (01261–)
Hotels and B&Bs: Park Hotel, Fife Street (–833001); Kathleen Grieg, 11 Gellymill Street (–833314); Monica's and Martin's, 21 Gellymill Street (–832336); Knowes Hotel, Market Street (–832229).
Banff (01261–)
Hotels and B&Bs: Banff Links Hotel, Swordanes (–812414); Banff Springs Hotel, Golden Knowes Road (–812881); Country Hotel, 32 High Street (–815353); Fife Lodge Hotel, Sandyhill Road (–812436); Carmelite House Hotel, Low Street (–812152); Montcoffer House, Montcoffer

(–812979); Mrs Monica Mackay, 13 Fife Street (–812509); The Orchard Duff House (–812146); Mrs Watt, Bellevue Road (–818241); Morayhill, Bellevue Road (–815956).
Camping: Banff Links CP (–812228).

WATCH OUT FOR!
Mounthooley Doocot. Castellated doocoot and good views just beyond Rosehearty.

Macduff Marine Aquarium, 11 Shore Road, Macduff (01261 833369).

Duff House (HS), Banff (01261 818181). Georgian Baroque house designed by William Adam contains an outstanding collection of art and furniture. There is a tearoom and the gardens are worth exploring.

BANFF TO TURRIFF (12 MILES)
Return to bridge over the Deveron between Banff and Macduff. Take the A947 for Turriff on the Macduff side of the river. After about one mile follow NCN1 to the right. Alternatively you can follow the tracks through the woods south of Duff House to Alvah Bridge, the route is unsigned; pick up a map at Duff House. Follow NCN signs and follow Deveron upstream to T-junction with B9025. Turn left into Turriff. At the end of Church Street turn right into Market Street. Follow road round to the right onto High Street.

Terrain: Wonderfully varied gradients that are never especially challenging.

ACCOMMODATION
Turriff (01888–)
Hotels and B&Bs: The Gables, Station Road (–568715); Fife Arms Hotel, The Square (–563468).
Camping: Turriff CP, Station Road (–562205).

WATCH OUT FOR!
Old Bridge of Alvah. Beauty-spot that can be reached via the Duff Estate or from NCN1 at Montcoffer; however, the approach roads are very rough.

TURRIFF TO ALFORD (30 MILES)
Follow High Street west for Aberdeen, A947. Go left at ostentatious Mercat Cross. Descend over stream and turn right for Huntly, B9024. Turn left immediately for Thorneybank. Follow road all the way to T-junction with B9001. Turn left and then after 200 yards turn right for Logie

Newton and Fisherford. Follow road to T-junction at Fisherford. Turn right. After 200 yards go straight on for Culsalmond when main road bends to the left (Cadgers' Road). Go straight over A920 at Culsalmond for Williamston. Ignore turning for Williamston at Mosside, instead continue to T-junction with B992. Turn right and proceed to junction with A96. Turn left then right for Insch, B992. In Insch go straight through at cross. At railway station turn right. Cross railway line at level crossing and then after 200 yards go to the left for Auchleven and Whitehouse. Follow the road through Auchleven and begin long climb. After a long downhill you continue straight on through Keig, which means actually leaving the B992. From Keig follow road to Montgarrie. Turn left in Montgarrie for Alford. Follow road into Alford.

Terrain: This section is quite hilly. Although fairly easy to begin with, there is a long and at times steep climb followed by a long downhill between Insch and Alford.

ACCOMMODATION
Alford (019755–)
Hotels and B&Bs: Haughton Arms Hotel, Main Street (–62026); The Vale Hotel, Main Street (–62183); Bydand, 18 Balfour Road (–63613); Macbrae Lodge, Montgarrie (–63421).
Camping: Haughton CP, Montgarrie Road (–62107).

WATCH OUT FOR!
Picardy Stone (HS). An important Pictish symbol stone, two miles west of Insch.

Archaeolink Prehistory Park (01464 851 500). Everything you need to know about pre-historic times, three miles east of Insch on the B9002.

Grampian Transport Museum, Alford (019755 62292). Classic vehicles and steam engines.

ALFORD TO DYCE (32 MILES)
Retrace route through Keig and back towards Insch. After a short distance turn right for My Lord's Throat. Follow the Don downstream to T-junction. Turn right for Monymusk and then turn right again for Monymusk. At crossroads turn left for Monymusk. Continue through Monymusk to T-junction with B993. Turn left. After 200 yards turn right for Cluny and Sauchen. Follow road for two miles to crossroads then turn left for Kemnay. Follow road through Craigearn and back to B993 (purpose of loop is to take in Castle Fraser, watch for right, unsigned in this direction). Turn right and follow B993 into Kemnay. The B993

becomes the B994 which we follow through Kemnay and for two miles on the other side. Turn left off the B994 for Kintore and Caravan Park. At next T-junction turn right and follow Forest Road into Kintore. Opposite post office turn right. At Kintore Arms go off left for Hatton of Fintry. When B997 goes left for Hatton of Fintry go straight on for Deystone. Keep left at Kinnella and at next junction follow road round to the left and proceed to crossroads with B979. Go straight over and then after short climb turn left. After half a mile follow round to the right, uphill. After three miles you come to a junction with a busy road and turn left then right. Follow road under railway line to T-junction and turn right. Follow to junction with Victoria Street and turn right. Follow signs off Victoria Street for railway station.

Terrain: There are lots of ups and downs. Especially at the beginning and at the end, some climbs are steep but they aren't sustained.

ACCOMMODATION
Kintore (01467–)
Hotels and B&Bs: Torryburn Hotel, School Road (–632269).
Camping: Hillhead CP (–632809).

WATCH OUT FOR!
Monymusk Church. Norman church that has been in continuous use since the twelfth century.

Castle Fraser (NTS) (01330 833 463). Extensive display of historic furnishings and paintings in fairytale sixteenth-century castle; between Monymusk and Craigearn.